Florida A&M University, Tallahassee
Florida Atlantic University, Boca Raton
Florida Gulf Coast University, Ft. Myers
Florida International University, Miami
Florida State University, Tallahassee
University of Central Florida, Orlando
University of Florida, Gainesville
University of North Florida, Jacksonville
University of South Florida, Tampa
University of West Florida, Pensacola

University Press of Florida

Gainesville · Tallahassee · Tampa · Boca Raton

Pensacola · Orlando · Miami · Jacksonville · Ft. Myers

EMBRACING

AMERICA

A Cuban Exile Comes of Age

Margaret L. Paris

May all your
journeys be
filled with
peace & light.

Margaret
Paris
1-31-03

Copyright 2002 by Margaret Paris
Printed in the United States of America on recycled, acid-free paper
All rights reserved

07 06 05 04 03 02   6 5 4 3 2 1

Library of Congress Cataloging-in-Publication Data
Paris, Margaret L.
Embracing America: a Cuban exile comes of age / Margaret L. Paris.
p. cm.
Includes bibliographical references.
ISBN 0-8130-2545-1 (cloth: alk. paper)
1. Borkland, Elena Maza. 2. Cuban American women—Biography.
3. Cuban Americans—Biography. I. Title.
E184.C97 B667 2002
973'.04687291'0092—dc21
[B]   2002027137

The University Press of Florida is the scholarly publishing agency
for the State University System of Florida, comprising Florida A&M
University, Florida Atlantic University, Florida Gulf Coast University,
Florida International University, Florida State University, University
of Central Florida, University of Florida, University of North Florida,
University of South Florida, and University of West Florida.

University Press of Florida
15 Northwest 15th Street
Gainesville, FL 32611–2079
http://www.upf.com

To the de la Maza family,
who generously shared their tragedies
and their triumphs.

Contents

Illustrations ix

Foreword xi

Preface xv

Chronology xxi

1. Leaving Havana; Resettling in Albuquerque, New Mexico 1

2. De la Maza and Caturla Family Histories in Cuba 27

3. Mrs. de la Maza and Cecilia's Flight to the United States; Together in Albuquerque, New Mexico 54

4. Starting Again in Arlington, Virginia 81

5. Introduction to Art; the Hippies' Life of the Sixties 106

6. Discovery of Tai Chi; Grandfather and Aunts Leave Cuba; Other Family Events 128

7. Cecilia's Dilemma 151

8. Raising David; Rediscovering Tai Chi 164

9. Elena's Art; Return to Cuban Heritage 175

Appendix 205

Notes 207

Illustrations

1. Mr. de la Maza and his daughters, on a family vacation at the Vanderbilt Hotel in Miami Beach, 1953   6

2. General Francisco Carrillo and his staff, including Othon Caturla, War for Independence in Cuba, 1898   33

3. Mrs. de la Maza and her four daughters, 1953   41

4. Cecilia and the trained cats on her sixth birthday, 1957   46

5. "Gingham dress" birthday party, 1953   47

6. De la Maza family, February 4, 1961   48

7. Elena's first communion, 1954   51

8. 1405½ Roma Street, the de la Maza's first rental house in Albuquerque, New Mexico   61

9. Elena and Cecilia celebrating Independence Day of Cuba, May 20, 1962   68

10. Elena in costume for the production of *Brigadoon*, 1963   86

11. De la Maza family in front of their house in Arlington, Virginia, 1966   88

12. Portraits of the Maza sisters used for their residency application in 1964   93

13. 16806 Excaliber Way, Elena and Herb's house in Sandy Spring, Maryland   108

14. Elena and Herb's Christmas card, 1973   137

15. Elena and Herb's Christmas card, 1974   138

16. Beatriz and Sergio del Castillo's wedding, 1972   147

17. Portrait of Cecilia at thirteen   152

18. Elena, Herb, and David on vacation in Florida, 1986   166

19. Elena demonstrating the tai chi movement "snake creeps down"   169

20. Elena on the Great Wall in China, 1988   171

21. Tai chi students from Dennis Brown's studio in Chen jiago, Henan province, China, 1988   173

22. David, Herb, and Mrs. de la Maza, Christmas, 1997   176

23. Elena with Norman Parish, owner of Parish Gallery, 1994   183

24. Elena and her mother, Olga Caturla de la Maza, at the reception for Elena's solo show, *Various Splendor*, 1996   191

Foreword

It was raining heavily on the afternoon of August 22, 1961, when I arrived in Miami with my sister, Raquel, and my cousin Maria de Lourdes. I was seventeen years old; my sister and cousin were fourteen. We thought at the time that we would be back to Cuba soon. That was forty years ago.

Our experience was not unique. It was the lot of thousands of unaccompanied Cuban minors who left their homeland under the auspices of what came to be called *Operation Pedro Pan* during the traumatic first few years of the Castro regime. Many, if not most, of the passengers on our flight that rainy August afternoon were children. One of them—he could not have been more than four or five—had a sign with an address in Miami pinned to his clothes.

Like my sister, my cousin, and me, Elena Maza Borkland and her sisters Beatriz and Silvia left Cuba as unaccompanied minors in 1961, leaving behind a fractured family. Parents and a younger sister, Cecilia, remained in Cuba waiting for Castro's downfall or, failing that, an eventual family reunification in exile. The future, once predictable, now became one big question mark: lifetimes would unfold under circumstances no one had anticipated, let alone prepared for.

I have often wondered what mysterious mechanism, what strange Pied Piper could have triggered the unique Cuban children's exodus of the early sixties. I have also wondered whether, under similar circumstances, I would have sent my own children away. Probably not, but then, who am I to judge? Fortunately, life has not presented me with the same painful dilemma that confronted my parents, the de la Mazas, and thousands of other Cuban parents forty years ago.

One thing is certain. At least for me, the experience of being young and free in America was exhilarating. What my life would have been like had I remained in Cuba is a question for which there is no answer. I do know that I have lived my life in freedom and that I would not have wanted it otherwise. What might have happened—or not happened—in Cuba had the elite social and economic groups represented by the Pedro Pan children remained there is, of course, a fascinating speculation.

There are as many Pedro Pan stories as there are Pedro Pan exiles. Some are tragic, some are joyful, some are depressing, and some are inspiring, but none is boring. The late Ana Mendieta, the brilliant but star-crossed sculptor, was a Pedro Pan child. So is Mel Martínez, the current secretary of housing and urban development, the first Cuban-American to serve in the president's cabinet. This book is Elena Maza's page in that great collective story, masterfully captured in a series of interviews with Margaret Paris. It is a great read and an important contribution to the literature of exile and immigration in America.

The Mazas were an established Cuban family. The paterfamilias, Aquiles, was one of the island's top architects. A cousin, composer Alejandro Garcia Caturla, was a pioneer in the fusion of African elements into mainstream Cuban music. García Caturla, who maintained a public, stable relationship with an Afro-Cuban woman and later with her sister, was also a judge. He died a tragic death, murdered by a disgruntled litigant.

The world the Mazas found in the United States was one very distant from that of their Cuban traditions. This is the story of Elena's—and her family's—survival and adaptation to life in a United States that was undergoing societal changes as profound and, in many ways, as unsettling as anything happening in their island home. Ironically, Elena left a Marxist-Leninist revolution only to encounter a sexual one, a civil rights struggle, an anti–Vietnam War insurgency, a women's movement, and the drug culture of the sixties and seventies—all within the space of a few years.

Encompassing a difficult exile in New Mexico, her experience of Woodstock, the rediscovery of her Cuban identity, a loving and happy marriage to an American, the suicide of her sister Cecilia, bringing up Cecilia's troubled child, exploring oriental wisdom, earning a respected niche in the Washington, D.C., arts and community advocacy scene, Elena's fascinating odyssey unfolds. It is a story at once heartrending and inspiring, exploring with utmost candor the pain of exile and re-settlement and the ongoing conversation with Cuba and Cuban identity that is so central to the Cuban-American condition. Once begun, this book is hard to put down. It carries the power of personal testimony and the sweeping scope of family saga; it is at once an elegant text and a lasting contribution.

Miguel A. Bretos
Senior Scholar
Smithsonian Institution

Preface

I met Elena Maza Borkland in early 1994 through the Washington, D.C.,
chapter of the Women's Caucus for Art (WCA/DC) at a meeting to
discuss a proposed show. The WCA/DC is part of a national organization that provides arts advocacy for women artists of all colors, back-
grounds, and abilities, enabling them to discuss issues, organize social
projects, and exhibit art. Elena Maza, the WCA/DC exhibition committee chair, had drawn up the proposal for the show *The Five Elements.*
When we met at her house, Elena explained the theme of the show: for
the Chinese the world is made of up five elements—wood, fire, earth,
metal, and water.¹ The show would include work by artists who addressed one or more elements in their work.

I immediately liked the quiet authority with which Elena spoke, and I
agreed to work with her on photographing the work that was juried into
the show. As we worked, she told me a little about her life: she was born
in Cuba and had come to this country in her teens. Her paintings were all
over her house—on the walls as well as leaning against them—waiting
to be sent to other shows or to be stored. I was surprised and intrigued by
the references to the Afro-Cuban culture in her work. "It's part of my
heritage as a Cuban and something I'm interested in," was the way Elena
explained it.

We had many quick and casual exchanges over the next year. In November 1995, Elena and I were gallery sitting for another Women's Cau-

cus show in downtown Washington, D.C., and I asked her to fill me in on some of the details of her life.

Elena and her three sisters grew up in Havana in a comfortable middle-class family. Her parents are referred to in this book either as Mr. and Mrs. de la Maza, a more formal designation, or as Mr. and Mrs. Maza. Elena and her sisters have used only Maza in the U.S. because this is what was on their passports. Her father had a private practice in architecture in which he did a variety of projects, including landscape architecture. He also worked for the Ministry of Public Works. Although the family had servants, Elena's mother—a trained teacher and poet—was very involved in raising her daughters. While she devoted herself to every part of her daughters' lives, often making them special dresses for birthday parties, Mrs. Maza continued to write poetry. There were daily visits with grandparents, aunts, and an uncle.

Elena and her sisters were thoroughly enmeshed in what Havana had to offer a family of their means: they went to private schools, took piano and ballet lessons, sang in their church choir, and took family vacations to resorts in the countryside. This way of life was significantly curtailed when Castro came to power. Their middle-class life began coming apart as Castro began a series of reforms that swept away their rental income and Mr. Maza's private architectural practice, both of which had helped to make this lifestyle possible.

In 1961, when she was thirteen—two years after Fidel Castro took power in Cuba—Elena came to this country with two of her three sisters to live with foster parents in Albuquerque, New Mexico.[2] They were part of what came to be called the "Pedro Pan," or "Peter Pan," airlift of Cuban children, a remarkable, yet relatively unknown piece of history in Cuban-American affairs.[3] For Elena, the normal turmoil and change experienced in adolescence was exacerbated by the separation from her family, her country, and her culture.

Elena's family was finally reunited in Arlington, Virginia. Elena went to college, becoming involved in the counterculture of the late sixties and early seventies. The family tragedy of her sister Cecilia's death became interwoven with Elena's own journey of marriage and with her becoming a tai chi master, an accomplished and recognized painter, and a community activist for the arts and Cuban culture.

Several days after she shared some of her life story with me, I asked Elena if she would consider my interviewing her for an oral history/biography.

I currently teach at Duke Ellington School of the Arts, the arts high school in Washington, D.C., and part-time at Georgetown University, which is several blocks from Ellington. For nine years in the seventies and early eighties, I edited *Cityscape*, one of the oral history/writing projects modeled on the *Foxfire* magazine and books: interviews by students with members of the community were taped; the tapes were transcribed and then edited and laid out with photographs to become stories.[4] The experience with *Cityscape*—one of the first high school publications to be recognized by the Robert F. Kennedy Journalism Awards—helped prepare me to tell Elena's story.

On New Year's Day in 1996 we began. After our first interview, I knew we had easily established the rapport needed to do the project. Over the next two years, Elena and I filled up thirty-one tapes with questions, responses, and memories. These tapes were transcribed and extensively edited to create the text for *Embracing America*.

When I was working on the endnotes for *Embracing America*, I knew it was important to include some factual information about the airlifts called Operation Pedro Pan. Elena knew many people on the East Coast who had come to America through the airlift, so there were abundant anecdotal stories, but I had difficulty in locating statistics about Operation Pedro Pan.

On January 12, 1998, the *New York Times* ran a front-page article about some of the people who as children had been part of the Pedro Pan airlifts. At the end of January an article on the airlifts appeared in the *Washington Post*.[5] The *Times* article mentioned the role of Father Walsh and the Catholic Charities organization; it also mentioned that Professor Maria de los Angeles Torres, a political science professor at DePaul University in Chicago, planned to sue the CIA to force the agency to release its files about Operation Pedro Pan.

Through her extensive network of Cuban friends, Elena knew that Yvonne Conde was getting ready to publish a book about the airlifts. In March 1999, Ms. Conde told me in a telephone conversation that the *Times* article was serving as the catalyst for the June 1999 publication of her book, *Operation Pedro Pan*.[6] Conde's book is a comprehensive history of the airlifts that also profiles some of the participants, including herself: more than 14,000 children were flown out of Cuba in this operation carried out by the Catholic Church and (unofficially) by the United States government. Later I discovered that one year earlier, Victor Triay had published *Fleeing Castro: Operation Pedro Pan and the Cuban Children's Program*, an informative book that also deals with Operation Pedro Pan.[7]

The airlifts were fascinating and historically important events. Equally important to me was the story of this individual woman's life. When I began interviewing Elena, I had just finished a five-year project—*Valued Woman: A Photo Essay in Celebration of Women Over Forty*—which was exhibited in New York and Pennsylvania and at three locations in the Washington, D.C. area. This project, both an exhibit and a catalogue, focused on fifty-six women—primarily from metropolitan Washington, D.C.—who were over forty and who had been able to extend their lives in special ways beyond the traditional expectations of women in our culture.[8] The large-format portraits of each woman were accompanied by hand-lettered statements by myself and each of the subjects about what it meant to be of the age when women are sometimes dismissed. When I had the opportunity to hear Elena's story in detail, I realized that focusing in detail on one woman could be a next logical step in my exploration of women in our society.

Embracing America, then, came about because it is the story of a remarkable woman who was a player in a significant historical event. Elena Maza emerged from her triumphs and tragedies as a whole, engaged woman: a wife and a mother, a successful artist, and a community activist. She is able to look thoughtfully at her past and describe it with unflinching honesty while remaining totally committed to her family and her Cuban roots.

Acknowledgments

My thanks go to those who helped with this project: Dr. Miguel Bretos, who is now a senior scholar at the Smithsonian Institution and who was head of the Latino Initiative at the Smithsonian when I approached him about doing the foreword several years ago; Teresa Grana, who has diligently shepherded this project from the beginning and who has been an important connection with the Latino community in Washington, D.C.; Lucinda Paris, a writer and friend who gave long-term assistance and support; Phyllis Jacobs and Amy Mehringer for editorial advice; Susan Fernandez and Gillian Hillis of the University Press of Florida; Helen Dalrymple, senior public affairs specialist, Office of Public Affairs, Library of Congress; Daniel Freedberg, The Free Press; Dr. Paul Huntsberger, Two Eagles Press International; Mo Palmer, archivist, Albuquerque Museum; Dr. Richard Powell, Department of Art and Art History, Duke University; MacUpgrades and The Writer's Center, both in Bethesda, Maryland; Ionel Dinu, Parcel Plus, Rockville, Maryland; Deborah Warin, director of continuing education, Georgetown University; the administration of Duke Ellington School of the Arts, Washington, D.C.; many, many friends and my family, especially my daughter, Simone Booth, and my aunt Eleanor Anne Hammond, who worked for seventeen years as a librarian in St. Petersburg, Florida, ten of those years as head of circulation. It was a privilege to be able to use the library resources of Montgomery County, Maryland, where I live. My admiration and thanks go to the reference librarians at the Davis and Rockville libraries and especially those at the Wheaton Regional Library. Their patience and professionalism were outstanding in helping me track down various material for the endnotes.

Chronology

1895 José Martí, the Cuban writer, patriot, and revolutionary, signs the order for the third rebellion to begin on February 24, resulting in the War for Independence (Spanish-American War).

Othon Caturla, Elena's Maza's maternal grandfather, joins the *mambises*, the liberation army for the War for Independence. He serves under General Francisco Carrillo. After the war he attends and finishes medical school at the University of Maryland, Baltimore, and returns to practice in San Juan de los Remedios, Cuba.

1901 Juan José de la Maza y Artola, Elena's paternal grandfather, is elected to the Constitutional Assembly and forms the Moderate Party in the new Republic of Cuba. He is elected to the Senate in 1912.

1905 Aquiles de la Maza, Elena's father, is born in Havana.

1906 Alejandro García Caturla, a cousin of Elena's mother, is born in Remedios. He would become one of the pioneers of avant-garde music in Cuba, incorporating percussive and syncopated Afro-Cuban sounds and rhythms.

1911 Olga Caturla, Elena's mother, is born in Remedios.

1925 Gerardo Machado is elected president of Cuba. While Machado promises liberal reforms, his administration is soon corrupted by excessive graft and the increasing presence of the military in civil service positions.

1928 A constitutional convention gives Machado a six-year term without requiring his reelection.

1933 Machado resigns. Havana is infused with a progressive outlook, an atmosphere of hope and possibility.

1934 Colonel Fulgencio Batista takes over effective control of the government. Although Batista does not officially become president until 1940, he wields power behind the scenes after the fall of the dictator Machado. Once president, Batista rules with repressive military forces.

1935 A typhoid epidemic in Remedios kills the Caturla son, Othon. His father, Dr. Othon Caturla, moves his family to Havana.

1940 Alejandro García Caturla is assassinated.

1943 Aquiles de la Maza and Olga Caturla meet; they marry in 1945.

1946 Beatriz, the first of four daughters, is born. Elena follows in 1947, Silvia in 1949, and Cecilia in 1951

1958 On December 31, Batista flees after the scattered but impressive victories of Fidel Castro's revolutionary forces.

1959 On January 1, Castro begins to move across the island. He stages his victory march into Havana on January 7.

The Agrarian Reform Law is announced. At first this law is applied only to the nationalizing of large plantations, but gradually it is extended to include all income from private rental property and income from private professions.

1961 On March 29, Beatriz, Elena, and Silvia leave Havana as part of the airlifts later named Operation Pedro Pan. They are placed with foster families in Albuquerque, New Mexico.

On April 17, the Bay of Pigs invasion to topple Castro is led by trained Cuban exiles. This effort fails due to miscommunications, equipment failures, and lack of air and sea support by U.S. forces.

In August, Mrs. Maza and Cecilia leave Havana; three months later they move to Albuquerque, New Mexico.

1962 In June, Mr. Maza leaves Havana and goes to Opa Locka, a Florida airport where part of a former military installation was used as a processing center for Cuban men. He moves to Arlington, Virginia, where he had been offered a job as a draftsman. The entire family is reunited there several months later.

In October, the Cuban Missile Crisis occurs after U.S. reconnaissance flights detect that the Soviet Union has begun secretly building missile-launching sites in Cuba. The United States imposes a naval blockade and demands the removal of the missiles. A tense standoff follows, and negotiations result in the United States agreeing to withdraw its missiles from Turkey and in the Russians agreeing to withdraw their missiles from Cuba.

1964–65 Elena continues her studies in music with Mrs. May of the Friday Morning Music Club.

1965 Elena graduates from high school and enters James Madison University in Harrisonburg, Virginia, as a music major. She stays for one year.

1967 Elena enters Catholic University in Washington, D.C., as an architecture major. She stays for two years.

1968 Riots in Washington, D.C., erupt after the assassination of Dr. Martin Luther King Jr.

1969 Elena meets Herb Borkland.

Elena attends the famous rock concert in Woodstock, New York.

1970 Elena and Herb attend one of the large peace marches in Washington, D.C., to protest U.S. involvement in Vietnam.

1972 Herb and Elena begin studying tai chi.

Sarah Caturla, Maria Victoria Caturla, and Dr. Othon Caturla —Elena's aunts and grandfather—leave Cuba and relocate near Elena's parents in northern Virginia. Dr. Othon Caturla dies five weeks after arriving in the United States.

Beatriz marries Sergio del Castillo.

1975 Elena marries Herb Borkland.

1976 Sylvia marries Bill Heron.

1977 Cecilia gives birth to David.

1978 Elena becomes a citizen of the United States of America.

1979 Aquiles de la Maza, Elena's father, dies.

1981 Margaret Borkland, Herb's mother, dies.

1983 Cecilia succumbs to mental illness.

1984 Elena becomes the guardian of Cecilia's son, David. David begins studying tae kwon do.

1985 Herb resumes studying tae kwon do.

1986 Elena's first solo show of watercolors is held at Brookside Gardens, a Montgomery County park in Maryland.

Herb, Elena, and David move to Sandy Spring, Maryland.

1987 Elena begins studying tai chi again.

1988 Elena goes to mainland China for a month with an American tai chi group.

1991 Elena starts Olney tai chi classes in her downstairs studio.

1994 *Afro-Cuban Paintings*—a solo show of fifteen of Elena's paintings—opens in January at the Parish Gallery in Georgetown.

Elena becomes exhibition chair of the Women's Caucus for Art of the Greater Washington, D.C., area. In 1996 and 1997, she serves as president of this organization.

1994–95 Elena curates *A Collage of Cultures: Many Visions, One Community*—an award-winning exhibit with related catalogue—at the Dover Art League in Dover, Delaware.

1995 Margaret Paris, the author of *Embracing America*, and Elena discuss Elena's life in detail.

1996 Margaret Paris begins taped interviews with Elena.

Various Splendor, a solo show by Elena, is held at the Dover Art League.

The Cuban American Cultural Society is organized by Elena Maza, Lucía Vassallo, Oilda del Castillo, María Bertrán, and M. Joaquina Díaz.

1998 Elena exhibits with Santiago Caballero in *Two Capital Painters*, a two-person show at the Alfredo Martínez Gallery, Coral Gables, Florida.

Elena is awarded residency from August to November at the Mill Atelier, Sante Fe, New Mexico.

2001 A book of Olga Caturla de la Maza's poetry, *Todo el mar para mis sueños* (All the sea for my dreams), is published by Two Eagles Press International of Las Cruces, New Mexico. Elena serves as the editor and translator for this book.

Leaving Havana; Resettling in Albuquerque, New Mexico

After going through customs we went into a big room; glass doors closed behind us. That was it. You had crossed the line. Everybody else in your family was outside. I could see my parents and my Aunt Sarah on the other side. I didn't want to look back. I was afraid I would break down and start crying. I didn't want them to see me cry.

Tears run down Elena Maza's cheeks as she describes the day she left Cuba as a thirteen-year-old with her sisters Beatriz, fifteen, and Silvia, eleven. Thirty-five years have not diminished the pain she felt at the separation from her country, her adult family, and her youngest sister, Cecilia.

She is quiet for a moment. We both look out at the snow-covered yard around her spacious house in Sandy Spring, Maryland. She says she always cries when she talks about this day.

This was probably the worst day of Grandfather's life. He was already seventy-six, and he had given so much to his country. He had fought in the War for the Independence of Cuba, what Americans usually call the Spanish-American War. And now the exodus of his family was beginning. He was so devastated that he didn't come to the airport. My aunts and mother were concerned about him. In fact, my Aunt Sarah, who was the one person in our family who could drive, was so upset that she didn't feel she could drive to the airport. My father hired Antonio, a taxi driver who sometimes worked for my father as a chauffeur, to drive us.

Beatriz and I were very frightened and were trying to hide it, especially from Silvia. We were being very protective, trying to distract her and do whatever we could to make her feel better. Having grown up in a close family, it was sort of an instinctive thing to do. Aunt Sarah and my parents stayed with us for an hour, then left, assuming we'd be taking off soon. I remember turning around; I could no longer see them through the glass doors.[1]

The flight was supposed to leave at 4 or 5 P.M. We got to the airport around 2 P.M. because we knew the officials were going to search some of the people. We were not subjected to a body search as some of my friends were. These body searches were done systematically to humiliate those leaving. I had one friend who was about twenty at the time. She was a very pretty young lady, engaged to be married. She was sent out by her parents to join a sister in the U.S. who had just had a baby. She told me that every body cavity had been searched by one of the female militia members, just to mortify her because they knew she was a virgin. Many young women of that age were subjected to that. We were lucky we weren't.

Our only other concern was when they asked us to open our bags. Although we were not carrying anything that was considered contraband, we were worried they might want to take something out of our bags.

We had been told not to say anything at the airport. Our official story was simply that we were being sent to the U.S. because our school had been shut down, and that we were going to improve our English. When we finished high school, we would come back. Our parents had instructed us not to say anything about politics or anything against the revolution because that would obviously make us suspect.

Elena describes the events that led to her mother's decision to send three of her children to the United States.

Fidel Castro had been in power two years. Beatriz and I had been attending Ruston Academy, a bilingual American school. The elementary school we'd gone to was also bilingual, so we knew English well.

Castro ordered all Americans to leave by the end of December 1960.[2] Mr. Baker, the principal of Ruston, called in all the parents of his students before turning the school over to the authorities. He wanted to start the same school in Coral Gables, Florida. Mr. Baker was going to take a group of students with him; he asked my mother if she wanted Beatriz and me to go with him. My mother declined the offer, but she decided she would take us out of school when Mr. Baker left.[3]

Elena becomes serious as she describes a particular teacher at Ruston.

I had one social science teacher who was decidedly communist; he was conducting the class in such a way as to elicit certain responses. He tried to convince us of the justice of the Agrarian Reform Law.[4] A *latifundio* is a large parcel of land held by one owner or a consortium. Castro's agrarian reform broke up this monopoly, so that the peasants would finally have some land. At first we supported it. The problem arose when all land was declared part of this reform, even very small plots. My mother's father had inherited four small farms in Las Villas. His rents were reasonable and produced some income for his retirement. There were tenants on these plots who had lived there their entire lives. The largest farm was ten or twenty acres. We felt this land—such small plots—shouldn't qualify. My grandfather lost his land.

Then my father lost his boyhood home, a townhouse where he had his architectural office and where he rented some rooms as offices. That rental money had to be turned over to the government. My dad couldn't have a private practice anymore; he could only work for the Ministry of Public Works. He'd always worked there as an architect in addition to his private practice.

These changes occurred over a two-year period. There were other families of students at Ruston who were also being divested of everything they owned. The teacher was trying to convince us of the justice of this, but it was hard for us to feel any justice in what was taking place. We were aware enough politically at that time to know that he was trying to influence our thinking. We were doing everything we could to resist his influence without jeopardizing our grades.

I had read Orwell's *Animal Farm* after Castro's rise to power, on the recommendation of my Aunt Toya.[5] The parallels about the rise of a totalitarian system were inescapable.

I ask Elena if her parents felt that they could wait it out, that things would change.

My dad was convinced that Castro wouldn't last. Everyone felt that they had outlived some other horrible dictators, that it was just a matter of a couple of years before something would happen and Castro would be taken out.

Before Mr. Baker left for America, he called my mother in and told her that the Cuban authorities had looked through all the records, and that they had spotted Beatriz and me as possible candidates to go to the U.S.S.R. for schooling. That really panicked my mother.[6]

On the last Christmas Elena's family was together in Cuba, they had the Nochebuena *banquet and went to Mass, as always, but there weren't as many presents and there was no Christmas tree. Elena smiles as she explains that Castro felt the American-style Christmas with the tree and especially Santa Claus was imperialistic.[7] He asked that no Cubans have a tree. For Santa Claus he substituted a figure of the typical Cuban small farmer: Don Feliciano wearing a beard, a* guayabera *(a traditional Cuban pleated shirt worn outside the pants), and a straw hat.*

We never went back to school after the Christmas vacation. Shortly after January 1961, there were rumors that we were going to be invaded by the U.S. My parents wanted to get us out before a war started. Already the exodus had begun; people were beginning to panic. It had really been noticeable during the school year. Every week there would be one fewer person in my class.

Our lives were consumed with our own preparations to leave. By January 1961, we started getting all the papers and passports ready. It was still relatively easy, but it took us three months. We were to be part an airlift organized by Mr. Baker and the Catholic Church.[8] This idea of the airlift was to get as many children under the age of eighteen out of Cuba as soon as possible. My mother had outfitted us with winter clothes that she thought we might need. We weren't sure where we'd be located in the U.S.

Beatriz, Elena's older sister, has recorded her own memories of the departure in her unpublished "Memoirs":

> *There were rumors of a law to be passed which would turn parental rights over all children to the state. This is when my parents made the decision for us to leave. The National Catholic Relief Services had set up a refugee camp outside of Miami for children and adolescents who left without their parents, until they could be more permanently placed in foster*

homes.[9] *Nuns from a girls' school in Havana and a married couple chaperoned and took care of the refugees. However, very little was known about
the details of the place on the other side of the Straits of Florida, since
inquiries could only be made indirectly.*

*It is only now that I am a mother that I can even begin to understand how
difficult this decision must have been for my parents, especially knowing so
little about the hands in which they were going to place us, having nothing
but faith to turn to, and knowing that they might never see us again.*

*It was partly an adventure, freedom from a situation that was becoming
unbearable, not because of the scarcity of food—this wasn't yet a problem—but because of the repression, the constant subtle and not so subtle
"brainwashing" in the media, the feeling that walls had ears. I worried
that something I might write on a test in school might land my family or me
in prison. I never doubted that our exile would be for a limited time, the
regime could not last.*[10]

Elena continues to describe their departure.

My parents had obtained visas from the Jamaican embassy. In case the
plane tickets to the U.S. didn't come through, Jamaica would be a way
station to come into the States. At the last minute we received a waiver
from the U.S. government, so we could enter.[11] The word that we had
the plane tickets didn't come until three days before we left. When the
news came that we were cleared to go, it was just a matter of packing the
suitcases. My mother gave us last-minute instructions—the usual things
mothers tell their daughters—"If strange men come up to you, don't
talk to them; don't let them touch you."

*Beatriz added this in her "Memoirs": "One of the last things my mother
said to us was that I would have to look after my sisters, be like a mother to
them, and that they were to obey me. I took it very seriously."*[12]

Elena continues.

We had been so busy with these preparations that when it was time
to go, it was a shock. I remember thinking, "It's finally happening." I
didn't want to think about it. I wanted it to be a perfectly normal trip like
the ones I'd made before.

*Elena was four and a half years old the first time she visited the United
States. She and Beatriz took a summer trip to Miami Beach, staying at the
Vanderbilt Hotel with their grandparents and aunts. When she was six, the*

1. Mr. de la Maza and his daughters on a family vacation at the Vanderbilt Hotel in Miami Beach, 1953. *Left to right:* Silvia, Cecilia (in water), Elena on her father's shoulders, and Beatriz.

whole family came for a vacation. For Elena, the highlight of both trips was getting on the airplane and flying.

Elena tells me that on the day in 1961 that the three sisters left Cuba, contrary to what her parents thought, the flight did not leave immediately. She and her sisters waited for several hours.

We entertained each other. We played childish games. We sang songs. The room was full of kids and a few chaperones. We talked to a lot of the other kids to see which schools they had gone to and if we had any friends in common. It turned out that we didn't. We waited for what seemed to me a long time, although Beatriz has reminded me that it was only two hours. The delay was probably because of problems with other people who were trying to get out.

Beatriz remembers that when we boarded the plane a button saying "National Catholic Relief Services" was pinned on each of us, so we would be identified when we arrived.[13]

After we boarded the plane, the captain announced, "We are a little overloaded. Our capacity is 114, and we are carrying 120 people."

Elena says that apparently a few people, passing as escorts for the chil-dren, had sneaked in without legal papers. When the children were called to check in, the child's name and "companion" would be called. Finally, Elena says, their plane took off.

The minute we hit the air everyone cheered.

I quickly interject the obvious question: When you were in the air did it seem like the sweep of history or did it seem like a separation?

It was a mixture of both. Everyone needed to release the tension. Be-fore boarding the plane, everyone including myself wondered if we would be turned back and not allowed to leave because they caught someone trying to sneak out. It was a day none of us on that plane would ever forget.

Beatriz wrote this rather poetic observation: "As I looked back, thick and ominous dark clouds had gathered in the horizon. Until then, I had never doubted that our exile would be short, that the regime wouldn't last. But at that moment, with the gathering storm behind, in the distance, I was sud-denly overcome with a strange feeling that this was going to be for much longer. Somehow, the impending storm was about to wash away the bridge to my past, that, perhaps, I would never see my country again."[14]

The flight was uneventful; it took about one hour to fly to Miami. It was a calm night. When we landed, we were met by a nun and the Prunas, the people who helped run the camp that was part of the airlift. They helped us through customs.

From the airport we were taken to an old hospital building that had been donated to the Catholic Relief Services as a way station. This camp was in a rural section southwest of Miami called Kendall, which has since become a well-to-do suburb.[15] We three were put in a little room away from the rest of the children in the camp. It was 11 P.M., but it seemed much later to me.

We had never spent even one night away from home. Sleepovers weren't done in our family. We had friends who had wonderful ranches and farms out in the interior of Cuba, and every Christmas or Easter vacation they would invite us to come and stay. My mother would say, "Oh, I don't want you girls to sleep away from home."[16]

The first day at Kendall, they let us sleep late. When we woke up, all these girls were coming in and checking us out, asking, "Where is your family from?" Most were around my age, but there were some that were as young as seven years old and some as old as seventeen.

They began to tell us what the camp rules were and what the schedule was. School was held in the morning. This mostly consisted of reading the Bible in English. After lunch we would be assigned bunks in a long room with two rows of bunk beds. There was a foyer, which was kind of like a playroom. On either side were the two large bunkrooms, boys in one and girls in the other. Each had a communal bathroom. A priest was in charge of the boys and a nun in charge of the girls. The total was probably seventy-five girls and seventy-five boys. There was just one building, with a little outbuilding in the back for washing clothes that was called the "Clubhouse." On the other side of the road were a convent and a chapel. The youngest children stayed here at night with the nuns. There were three nuns who slept in the barracks with us.

Everybody there had chores to do. We were assigned different duties on a rotating basis—serving in the dining hall, mopping, washing dishes, that kind of thing. We had to make our beds every morning. Our bunk beds were tiny; the mattresses, I think, were only two inches thick, and they sagged.

Getting to sleep was hard. They enforced incredible hours—lights-out was at 9 P.M., and we got up at 6 A.M. Since we hadn't been in school for three months, we had gotten used to the good life of staying up late and sleeping late. The first few days were the roughest.

This was the first time we had ever had to take care of washing and ironing our clothes. There was a rite of initiation connected to this: everybody knew you would ruin the first piece you tried to iron, that you would scorch it. It happened to me; I scorched a white blouse.

Many of us attended the daily service in the chapel. It was a place to go, a quiet time, and it tied us to home. Aside from prayers and the Bible reading, we were pretty much on our own; we had to entertain ourselves. My sisters and I had learned to sing harmony in Cuba, and our singing talents came in very handy. One girl in the camp had a guitar, and we would sit around and sing and talk about things at home.

There were rumors flying constantly, especially about the invasion. All Cubans thought the Americans would invade Cuba. Even before we left, our mother would drill us about what to do if we were gassed, if we were caught in the middle of the street: "Get down on the ground and don't get up." Someone in the camp had a short-wave radio—as did people in Cuba. So the rumors would start: "Castro is dead," or "the invasion has started."[17]

Elena mentions that they met the boys in the community room, but that a lot of the girls were shy. This topic leads Elena to a discussion of her social experiences in Cuba.

At thirteen, I had just become interested in boys. We had attended a girls' elementary school, so during that time we had been totally segregated from boys. Ruston was co-ed, which was a change for us. This was part of the reason everyone was dying to go there. Ruston introduced us to a number of American customs. Every week there would be some activity—a mixer, a dance, or a movie. I remember seeing *Viva Zapata* at one of these.[18]

The dancing was important. Cubans love to dance. We already had a small group of girlfriends who would have dances at each other's houses. These were co-ed parties, well chaperoned by at least three mothers. This was typical for girls at that age.

So at Kendall suddenly you were in this situation where there weren't the three mothers, and you became shy because you didn't have the structure?

Part of it was that. I remember one of our parties in Cuba, the boy I invited was almost the "boy next door"; his house was a block away. My mother had gotten to know this family when I was in a stroller, when she took Beatriz and me on jaunts. This family had five boys. I can still remember when my sister Cecilia was born, and I was three and a half or four. We had wanted to have a baby brother, and this other family had wanted to have a baby girl. Their new baby had turned out to be another boy. When our families visited each other for the first time, we went up to Mom and said, "Hey, can we trade?" The mothers thought this was a riot, but we were quite serious.

Elena brings out some writing she has done recently after looking through some of the hundreds of family photographs taken in Cuba and the United States. In the section on Kendall, she writes of a special new discovery made there.

When I was about seven or eight, I heard my father say to my mother that he had seen *neblina* that morning on his drive out by airport at *Rancho Boyeros*. I'd never heard the word before. I asked him what *neblina* was, and he attempted to describe mist or fog for us. It was a pretty rare thing in our part of Cuba. It sounded as mysterious and romantic as what it was supposed to describe. For several mornings after that I looked carefully upon awakening, hoping that it would appear in our yard. It didn't, and I forgot all about it.

One morning shortly after our arrival at the Kendall camp, I awoke to see the world had completely vanished—the pine trees, the road, the building with the chapel, gone. Everything outside was a soft, grayish white. I rubbed my eyes, thinking I must still be dreaming, but it was real. We got dressed and started walking across the road to attend Mass at the chapel. As I walked, gradually the road emerged, then the trees and the building. Finally it dawned on me—this must be the fabled *neblina*. The fog was as thick as the inside of a cloud. By the time Mass ended, and we went back for breakfast, the fog began lifting, and the world resumed its normal outlines.[19]

Elena continues talking about her new life at Kendall.

Some of the older girls were a little rambunctious. After lights were out, there was one who would put a towel over her head, and in silhouette she would look like a nun. In her sternest voice, she would say, "I'm going to turn you all in" and scare the life out of us. But there weren't any real discipline problems. Most of us wanted to be good kids because we were so scared. When the younger girls would cry, the older ones would try to comfort them.

Elena and her sisters remained at the camp for two weeks.

It seemed longer. I was getting tired of the whole camp routine. I wanted to get on with my life. This was like being on hold forever.

She explains how they were able to leave the camp once they had been placed with families.

The word had gone out among the Catholic dioceses that there was a great need for families to take the children from the airlifts.[20] Catholic Welfare investigated the families to see if they had enough income to provide decent housing, decent meals, clothing, and medical care. Families volunteered to be foster parents.

Once a day there would be a community meeting with the nuns. There would be assignments available with different families in different places. They wanted to keep the group circulating so more could come in. The nuns would go through a list and say, "We have room for two in Arlington, Virginia. Would any of you like to go?" We were given some choice, but for those of us with siblings, our primary consideration was that we not end up in different cities with different families.

The first place for three was with a family in Oregon. Beatriz and I thought about it for a while; then the nun said we would go to the same city but not to the same family. We thought it was too far away, maybe too cold, and we wanted to stay together. They could not force you to leave if you didn't want to.

One evening when the nun read the assignment list, there was a place for three in Albuquerque.[21] My sisters weren't around. I said, "Would you put us down for that?" I had no idea where Albuquerque was. When they told me it was New Mexico, I thought, "There must be some Spanish-speaking people there." I really had only a vague idea geographically where it was. Then I went and found my sisters and told them about it. In later years Beatriz would throw it in my face: "You went ahead and signed us up without consulting me. I was supposed to be the mother!" I told her I did it because I was afraid someone else would take it.

In a day or two it was set. Catholic Charities bought the tickets. At 9:30 or 10:00 P.M. we boarded the plane to Chicago and got to Albuquerque the next morning. Our flight was fourteen hours. Along with me and my sisters was a brother and sister who had been at the camp. It was not the best flight. We hit a really bad storm over Cincinnati. I was sitting next to the brother, and we saw one of the plane's engines flaming out. I asked the stewardess if we'd lost an engine.

She said, "Yes, but we have three more."

In addition to this scare, Silvia was getting horribly airsick. We couldn't figure out what was wrong. We'd never seen motion sickness before. We thought at one point that something was seriously wrong with her.

When we got to Chicago, it was bitter cold. It was one in the morning. It was the coldest place we'd ever been. Beatriz and I wondered if we would see any gangsters. The only thing we knew about Chicago was from the movies: Al Capone had lived there. Anytime we saw anyone in a trench coat, we would say, "Could that be one?"

Elena has made coffee. We are sitting in her formal living room. She points to the furniture and says that this is the "Borkland legacy." She is referring to her husband Herb's family. I smile to cover my ignorance. When I had said I would like the interviews to take place here instead of in the more modern and informal family room, I had thought this furniture was from Cuba, forgetting that Elena had told me earlier that her sisters and her parents had left with only one or two suitcases of clothes.

When I ask Elena to say more about the furniture, she tells me it was her mother-in-law's special pride. On each side of the Chippendale couch are two mahogany end tables with antique lamps. To the right of the couch, two chairs frame a larger mahogany table. Elena says these are the "grandfather" and "grandmother" chairs, sitting chairs from the Victorian era. On the wall opposite the grandparent chairs is a spinet piano that Elena's father bought when she was in high school. To the left of the piano beside the entranceway to the dining room is an armchair covered in a subdued gold brocade. Above the chair on the wall is a distinctive silk-screen print of a man in front of an enlarged piece of music. On my first visit, I commented on this print and noticed that it was signed to Elena and her family.

This is my mother's cousin, Alejandro García Caturla. He was a composer who now, years later, is very well thought of as one of the pioneers of avant-garde music. We'll talk about him later.

When we got to Albuquerque, it was very clear. I had never seen mountains with snow on the top. As the plane flew over the mountains, I thought to myself, "What an interesting place." I was going to be able to touch snow, something I'd only heard about in Cuba. The closest we had ever gotten to snow or even to *escarcha* (frost) was what formed on the outside of the freezer compartment of the Frigidaire. I had loved scraping it off and eating it on hot days.

When the Maza sisters came to Albuquerque, it had a population of close to two hundred thousand. It is slightly more than two hundred miles from the Mexican town of Juárez. In the fifties and sixties, Albuquerque was the place where the famous and well-used Route 66 crossed U.S. 85, which ran from Mexico to Denver. The Rio Grande River runs through Albuquerque, separating it into east and west sections with the business district in the east and suburbs across the river in the western part. In the early sixties, its downtown was comprised of ten blocks of mostly low-rise buildings. An aerial view of the town taken in 1953 shows five or six high-rise buildings scattered among gridded streets. The Old Town was founded in 1705. The San Felipe Church, with records dating back to 1706, is still located on the plaza around which the rest of the city was built. North of the city are ruins of the Indian pueblos of Kuaua and Puarai that date to the sixteenth century. Farther north are the Sandia Mountains, which rise to more than ten thousand feet. Ski slopes and summer and winter trails were already in place when the Mazas moved to the area. The Newcomer Book: A Photographic Guide Book to Albuquerque for the New Resident of 1953 *boasts of the many schools, churches, and medical facilities in the area, as well as the new airport.*[22] *Elena says there were many military people in the area due to the proximity of the Kirtland Air Force Base.*

We were met at the airport by Helen and her husband; Helen was with the Catholic Charities organization. After we got our bags and sat down together on a bench, Helen gave us the bad news: "Sorry, there's been a miscommunication; the Garcías don't have enough income to properly care for three. What we've decided is that two of you can stay with the Garcías, and then the other one can come with me and stay with my family."

My first thought was, "Who's it going to be?" I realized we couldn't leave Silvia by herself because she was so little. I had been more independent so I said, "I'll go with Helen's family." It was hard for me to make the decision, but I felt like I needed to make the sacrifice. Beatriz had come down hard on me for making the decision to go to Albuquerque without consulting her. Of course, Beatriz and I had always gotten along well, but she loved to tease me. This teasing was hard for me to take. Sometimes I would get really angry, but at other times I would only pretend I was angry, so the teasing wouldn't continue. We had good sibling rivalry. Beatriz was always such an outstanding student, and I knew I could never compete with her grade-wise.

You had initiated the trip to Albuquerque. Choosing to leave your sisters and go with Helen must have been a hard decision.

Part of it was that, having done something Beatriz disapproved of, I needed to make up for it. But also I thought Beatriz was more temperamentally suited to reassure Silvia. In our family we fell into a certain pattern: Beatriz and Silvia sided with each other; they were natural allies. That they should remain together was totally fixed in my mind.

We drove first to the Garcías, where Beatriz and Silvia would be staying. Mr. García was a World War II veteran. He was retired from the military and worked as a postman. The Garcías were dear, dear people; they were grandparents in their sixties with one son who lived in Denver. They were of Mexican descent and knew a little Spanish. The Garcías had a small house in a slightly older section of town. Beatriz and Silvia shared a room with bunk beds.

The section that Helen's family lived in was the northeast part of the city. It was a typical suburb that seemed to me almost like a *Gidget* movie.[23] That was one of the things that made it seem sort of odd and comforting in a way to me, because I had seen that movie. At first it was really kind of fun. Helen and her husband were much younger than my parents, and they had four children—two boys and two girls—so there was a correspondence to my family. The youngest was six or seven. They even had one daughter who was almost the same age as me.

Helen's husband, John, was nice; he worked for the telephone company. They had a lovely home. Helen had a white car—a Chevrolet or a Ford with a red interior. They had a telephone in every room; they actually even had a telephone in the bathroom. I thought this was super neat.

Because of the bilingual schools I had gone to in Cuba, my English was fine. That first night I was the center of everybody's attention. When we sat down to dinner, everyone was full of questions. They wanted to know everything about Cuba. Their picture was that all Cubans had big sugar plantations, that we sat around these big verandahs with the men smoking cigars and waiting for the servants to do everything.

That first dinner conversation included other questions that seemed preposterous to Elena. The children asked if there was electricity in Cuba or if there were any schools there.

I commented that Elena probably knew more about the United States than Helen's family knew about Cuba. After beginning my interviews with Elena, I realized my own ignorance about Cuba. Elena lent me Hugh Thomas's Cuba, the Pursuit of Freedom.[24] *I was amazed at how seldom Cuba had been mentioned in the history courses I had taken in college, especially since there had been extensive lobbying in the United States and Cuba for it to become a state.*[25]

At Helen's everyone was on their own for making breakfast on Saturday morning. They assumed I knew how to prepare food, but I hadn't the slightest idea how to fix anything in the kitchen. My grandmother had never wanted us to go into the kitchen; my mother had fixed everything for us. When I found everybody making their own breakfast at Helen's, I said, "I'm going to skip breakfast." I was too embarrassed to say I didn't know how to fix anything.

I was very self-conscious about my weight. I was 5', 2" inches and weighed 130 to 140 pounds. You can see from the photos that I've shown you that I was chubby. I'd noticed already that all the American girls were much slimmer. I wanted to lose weight; I felt very fat. Janet, the daughter close to my age, was as slender as a rail. So that Saturday I began my diet!

On her first weekend with this American family, Elena saw ice and snow.

We drove up to the Sandia Mountains for an outing. I wore a pair of lined black-and-white-checked wool pants that Mom had made for me, but I had no boots, so I wore saddle-type shoes and borrowed gloves. In mid-April the snow was no longer a pristine fluffy white but had the hard ice crust of much melting and refreezing and was still a couple of feet deep.

The kids in the family showed me how to slide down a steep slope on my fanny. We even found an old tire and took turns sliding down on that for a couple of hours until the melting snow refreezing on my fanny, thighs, and knit gloves finally made me so cold I couldn't stand it any more. My feet had long since gone numb. We drove back for a hot lunch.

On the first weekend Elena was in the United States, the anticipated invasion of Cuba began. This invasion is named after the landing site of the invasion: Bahia de Cochinos, *the Bay of Pigs. The invasion was led by trained Cuban exiles. The initial landing was disorganized due to miscalculations and equipment failures. Using his intelligence network, Castro knew in advance where the landing was going to take place and had soldiers in the area. When the invasion forces were attacked, one ship sank and one was blown up. The remaining ships withdrew, and the exile forces were further thwarted by never receiving the expected ammunitions and supplies. Promised air support never materialized. Castro had one hundred thousand people arrested, including all the bishops, journalists, CIA agents, as well as any-*

one suspected of being a counterrevolutionary sympathizer. The Cuban government's reaction to the invasion was so devastating that Hugh Thomas writes that after this, it was unlikely there could ever be an internal rising against Castro.[26]

Thomas has represented the conventional understanding of what happened during the invasion. In Bay of Pigs: An Oral History of Brigade 2506, Victor Triay has a slightly different and more expanded view on this invasion. His day by day account provides a detailed history of the invasion interspersed with interviews of surviving members of the Brigade, a highly trained and highly motivated group that came from an ethnic and economic cross section of Cuban exiles, dedicated to overthrowing Castro—not the rag-tag, undertrained group of zealots sometimes portrayed in descriptions of this group. This is a brief and condensed summary of what Triay covers in 183 pages. The exiles in Brigade 2506 had a detailed plan worked out. After a surprise attack on Castro's small air force by the Brigade's B-26s, the exiles' planes would land at Trinidad, which had easily accessible beaches; nearby Casilda had a deep water port, ideal for the land invasion and necessary naval support. Their plan was vetoed by President Kennedy as "too spectacular." He was extremely concerned about provoking the Soviets. After asking for an alternative landing site, the president approved a night landing only in the area around the Bay of Pigs, a site that proved to be unsuitable, if not impossible. Some military planners considered this the first "fatal error made by President Kennedy." Castro, through his network of spies, knew in advance that the attack was going to take place but did not know where or when. The first air strikes by the Brigade's B-26s were canceled by Kennedy; subsequent miscues and accidents during the hazardous night landing alerted the local authorities that the invasion had started, and the landing site was communicated to Castro soon after it began. By daybreak Castro was able to launch an air attack, the exact reverse of what the exiles had planned. Castro was correctly concerned that if the Brigade landed and successfully established themselves, if only in a small area, they could be recognized as a provisional counterrevolutionary and democratic government by the international community. Therefore, the early attacks by Castro's air force and army were critical in the first days. The attacks made it impossible for supplies to be unloaded. The Brigade was ultimately "left defending a beachhead with a day's supply of ammunition, no naval support (the ships had withdrawn to international waters after the air attack started) and virtually no air cover," *all of which had been promised and all of which was withheld, on President Kennedy's orders. Due to the air attacks, the landing craft could not be used to ferry supplies from the ships to the land; the supplies were finally air dropped, a futile effort to compensate for the U.S. government's aborting of the exiles' original plan. Most of the supplies went into the swamp and the sea. In spite of these dire circumstances, the Brigade, at a ratio of 370 to 2,000 Castro forces, fought valiantly. President Kennedy did not want the United States directly involved any more than it had been. Reluctantly he agreed that the Brigade's B-26s, flown by one exile and three members of the Alabama National Guard who had trained the Brigade, plus American fighter jets could provide relief for the stranded Brigade for one hour. As the jets unfortunately arrived after the B-26s, two of the three B-26s, with no air cover, were shot down and their crews killed. For days the Brigade was pursued by Castro's army, and the U.S. jets available then were denied permission to "even fire over the heads of the Castro forces pursuing Brigade members who were seeking rescue."*[27]

All of a sudden all the world's attention was focused on Cuba. The first thing that happened was that all communications stopped between the United States and Cuba. For about a month I didn't know anything about my family, and they didn't know where we were either. The news that I was hearing terrified me. My dad could have been arrested. Many people were arrested who'd done nothing but were just suspected of sympathizing. I had no idea what was happening. You could not call by phone, or send or receive letters. That's when the enormity of it all began to sink in, because I was really cut off.

I found that Graciela, a good friend from Cuba who had been part of the airlifts, had ended up in El Paso, so we started writing each other. For that one month that we were *incommunicado* with our families, we wrote each other.

The only other people I could talk to about this were my sisters. We called each other up and asked over and over again: "What do you suppose is going on? Do you think Mother and Dad are O.K.?" It was a matter of waiting patiently. I hoped that because my parents were quiet, middle-aged people, they wouldn't be in too much danger.

I tried to find a gentle way to ask Elena if she ever considered the possibility that she might not see her parents again. When she answered, she didn't flinch.

Very definitely. At that point I thought, "Maybe, this is it; maybe it will just be the three of us. And we'll never see our parents or sister again." That was very, very scary.

This first interview I had with Elena was on January 1, 1996. She had showed me family photographs, talked about her early life in Cuba, and finished with a tour and commentary about her paintings in the formal living room and dining room. I had put away the tape recorder and was reaching for my coat when Elena came up close and looked directly at me.

Leaving Cuba was the best thing that ever happened to me.

My eyebrows raised. I knew we had to talk about this, but it was already late in the afternoon. When Elena had agreed to be interviewed for an article and possibly a book, I had promised her that the interviews would be done to fit her schedule and that none would be longer than two hours. I put my hand on her arm. Next time. I promise we'll start there. You won't forget?

Elena was completely serious.

I'll never forget.

Our next interview began with this.

Coming to the U.S. and immediately facing such a crisis changed me in ways I could never have anticipated. I was a very spoiled kid in Cuba. I had what my family called a "strong temperament"; I was high-strung. I used to have tremendous arguments with my dad because he would try to get me to engage in civilized behavior at the table. I would talk back to him in every possible way. I got outrageously out of line. But my parents put up with this because I was their child.

So the big change for me was finding myself with a family that wasn't my own and realizing, "Oh, they're not going to put up with this from me. I can't do this anymore." With Helen's family I knew I had to be on my best behavior at all times, or they might even throw me out. Right away I knew I had to keep a grip on my own emotions. I became a more disciplined person in terms of not indulging in the sort of displays of temper that I had come to think of as not only natural but as my right. It taught me to be more accepting and cooperative in general.

It is difficult for me to think of Elena as being self-centered and high-strung. She is energetic and spirited, but she is giving and cooperative. We first met when we photographed the art in a show sponsored by the Washington chapter of the Women's Caucus for Art. We did the photography in

Elena's tai chi studio in the basement of her house. To do this, we had to figure how to block off the daylight from the large sliding doors in a way that could be easily repeated over several sessions, to set up and balance photo floods, and to check exposures before any of the photography could begin. Elena was shooting filtered color slide film, and I was shooting black-and-white. Because of the difference in the films, each camera required a different exposure. We were confined to the two morning hours I had free once or twice a week. Doing this project right required careful joint planning and patience. It was a situation where self-centeredness and emotional extremes would have thwarted our completing the project. Elena was a perfect partner in co-operation and good humor.

Elena talks more about her life with Helen's family.

They had their family routine, and they integrated me in it. Everyone was expected to do chores. I shared a room with Janet, their daughter close to my age.

It was now the first week in April, and I had to get back to school. My sisters and I hadn't been in school since Christmas break. I was enrolled at the parochial school near where Helen lived; Beatriz and Silvia went to the one close to the Garcías. I finished the eighth grade there and went through the graduation ceremony just like the American girls. We got all dressed up. I had a pair of incredibly high stiletto heels that I had inherited from a cousin of mine in Cuba who was a little bit older. That pair of shoes was one of my treasures, and I insisted on wearing them to this graduation. As the shoes were actually a little small, my feet almost died.

I started my menstrual period probably a month before leaving Cuba. Janet started her period the summer after I came to live with them. When Helen and I were going somewhere in the car—just the two of us—she said to me, "Oh, my baby has become a woman." She told me about Janet getting her period. Janet was too self-conscious to tell me.

After the beginning of their menstrual periods, were girls considered "women?"

Yes, that's the way we identified this rite of passage. We were considered late in our family—Beatriz was fourteen, I was thirteen and a half. Many of the girls started early—in the sixth grade. I remember a friend, Carmen, saying to me when I went to her house, "My cousin just became a woman." She was only nine.

So I was a woman! Helen would look at me and say, "Oh, you are already so developed." I did have breasts and was already transformed into a woman with a full figure.

I had brought a bathing suit from Cuba, and that suit, probably made of cheap material, disintegrated within a month of constant use in the neighborhood pool. I was too embarrassed to ask Helen to buy me a new bathing suit. She saw I needed one and gave me one of hers. I remember going with Janet that summer to buy a bathing suit. She must have tried on a hundred.

Elena pauses and looks beyond the sheer curtains, out the living room window.

I'm just remembering something I lost at the pool. Beatriz and I had initial rings that our grandparents had given us. Mine had two initials— EM. They had given them to us on our twelfth birthdays, a sort of coming-of-age present. Maybe it was a family tradition. My mother says that her father gave her a ring that had been a family heirloom when she was around that age. Ours were made up especially for us. When I was at the pool in Albuquerque, that ring was stolen and was never found. I felt really bad at losing it. I had brought so little from Cuba. Besides the clothes, there was only that ring and a pair of earrings. Later the earrings were lost when my sister cut my hair. We were outside; the earrings got caught in the hair that fell to the ground. We searched for days afterward but never found them.

You know the strangest thing; I didn't have a photograph of my parents or of our house in Cuba. That had been a blind spot. My mother's concern was that we have enough clothes, especially warm winter clothes because we might be in a really cold climate; we each could bring only two big suitcases.

I was becoming Americanized. I was in a big hurry to be as much a part of this new country as possible. At first my relationship with Janet was OK. I tried to pal around as much as possible with her girlfriends. I went with her to a lot of slumber parties, and we did the typical outrageous things. We always had to have the water balloon fight. We talked about everything we knew about sex and boys. It was sort of exciting to me. Some of the things that the girls chose to talk about did strike me as a little off-color, distasteful; but on the other hand, I wanted to be accepted as part of the group.

I was so used to being in a tight-knit family, and I thought that this was what Janet would want me to do. But this was exactly what she didn't want me to do. Our friendship started coming apart over the summer. I guess she felt I was encroaching on her territory.

By the time the next school year started, without consulting me or saying anything, Janet told her mom she wanted me out of her room. The next thing I knew, all my things were being moved into the room of her nine-year-old sister Cathy. Janet would ostracize me, not talk to me, even in school; she wouldn't walk with me to school. I had to walk to school with the little kids.

Elena says she was going through a lot of changes. Most notable was that she was not able to see the blackboard in school. She had become nearsighted. Helen took her for a medical examination, and she got glasses.

I felt so strange having these chunky old glasses, but I couldn't see without them. When I was examined for the glasses, I got a complete medical examination. A funny thing happened. I totally misunderstood that they wanted a urine sample; I thought they wanted a stool sample. They did this in Cuba routinely to check for parasites. I went into the bathroom and I struggled to produce it. Then I put it through the little window. Helen explained, and we all laughed.

There was another little Cuban girl who got a medical examination at the same time; part of this was a genital exam. They probably just wanted to make sure she was developing normally, but when they asked this girl to open her legs, she was outraged. She complained to me for days, asking, "Did they do that to you?" I tried to reassure her by saying, "No, but I'm already a woman."

Most of us were made aware that ladies always sat with their legs closed. You didn't want to make a display of yourself. I'm sure that along with all the other advice they gave daughters before they left Cuba, many mothers said, "Just keep your legs closed."

Elena says that she was trying to act as American as possible, and that at some level she succeeded. In spite of feeling self-conscious about the glasses, she was elected "Most Friendly in the Freshman Class." I ask her, if, even with this honor—the kind so important in high school—she experienced any prejudice because she was Cuban.

No, I didn't feel that way. Great curiosity—I was like the new toy, the new novelty on the block. When we got to Albuquerque, there was one other Cuban exile girl, Maria Elena. She was the first Cuban in the school. She wasn't developed yet; she was very small, so she looked young. I'm sure the kids must have driven her crazy asking questions. Some of the questions were insensitive—like about electricity—and seemed to imply we were backward. You had to stand up for yourself. Maria Elena had a feisty temper, and she was a fighter, too. That was good, because otherwise I don't think she could have survived.

We were the second group that came to Albuquerque. Then more and more kids came. Some of these I encountered in the high school. All the Cuban girls would look to me because I was one of the first, asking, "How do I deal with this? What do I do?" Some of them did not speak English very well.

At the end of the summer Elena's mother was finally able to leave.

My mother left Cuba in August 1961 with Cecilia, my youngest sister. When she got to Miami, she couldn't, of course, be adopted by an American family. She spent about three months in Miami. My mother left Cuba with almost nothing. She did what all the Cubans who left did. They went to the Catholic Charities organization and were given so much to live on per month. Because my mother had my sister with her, she was getting one hundred dollars per month. They had to pay for all their expenses out of that. She found a cheap hotel room. The problem was they couldn't cook there, so they had to buy their meals elsewhere. She put Cecilia in the parochial school in the area, where she got a free breakfast and lunch. My mother had budgeted exactly one dollar for the evening meal. She would go to Walgreen's and get the one-dollar blue-plate special; she would let Cecilia eat most of it since she was the child. My mother was never a thin woman; by the time she came to Albuquerque, she was the thinnest I'd ever seen her. She was literally starving.

She went every day to an agency to see if there were any jobs, but she never found one.

In Albuquerque, Beatriz and Silvia were going to Saint Vincent's, a girls' school. In November, one of the teachers in the high school at Saint Vincent's became ill; a position opened for a teacher. Beatriz, whom Elena describes as an A student, very responsible and respected, thought, "My mother is a teacher. Here's a job for her."

We were corresponding with my mother, of course, and knew where she was and that she was looking for a job. Beatriz talked to the headmistress of the school and told her that our mother was a wonderful teacher, desperate for a job, and that if they would guarantee her a job, then maybe someone would get her a plane ticket so she could come. The headmistress agreed and said Catholic Charities could probably buy the two plane tickets for my mother and sister. Soon the whole thing was arranged.

Although Elena knew that her mother would be coming to Albuquerque soon, she still experienced intense anguish at all the changes she'd been through in the nine months since coming to the States.

My mother came at the end of November. I went through a terrible time right before that. When Helen's family celebrated Thanksgiving, I was so depressed that I spent the entire day crying. I did nothing but go in the corner and cry. When they asked me what was wrong, I had so many emotions that I had no vocabulary to describe my feelings. The best I could do was say, "I'm so homesick."

Besides missing my parents and my life in Cuba, there were other things taking a toll on me. I was doing a lot of the comforting and advice giving for the other Cuban exiles in Albuquerque, but I was also making mistakes. Some kids had been calling me with prank phone calls. When I got another phone call that I thought was from them, I told them off with some nasty things. Later Helen told me: "The person you told off is one of the ladies that works with me at Catholic Welfare. She was the one who helped place you." She made me call and apologize. I was embarrassed to death.

I ask how Beatriz and Silvia were doing at this point.

They didn't seem to be having the same problems. I guess because the two of them were together and they didn't have any other siblings to compete with. There were four children in Helen's family. To make matters even more complicated, within about two or three months of my arrival, a large family of kids from Camagüey, a city in eastern Cuba, came to Albuquerque. Helen had to struggle to place all seven of them. They couldn't go to one family. The older girl went to a couple who lived in the center of the city in an older home. That girl used to call me constantly, complaining how unhappy she was. I was sort of the intermediary between her and Helen. She knew that Helen was in charge. Helen had a really hard time placing the two youngest girls. She brought them into her house too. All of a sudden there were seven kids.

Last March 29, 1996, Beatriz, Silvia, and I went out to celebrate the thirty-fifth anniversary of our arrival. We got to talking about things. My sisters were surprised to hear me say that I'd chosen to go alone to the Helen's house because I'd felt the need to make a sacrifice, to make up for signing all of us up to go to Albuquerque. In all these years, it had never occurred to them. They'd thought that I'd been more interested in this family for the economic advantages and because the parents were younger and attractive.

In fact, Silvia told me that Mrs. García, the poor dear, thought that I'd chosen Helen because she was young and pretty and Mrs. García was an "old lady." I guess I never really told my sisters much of what was going on there. When Helen asked if I would like to go live with the Garcías after the other two Cuban girls arrived, I was so upset that I cried. Not that I was that anxious to stay with Helen's family, but I just couldn't handle one more resettlement at that point. I told them that I had gotten used to them and didn't want to leave.

After our first interview, I kept wondering if Elena had any kind of truly personal and private things that helped hold her life together during these nine difficult months. I noted this question in the transcription of the first interview with the word Privacy, *planning that this would be where we would begin when I met with Elena in two weeks.*

In spite of all the difficulties she has experienced in her life, Elena is a very positive, even radiant person. She has an enthusiasm for anything she does, including talking about her life. When I returned, I hardly had my coat off and the tape recorder set up when Elena began talking.

I almost called you up the day after the last interview to say that there was one important detail I totally neglected to mention—that was the piano and music. While I stayed at the Helen's, that's really the one thing that sustained me.

How typical it is and maybe even necessary that we temporarily forget the sustaining things and focus on the things that almost undo us. Perhaps it's part of our reflective self-preservation to be most aware of what hurts.

The piano was very, very important to me, and it sustained me because it was the only way I could express my emotions acceptably at that age. I didn't have the vocabulary to express what I felt, but obviously I felt a tumult of emotions. Being an adolescent is bad enough, but I had no way to sort through all the things that I was undergoing. And suddenly here was a piano. No one knew I had been taking piano lessons since I was four. It was serendipitous. Janet had been taking lessons to learn popular jazz.

Among the few things I had brought with me when leaving Cuba was Chopin's *Etudes*. I had just developed a great passion for Chopin. During the last three years that we were in Cuba, we had developed a very strong friendship with two other young girls who took piano lessons from the same teacher: Graciela, the one who came to El Paso, and Vivian, who was sort of Beatriz's bosom buddy. Graciela was pretty good at the piano. I loved to compete with her. She would stimulate me, so that when she practiced, I said, "Oh, I've got to practice to keep up with her."

Vivian had begun to learn this beautiful Chopin etude, which I thought was wonderful. My mother had bought me the whole book of the Chopin *Etudes*. This was the other personal thing that I had brought with me besides the ring, the earrings, and the stiletto-heeled shoes. When I was at Helen's and had nothing else to do, it was not unusual for me to spend hours playing. That's what kept me sane—being able to play the *Etudes*. That provided the emotional solace that I didn't have anywhere else. It did wonders for my piano playing, because all of a sudden I was sitting there practicing for two or three hours at a time and four hours on Saturday. I just got a whole lot better.

I ask how Janet handled the fact that Elena came into her house with a skill more developed than hers.

It was another source of friction but one that wasn't expressed. She admired my playing. What she was working on was completely different. I actually sat around in the background pretending to read a book when the teacher came just to see how they taught here. Janet tried to teach me how to do a bass walk. My left hand was much weaker; I didn't do very well. I didn't try to learn any of the pieces she was playing and to compete with her. She really didn't have much of an interest; it was just something her parents wanted her to learn. For me, the piano really was my private solace.

Helen's family admired my playing, so I got that reinforcement. I think at that point I was so desperate emotionally that it didn't matter whether everyone thought I stunk or what; I had to play. It was my thing, and it was also a tie back to home.

I used to wonder why I concentrated on Chopin.[28] He was a very feminine kind of guy. The mazurkas and the polonaises had been his tribute to his homeland. Years later it occurred to me that there was a tie —he was in exile and here I was in exile. Maybe we had felt some of the same emotions.[29]

De La Maza and Caturla Family Histories in Cuba

There was no legacy of antique furniture; there were no "grandfather" and "grandmother" chairs for Elena. There were two sisters across town in Albuquerque; a ring and a pair of earrings, both lost; a pair of too-small, hand-me-down high-heel shoes; and a copy of Chopin's Etudes. *The remembered details that Elena shares express her connection to the hundred-plus years of the lives of her sisters, parents, cousins, aunts, uncles, grandparents, great-grandparents in Cuba. The wealth of Elena's heritage is in her memory.*

Elena lent me a translation of an article about her paternal grandfather that Carlos Márquez Sterling wrote in 1984 for Diario Las Americas, *the main Spanish newspaper in Miami.*[1] *The following summary of Maza y Artola's political life is based on this article.*

Juan José de la Maza y Artola was born in Havana in 1867. He graduated in law from the University of Havana. While in Paris on a post-graduation tour of the Europe, he was approached to fight in what Cubans call the War of Independence and what Americans call the Spanish-American War. Spain was defeated in the war and, among the resulting hemispheric changes, Cuba became a republic. Maza y Artola formed the Moderate Party and was elected to the Constitutional Assembly of 1901. He began a career as a distinguished legislator and spokesman for many causes. He initiated legislation to create the Normal Schools, which mandated that the public universities train teachers. Through legislation he did two important things for the workers: he helped to create Worker's Day, or Labor Day, in

Cuba on the first of May; and he helped to construct housing for them, which benefited hundreds of poor families.

The following anecdote from the Márquez Sterling article illustrates Maza y Artola's humor and clever use of words.

"Maza y Artola, in addition to being a good orator, was also a parliamentarian who had very sharp quips. One day, in answering a senator of little culture and much verbosity, Maza began by saying, 'My . . . colleague who is distinguished by his pamphletic erudition.'" [2]

Elena adds that she loves the part in the article where Márquez Sterling says there were two parties, the Liberals and the Conservatives, and then there was Maza—"dead center in between," as Elena describes. He was a party unto himself.

She continues with the rest of story about her grandfather.

My grandfather retired from politics in the mid-twenties. He had tenure as a Greek professor at the university. Piedad, his daughter, had studied at the university and had become very interested in methods of teaching that were developing in Cuba at that time. She developed a specialty in pedagogy and then became a teacher at the university. When my mother was there, she was a student of Piedad's. This would have been during the time of Batista's first rule in the mid- to late 1930s.

At that point somebody in the government wanted to get my grandfather out of the university. They got the idea of organizing a boycott of his classes and talked to the students in the School of Letters. The idea was to prove that he had no popular support at the university, and that therefore his post should be eliminated or given to someone else. My mother and Piedad were among the few who dared to cross the picket line around his classroom. He was finally forced out. This probably happened because someone else wanted his job, not because of his political views; he had already made his bid for the presidency. When he retired from public life, he had a lucrative private law practice. He was very respected because of the people who knew him and his politics from the old days.

But being forced to resign from his university must have had an effect on him. Shortly after that he developed Alzheimer's. He went through two or three years of steadily declining mental abilities and then passed away in 1940. He was close to sixty-eight.

This was before I was born. I knew that he was a very magnetic figure; when I met people as a child and they heard the name de la Maza, they would ask, "Are you Juan José's granddaughter?" They would comment about him and what an extraordinary person he had been. The fact that they were impressed told me that he must have been a pretty important guy. I really didn't understand the extent of his importance in politics until I read the Sterling article as an adult. I never knew that he had presidential ambitions and that there were people who thought he would have made a terrific president.

Elena's father was the youngest of four children. His mother, Piedad de los Santos, had been married before. Her first husband died when her daughter, Elena, was two years old. After a period of mourning, Piedad married Juan José de la Maza y Artola. Three children were born to the new marriage: Juan, then Piedad, and finally, in 1906, Aquiles, who later became Elena Maza's father.

They lived in a house in old Havana on San Rafael Street. It was a very narrow townhouse, four stories high. One of my father's vivid memories of his early years was of watching Halley's comet from the rooftop of their house in Havana. It was in May 1910. He was not quite four years old at the time. He remembers being taken up to the *azotea*, the rooftop terrace, which all the houses in Cuba had. He was wrapped in a blanket. In those days my father suffered from asthma.

He remembers that the comet was beautiful, but he had been hearing people comment that the comet was going to fall on the earth, and that everyone was going to die. In childhood innocence, he believed them. After it passed over them, he asked, "Well, are we all going to die now?"

My grandfather had a handsome library. That's the personal relationship I have with him. I was fascinated by the library and always wanted to go in there. There were some old valuable books, so my father would always say, "No, you can't go in there by yourself and get the books. When you want something, you have to ask." As I got older I was able to have more and more access to it. Juan José had been a charter member of the National Geographic Society. Looking at those magazines [*National Geographic*] was one of the things I loved about his library. He had every issue, going back to the founding date in the 1890s. Whenever I could, I would go back and look at all those issues. Even after my grandfather died, my father kept up the membership, so there was a complete set until Castro closed things down.

He had an incredible collection of art books that were published around the turn of the century; they had beautiful leather bindings. I never got to look at those. These were, of course, very valuable; they had been kept in good condition. They were probably sold off by the Cuban government when they took over the house.

As I arrive at Elena's for one of our scheduled, twice-monthly meetings, Herb greets me at the door in his bathrobe to tell me that Elena's Aunt Sarah, whom they call Nina, is seriously ill. She has had a heart attack, and Elena and Herb were up very late the night before. Herb, ever gracious, brings me a cup of coffee. When Elena comes down, I offer my condolences and suggest leaving. She says she wants me to stay. It occurs to me that she may want to talk about Sarah. In spite of the grief and fatigue I see on her face, Elena is characteristically animated.

My Aunt Sarah was born on May 6, 1910. My mother was born slightly under a year later on May 2, 1911. They've always been very close as sisters. With Sarah there has been tremendous sibling rivalry, the kind that lasted a lifetime.

Elena laughs as she says this.

Sarah was perceived as being sickly and delicate, so she was always spoiled. Whereas my mother was thought to be strong physically, willful, and rebellious, so she was squelched.

My grandmother got pregnant soon after Sarah was born. Sarah blamed the fact that she was malnourished as an infant on my mother. My grandmother ran out of milk, so she couldn't nurse Sarah. She farmed Sarah out to a black lady who was also nursing her own infant, who was almost the same age. This was not at all uncommon. My grandmother caught her giving her own child preference while she was nursing both. Sarah blamed this lady for the fact that she grew up to be petite and frail. I think the whole thing is preposterous. My mother and Sarah are obviously two different constitutional types.

Elena's grandmother felt that Sarah could do no wrong; she was allowed to dominate and boss all the other siblings. Elena's mother, Olga, was considered rebellious because she wanted an education. Olga had always been interested in everything around her, but her mother determined that she would be the showpiece, the beauty of the family, that she didn't need to be educated.

Elena's Aunt Victoria, the youngest daughter, was very timid and submissive. The only thing she could use to assert herself was what she would eat and wouldn't eat: she was anorexic for many years. If her mother forced her to eat, Victoria would get sick. Their brother Othon died of typhoid before he was twenty.

My grandmother doted on Sarah because she saw Sarah as the mirror of herself. She encouraged Sarah's bossiness and her desire to lay down the law for everyone else. My mother didn't respond; she's a great expert at passive resistance. When she doesn't want to do something, she is not aggressive; she just quietly goes about doing what she wants.

Sarah acquired the nickname Nina because, when my oldest sister Beatriz was born, Sarah became her godmother, and the word for godmother in Spanish is *Madrina*. Beatriz couldn't quite say that, so it came out sounding like Nina. I heard Beatriz refer to her as "Nina," and I thought that was her name. She became Nina; even her great-nieces and nephews call her that. Toya is our nickname for Maria Victoria.

Elena's maternal grandmother's family, the Brus and the Seiglies, had come via eastern Europe. They were considered Italian because in those days the area in eastern Italy was called Trieste; today it is Dubrovnik. They sent their sons away to escape the many wars being fought in the area. When Elena's grandmother's grandfather was about eighteen or nineteen, he was sent to the New World. His family had given him a money belt. The ship he was on was wrecked somewhere in the middle of the Atlantic, but he managed to cling to wreckage for a day or two until he was rescued. Because he had the gold coins in the money belt, he was able to establish himself when he came to Cuba. He ended up starting a brick-making factory in Remedios.

He didn't know anything about this before, but he realized that building materials were needed and that he could make a decent living this way. He hired the locals and provided the capital and managerial skills to keep it going.

Elena says that her great-grandfather was from Spain. He had come to the New World as a general to fight for the Spanish in Colombia. He had been a career military officer and had fought in the Napoleonic wars. Because of the resistance his regiment had offered during the siege of a town in Spain, he had received promotions and risen in the ranks. He came to Cuba in 1812 and helped work out some of the terms of the peace.

In fact, one of my mother's cousins in Puerto Rico had the presence of mind to take out the original draft of those handwritten documents that were still in the family when we left Cuba.

My great-grandfather ended up finding a very wealthy widow by the name of Rojas. Her family had left her vast amounts of land in Las Villas, one of the central provinces. They married, had a couple of sons, and the property began to be split among the family.

Othon, my maternal grandfather, grew up at his family's sugar mill, a complex of buildings much like a farm. He was the fifth child in the family. His father died when he was fourteen. He had an older sister who was married and already had a child. There was quite an age spread. There is a photograph in which you can see the youngest child as only two or three and the oldest daughter's child, one year old. The older brother took over the sugar mill.

This was 1894; for the third time, the Cubans were starting the movement for independence from Spain.[3] The first of these uprisings for independence took place in October 1868; it was called the *Grito de Yara*. These uprisings for independence came to be called *Grito* (literally "shout") followed by the name of town where it occurred.

Elena interrupts the chronology to comment that on February 24, 1996, the anniversary of the third of these uprisings for independence, Cuba shot down two of the planes of the Brothers to the Rescue, an exile group in Miami. Jose Basulto, the co-founder of the group, flew the lead plane that allegedly violated Cuban airspace. The three planes were unarmed; two were shot down. Basulto, in the third plane, was able to return to Miami. We speculate at the coincidence. Elena says it must have been in Basulto's mind to use the date to call attention to the lack of independence in Cuba. She shakes her head.

No Cuban ever forgets February 24![4]

To register their intense displeasure with the Castro regime, Brothers to the Rescue has flown a number of missions into Cuban airspace. This group also has rescued Cubans who are trying to reach the mainland on flimsy rafts in the Florida Straits. Basulto is a veteran of the 1961 Bay of Pigs Invasion. To protest Castro's regime in 1962, one year after the invasion, he went so far

2. General Francisco Carrillo and his staff during the War for Independence in Cuba, 1898. Othon Caturla, Elena's grandfather, who was seventeen at the time, is in the front row, far left. Photograph by James H. Hare, in "Our Expedition to Gomez's Camp," *Collier's Weekly*, May 28, 1898.

as to take a high-speed boat into Havana Harbor and, with a semi-automatic cannon, to shell a hotel where he believed Soviet advisors were staying.[5]

Elena continues talking about her mother's family, describing a conspiracy among the Creole families. In the 1890s, a distinction was made in Cuban society between those Cubans who had been born in Spain and those who were from families long-established in Cuba, the Creoles. The Spaniards who maintained direct ties with the government in Spain were the ruling aristocracy, and they enjoyed certain political and economic privileges that the Creoles were completely denied.[6] *Elena describes the Spaniards as enacting an almost parent-child relationship with the Creoles. Therefore, the Creoles were at a disadvantage in spite of the fact that they owned vast amounts of land. They did not generally hold political offices. There were many Creoles who supported the idea of independence; they felt it was long overdue.*

My maternal grandfather felt that way: he wanted to join the guerrillas. Men or boys couldn't just go out into the bush and join up; they were inducted secretly. They would buy a ticket to a particular destination, so that it would appear they were going on a business trip or to visit a friend. About halfway there, at one of the unscheduled stops where the train fueled, they would get off. They would be met by a contact, taken to that person's house and provided with horses, then taken to where the liberation army was. The *mambises*, as the liberation army was known, had an extensive network; there were a lot of women among them.

My mother told me that the lady who helped to get my grandfather inducted into the liberation army when he and his brother decided to join was the mother of Urrutia; he became the interim president for a year when Castro took over. His family had been very involved in the guerrilla army of the 1890s; they raised money and procured clothes. This is how my grandfather joined and fought in 1895.[7]

The Americans didn't get involved until 1898; then the conflict was over in three months.[8] My grandfather served under General Francisco Carrillo. This man developed a real fondness for my grandfather; my grandfather became the general's aide-de-camp and would help take care of the sick. He would reminisce when he was old that when he went around the Remedios area, he would meet these old veterans who would say, "You set my leg and it is still fine." This is before he went to medical school and was probably part of the reason he studied medicine. He had found out he had an affinity for it, and it was a skill that was desperately needed.

After the war was over, Elena's grandfather went back home. He was of the age to go to the university. He asked his family, which was well-off, if he could come to the United States and study. In 1903, his family sent him to live in New York City with some relatives so he could learn English. The next year he went to Baltimore to attend the medical school at the University of Maryland. He finished in four-and-a-half years.

He went back and forth to Cuba several times while in medical school. As soon as he graduated, he came back to Cuba and immediately married Elena's grandmother. Elena is sure that this had been prearranged, but that he didn't want to wait for a fancy wedding.

Once Elena and I had established that the interviews would take place in the formal living room, we always sat on the Chippendale couch in the same places. I faced her from her right. The dining room was behind her, and near her left shoulder was the silk-screen print of her cousin Alejandro García Caturla. I saw this print as background during all of our interviews.

Alejandro García Caturla was a composer; today he is considered one of the pioneers of avant-garde music in Cuba. Castro has used him a great deal for propaganda purposes because he incorporated percussive and syncopated Afro-Cuban sounds and rhythms into his music. Hugh Thomas writes that by 1920, intellectuals and writers tended to identify the "real" Cuba with the Afro-Cuban descendants of the slaves who had built the sugar and rum industries. There was a growing awareness of their contribution to rhythm, dancing, and folklore, especially after the publication of Fernando Ortíz's 1906 book, Hampa Afro-Cubana, Los Negros Brujos.[9]

Alejandro García Caturla was born in San Juan de los Remedios, which is also where Elena's mother was born. This is a very old town, founded about the same time as Havana. It had remained a small, rural kind of place. Alejandro was precocious, learning to play the piano at an early age. In his late teens he entered into a liaison with a black woman, Manuela, who bore four children by him. Before Manuela died, he became involved with her younger sister and had another five children with that sister. Elena says that he supported them all.

When I ask if Castro was attracted to Alejandro because he had had black children, Elena agrees that was probably the case, that the racial aspect would have been important because Castro wants to promote Cuba as being free from the kind of racial prejudice that has been so much a part of the history of the United States.[10]

Alejandro's father was practical; he knew his sons had to have an education, and he sent both of them to the University of Havana. Alejandro had a wonderful time in Havana. While he was getting his law degree, he met a lot of musicians. He had a small popular band there in Havana. He spent one summer in Paris, where he studied with the famous composition teacher, Nadia Boulanger.[11] He composed, and he had his pieces played. As I said, he was incorporating Afro-Cuban sounds into his compositions. But his children had started coming, and he had to support them. He went home and took the examinations and went into law. He rose through the judiciary. Several times he went back to Havana to try to promote his musical career.

There was another contemporary of his, Amadeo Roldan, a mulatto, who also did similar things in his music. Dr. Charles White, now head of the Fine Arts Department at La Salle College in Philadelphia, Pennsylvania—where he's taught for many years—is writing a book on Alejandro. On one of his trips to Cuba, Dr. White got the silk-screen print of Alejandro and brought it to us. I have translated a chapter for him from the book *Music in Cuba* by Alejo Carpentier that contrasts Alejandro and Roldan.[12]

I ask how her family felt about his liaisons with the black women.

Because of his family's position in the community, it was the town scandal for a number of years. He became a judge in spite of it. It was not considered at all unusual for a white man to have a completely separate liaison with a black woman. For the woman, it was a desirable thing. She would get a rise in status among her own people. The white man generally supported her generously. Very often the white man would have a legal wife and a family that was the socially acceptable family. Alejandro never married. He only had one family—by the two black women. My mother says that when he came back from Paris, his parents threw him a big party. He started coming around to my mother's house a lot and played the piano for them. I suspect he was half in love with my mother, but they were first cousins. His parents were also first cousins. My mother admired his music but had no interest in him beyond that.

There had already been an attempt to assassinate Alejandro because of a different case several years before. Alejandro was a liberal judge who hated to see corruption in official circles. In the small towns most of the gambling was run on the sly by the police. His attacks on corruption did not sit well with some of the authorities.

Charles White told me that he had visited the town in Oriente where Alejandro had been stationed briefly as a judge. Alejandro had just walked out of his house and someone had shot at him. Fortunately the assassin missed. Charles told me that he had been to the house, and that you could still see the bullet holes.

Alejandro was going to try a case that involved a policeman who had beat up a young prostitute. The young girl was a girlfriend of one of Alejandro's sons, but he didn't get to hear the case. He had been called away to the Superior Court in Santa Clara, but the man who had been accused considered himself grievously wronged.

Every day when the post came on the five o'clock train, Alejandro walked from his office across the square to pick up his mail. He was walking back when the policeman who had been accused of beating the girl came up to him and said he wanted to talk to him.

Alejandro said, "We cannot talk here." He turned around to leave, and the man turned away from him. Suddenly, the policeman turned around again and said, "Doctor." He pulled out a gun and shot him. He was within two or three feet. Alejandro died twenty minutes later. Mom had moved to Havana and heard about it there.

Alejandro's mother and father supported his wives and all his children, and this was a large household. My grandfather was their doctor and said there were several people living there who seemed to be just hanging around, but Alejandro's father didn't want to hear anything negative about them. Another son tried to get him to disown them, but he considered them his grandchildren.

There was an aunt who'd been left a nice pension when her husband died. She gradually gave most of it to Alejandro's children. When she died, she had nothing left.

Did you ever meet any of them?

No, they lived in Remedios, which was a day's trip away. My mother kept wanting us to visit her relatives there, but my maternal grandmother had sad memories of the town because of death of her son Othon; added to this was the scandal of Alejandro's liaisons and the tragedy of his murder.

Charles White has met some of Alejandro's children. He got in touch with Alejandro's sister in Miami and found out about them. One lives in New Jersey but isn't in good health. Several are musicians in Cuba. Another was a dentist in Havana; she and several others have died.

Alejandro's house has been turned into a memorial. When he died in 1940, his family preserved his music room intact; they even had the suit he had on when he was shot. By the early sixties all of his family had moved away, and the house wasn't occupied. People started trying to take things out of it, especially his piano. A cousin of Elena's mother was outraged. She knew that Alejo Carpentier was a friend of Fidel Castro's, and she appealed to him. Alejo, an intellectual and a novelist, had been a life-long friend of Alejandro's. So the order came from on high not to disturb the house or its contents.

The print on the wall by the dining room is titled Museo de la Musica *(Museum of music). Under that is the full name: Alejandro Garcia Caturla;*

the third line is his birthplace: Remedios, Villa Clara, Cuba. This quote on the lower right of the print is taken from Carpentier's La Musica en Cuba:

> Alejandro García Caturla fue el temperamento
> musical mas rico y generoso que haya aparecido en la isla.[13]

> (Alejandro García Caturla had the most rich and generous musical
> temperament that has ever appeared on the island.)

I comment that music is an important thread that ties together several generations of the Maza family. Elena emphatically agrees.

Part of the reason music was so important was that this was the only entertainment you had. This was before phonographs. It was considered a social asset to be able to sing or play the piano. When you got invited to your friend's house, you could entertain them for the evening. This is part of the reason that my mother wanted us to have piano lessons. When she was young, she and Sarah took piano lessons from a local lady in the town; this teacher was very impressed with my mother. However, Sarah had no interest, didn't practice, and didn't make a good showing. My mother loved it and did practice and was a very good student.

The early twenties were called the "Dance of the Millions," referring to the profits reaped by the sugar industry during that time. Between 1918 and 1925, the price of sugar rose so high worldwide that every spare acre in Cuba was planted with sugar. The price of sugar was the highest it ever had been or would be until World War II. As a result, many people became well-off; however, by 1925 the price had fallen drastically.[14]

Due to the downward spiral of the economy, my grandmother had to tell her daughters she couldn't afford the piano lessons anymore. When they told this to the piano teacher, she took my mother aside and said, "You are such a good student, I want you to continue and I won't charge you."

Her mother said she couldn't possibly accept a favor for Olga that hadn't been offered to Sarah. They always had to be equal in everything.

When my mother grew up, the children of well-to-do families had tutors instead of going to the public schools. It would have been normal for all four of the children to study with a tutor. Then Othon, my mother's brother, would have had special studies with a tutor to prepare for the entrance exam to the university. That was a given, that the boy in the family would go to the university.

Once Sarah had finished the basics, she didn't have any interest in continuing, but my mother and Victoria did. So the three of them— Othon, Toya, and my mother—worked with a tutor so they could enter the university. At that time most families like theirs had libraries in their homes, so they used the one my grandfather had put together. It wasn't as big as the one in my father's house in Havana, but it was adequate.

There were periodic epidemics of typhoid fever in Cuba. There was one in Remedios in 1930. The whole family was ill. Othon died. My grandfather was devastated: he was a doctor, and he couldn't prevent the death of his only son. Even though he hadn't been the attending doctor, he felt that there was something he should have been able to do. In 1935, my grandfather moved the family to Havana.

The dictator Machado had fallen, and the country was emerging from the depression. Havana was infused with a progressive outlook, an atmosphere of hope and possibility. The move to Havana allowed Olga to finish high school and prepare to enter the university. She was twenty-four but determined to go on.[15]

This is a story that my mother tells about one of her examinations. In those days, even in high school many of the examinations were oral. You had to be really prepared because you didn't have any time to sit and think about the answer. One of the professors asked her what she knew about the French Revolution. It turned out that she had read about this in one of the encyclopedias that her father had in his library. One set of books he had was *Tesoro de la Juventud,* or *The Treasure of Youth,* a sort of a world book in Spanish.[16] It was twelve to twenty volumes.

My mother had read the section in this book on the French Revolution, so when she was asked about this, she was able to spout all kinds of things about it, including her own personal opinion. The professor marveled at the details in her answer, which was on the level of what a university student would give. When he asked, "How do you know so much about this subject?," she told him about reading in the *Tesoro,* and he was even more impressed by her inquisitiveness. She wasn't even aware of how much she had absorbed just by reading.

I used to read the *Tesoro* too. It had a terrific section on legends that was one of my favorites. These were old Spanish legends, illustrated by lithographs.

When my father's father died, my mother went to his house in San Rafael to pay respects at the wake. She had known his sister, Piedad, at the university, and she had met my grandfather as a student would meet a professor. She came on behalf of her family. She says that she may have shaken my father's hand; she doesn't remember.

It was at an exhibit of Cuban painters that Olga Caturla remembers meeting her future husband. He had been one of the exhibit's organizers. The day she went to visit, he was the only other person there; he asked if she had any questions. They had an interesting conversation, and she found him charming and informative. They didn't begin to see each other until after another chance meeting on a train coming back from Remedios.

There was another ironic thing about my parents' meeting. My father was involved with the restoration of a beautiful eighteenth-century church in Remedios, my mother's hometown. This project was carried out over a fifteen-year period under the patronage of Eutimio Falla Bonet, a very wealthy Cuban.[17] Remedios was largely unchanged since its heyday in the eighteenth century and was considered a small architectural gem. My father was a colonial architectural expert. In spite of working on this project for fifteen years, he had never met my mother.

After Elena's parents married, they lived with his parents. When Aquiles's father died, his mother no longer wanted to live in the townhouse. The de la Mazas bought a lot in a new development called Miramar, which was a suburb across the Almendares River, close to the sea.[18] Aquiles built a large house, and Elena's grandmother lived downstairs in a wing she shared with her son Juan. Upstairs Piedad, Aquiles's sister, lived with her husband and two sons. Aquiles, Olga, Elena, and her sisters had another wing downstairs in the back—a sitting room, bathroom, and one bedroom. Another bedroom was added when the girls began to be born. Mr. de la Maza also added a terrace outside as a playroom.

When I ask if it was typical in Cuba to have an extended family living under one roof, Elena answers affirmatively that it was the Cuban custom to share one big house.

My grandfather bought the first car in Remedios sometime around 1920 when he was feeling really flush. No one in the family knew how

3. Mrs. de la Maza and her four daughters, 1953. *Left to right:* Elena; Mrs. de la Maza holding Cecilia; Silvia; and Beatriz.

to drive it. They had a chauffeur. When they moved to Havana, they bought another car and had a chauffeur. When they had a string of bad luck with the chauffeurs, my Aunt Sarah volunteered to learn to drive. Sarah was very gutsy and ahead of her times in that respect. She was probably among the first women to take driving lessons in Havana. Victoria also learned to drive. They both became the family chauffeurs.

My mom wanted to share her children with her parents and her family—we were the only grandchildren they had. When Beatriz was born, she would go and spend the day with her parents in their house in Vedado, riding the bus in the morning and relying on Sarah or Toya to bring her back to the house.[19] It wasn't a far distance, but it was too far to walk. They were always were getting her home late, which upset my dad because he wanted his wife and baby home when he got home from work. My mother didn't have to make dinner because we had a cook.

After I was born, my mother suggested to her father, "Why don't you buy a lot in the same development? You could have your own house. It's better than renting a house."

Miramar wasn't too built up yet. He was able to buy a lot a block away. Then my father built my grandfather a house. As kids we were shared equally. This is the routine I remember: we would get up, and Mother made us breakfast in our little suite of rooms. Then it was playtime in our yard. Next Mom would take us for a walk around the block. We'd have lunch at her parents' house and play in their yard. We would come home to our house for dinner and have that with my dad, grandmother, and Uncle Juan. There was a late day ritual in good weather: we'd go to the beach near our house and watch the sunset.

Did you swim there, too?

No, there were too many sharp reefs, *dientes de perro* (dog's teeth); and it was rumored that there were a lot of sharks. Like a lot of families, we belonged to a beach club. The Biltmore Beach Club had an artificially created beach and had strong nets out in the water to keep out the sharks.[20]

When we started school, we attended a very unusual school named the *Artes e Idiomas* (Arts and languages). Everyone knew it as Margot Párraga's school. This lady, an incredibly strong-willed spinster, founded the school with her younger sister, Rosita. The two of them had been educated here in the U.S. in Boston. They spoke English beautifully with New England accents.

Margot had a very commanding physical presence: thin, wiry, bird-like, but with an incredible spirit and authority. Neither of the sisters had married; their mission in life was to educate young ladies—not of the richest families but of the *intelligentsia*. They really wanted the girls to be bilingual in Spanish and English. They also thought that French was not a bad idea. As early as kindergarten you learned your ABC's in Spanish and English. Rosita was the one who took care of the kindergarten; she would teach us phrases in English. You learned to say "please" and "thank you" in English and Spanish. She taught us English songs. The classes were very small. They accepted boys up to the first grade; then the boys got shipped out to other schools.

Later Elena asked her father why he sent his daughters to this school. He told her that the school had been in two old houses in Vedado, the same neighborhood that her grandparents had lived in. The two sisters who ran the school decided to join the two houses, and they hired Mr. de la Maza to design an auditorium that connected them. He visited the school when he was working on this design. He had been so impressed with what they were doing that he decided if he ever had any daughters, this is where he would send them.

I still have wonderful memories of Margot's school. I can still go through it room by room, first through seventh grade. I went to school mostly with the same group of girls. Many were from the area close to the school, and they walked to school. The tradition of Cuban schools, except for the really large schools, was that you ate lunch at home; you got a two-hour break at midday. My Aunt Sarah or Victoria took turns picking us up at noon and bringing us over to their house for lunch. The school day was for half a day until the second grade, when the day ran until 2 P.M. After the second grade, the length of the school day increased with each grade level.

Three times a week we had ballet after school. Ballet was the physical education of the school. Lots of girls in Havana from families like ours studied ballet. Most of us also went to Pro Arte, the performing arts society. Very few schools had ballet as part of our school curriculum. Our teacher, Cuca Martínez, was Alicia Alonso's sister. Alicia Alonso was the premier ballerina of our country and probably the only one from Cuba who was well known.[21] Martínez was quite a demanding teacher.

Besides the ballet, we were also taking piano lessons, as I've told you. When Beatriz went for piano lessons two doors down from where we lived, I threw a tantrum and said that I had to go too, that she couldn't possibly be the only one to go. She was almost six, and I was four. Finally my mother gave in. We went to classes together, and I went through the typical difficult kid stage. Several years later all of four of us were taking lessons there from Elvira. We could hear students practicing piano as we walked by. We called the music school Elvirita's Conservatory.

We learned on a regular-size piano. After a year we even learned to take musical dictation: the teacher would play certain notes, and we would have to write them down. We were quite advanced. The physical part didn't come as easy for me because I started so young and my hands were very small. When I was around nine or ten, my sisters and I instigated a mass rebellion in our house: we all wanted to quit the piano. As my parents always wanted us to play, they didn't quite know what to do.

This short rebellion was quelled by my mother in a very clever way. We had been practicing on a piano in my mother's parents' house just a block away. They had a player piano that had been converted back to a regular one. My mother went to my grandfather and said, "How about we buy the girls a new piano?" This stimulated our interest. Cecilia was the only one who refused to continue after that. She was about seven. I was ten. We had a ball going all over to shop for the new piano. We must have gone in every store and tried every piano in Havana. We ended up with a beautiful little spinet.

My mother had another new tactic. "I'll make a deal with you, too. You'll get a new piano and a new piano teacher. You need a new approach." Raisa, a younger and more enthusiastic teacher, had a little music school in an apartment. She and her mother lived in another apartment above the school. We liked the fact that she gave group lessons once a week. This added a degree of competition to the lessons.

Our teacher was associated with a guitar teacher who also taught in her apartment. The school would give twice-yearly concerts. When the guitar teacher's ensemble performed, she wanted everyone who was able to sing along. The guitar teacher taught us how to sing in harmony. We ended up learning quite a sizable repertoire of popular songs.

Elena pauses.
Beatriz reminded me recently about a place we used to vacation. When I came across some photos taken there, I remembered what a special place it was for all of us.

Beatriz describes San Vicente as a tiny resort in the mountains near the valley of Viñales, whose main attraction is sulfur springs of supposedly medicinal value.

We stayed in the Hotel Rancho San Vicente, the larger and more modern hotel. The focal point of this hotel was a large rectangular swimming pool. The water they served at dinner was this sulfur water—and believe me, my parents actually drank it. The rest of us requested bottled mineral water.

The valley of Viñales is famous for its "mogotes"; rock formations which rose almost straight up from the valley floor, with rounded tops.[22] They were green with grass and trees growing on them, some with the roots exposed, hugging the rocks. At dusk, a chorus, sometimes quite loud, as of thousands of tiny bells, suddenly rose in the peace and quiet. They said it was some sort of frog, which we nicknamed the "tilin" frogs.[23]

I ask Elena where the nickname came from.

It's an onomatopoeia. You know—a word that sounds like what it's describing, in this case, the sound of the frogs.

Beatriz describes their hikes around the valley. There was one special place they went called the Indian's Cave that had a small natural entrance, much like the front steps and small porch to someone's house. Inside, Beatriz writes, "there was a big room, full of shimmery crystalline formations colored white, peach and pale blue-gray. A natural balcony was a favorite spot for newlyweds to be photographed."[24]

Beatriz says she often dreamed of San Vicente and used to wake up full of the same yearning Heidi felt when she dreamed of Switzerland.[25]

Elena sighs.

We use to take such wonderful vacations together. Later we stopped going to San Vicente. Beatriz reminded me that it was because the last years of Batista's regime were so chaotic that we didn't want to be far from home.[26] So we went to the Cubañas, where my father had completed a motel.[27]

We had wonderful birthday parties. These were big affairs in Cuba.

Elena points to one of the photographs of Cecilia in front of some trained cats. There was a woman who brought these cats to birthday parties to provide entertainment. Mrs. de la Maza said that people would bring the woman

4. Cecilia and the trained cats
on her sixth birthday, 1957.

strays, and that she would work with them to see if they had potential as
performers. She and her husband had been in some European circuses; they
were World War II survivors who had resettled in Cuba. After her husband
passed away, she developed this act with the cats. She dressed the cats up as
if they were in a court pageant: one cat was the king, one was the queen, and
one was the page. She had a baton that she used to direct their performances.

Elena runs her hand over the photograph.

Cecilia loved those cats.

On my sixth or seventh birthday, I wanted a gingham party. I asked
my mother to make all of our dresses for it out of gingham. And all the
other girls came in gingham, too. I loved that party.

These photographs were taken at Beatriz's fifteenth birthday party. In
Cuba your fifteen birthday was a kind of "coming-out party." That was
in February, right before we left. Ordinarily this would have been a big

5. "Gingham dress" birthday party, 1953.

6. De la Maza family on Beatriz's fifteenth birthday (February 4, 1961), one month before three of the sisters left Havana on an Operation Pedro Pan airlift.

party—a dance with a band and lots of fancy refreshments, but we knew we were leaving soon; no one felt like celebrating. We just had a small party in the backyard. In this photograph are Beatriz's classmates from Ruston and our friends from the music school.

Ruston had a reputation as being one of the best new schools. Elena says she thinks her parents also liked the design, based on the American model of having a lot of glass. Each classroom had one glass wall, so the rooms were very light. The school also had beautiful grounds. Many of Margot's students attended there.

They made a deliberate choice not to send us to religious schools because, although she might not admit it, my mother probably thought they were too repressive, that they tended to squelch a girl's spirits. She always was a great believer in being as natural as possible. She wanted us to have a happy childhood.

Ruston had two different study programs. There was the *Bachillerato*, the Spanish high school, which was five years; then there was the traditional American high school, which was four years. The Maza girls were enrolled in the *Bachillerato*.

Let's go back to your mother wanting you to not be repressed by a religious school. What part did religion play in your life in Cuba?

There were many girls going to religious schools around us, but Margot's school was not religious as such. They had a priest come in once a week. We would have an hour of religious instruction with him. We would learn the catechism and to say our prayers. In Cuba the confirmation was very close to the first communion. We had to learn certain things for the confirmation ceremony. All of us sisters made our first communion. We all wore the same dress, altered slightly.

Elena laughs.

We were different sizes—some small and some not.

In Cuba, the majority of the people are Catholic or at least used to be. While the religion a lot of people practiced tended to be a social thing, with my parents it was very sincere. I can remember they took us to church every Sunday. My grandparents did not attend church. My mother tells me that neither of my grandparents was particularly religious. When she was young, they never attended church on a regular basis. After her brother died, she and Sarah particularly felt strongly drawn to the church. They became devout churchgoers. I can only presume that when you are a survivor of a terrible illness, you feel you have been spared for a reason. This can be the beginning of developing a spiritual life.

Sarah and Mr. and Mrs. de la Maza, as confirmed churchgoers, attended Mass at a small convent near their house or at their regular parish church.

Religion, as much else in Cuba, was inextricably tied to the unstable political situation. Hugh Thomas writes that by 1952, when Batista officially took over a second time through a coup, most Catholic laymen and priests did not support him. He was, however, congratulated by the cardinal.[28]

I ask Elena if her family ever talked about religion.

Not as an isolated subject. There was a strong social component to church. Many activities revolved around the church life: our first communion or singing in the choir. We were always discussing specific things about the service. A special delight for me was to be able to sing in the choir. We'd only joined it a month or so before we left. My dad, Beatriz, Silvia, and I were preparing some songs for the Easter service.

Holy Week in Havana is a big event, Elena says. There were processions where the altars were brought out on Good Thursday. The altars rested on pallets carried by large, strong men. There were incense, prayers, and people doing penitence, sometimes going up steep steps on their knees.

We went once and I was a little spooked by the whole thing. We didn't go again because Silvia was frightened by the experience.

The tradition that I loved was the stations of the cross. You went to a different church to do your prayers, one for each station. You had to do seven stations. For me it was wonderful experience. We'd go to some old, ornate churches; it was great fun to be able to light a candle in this beautiful, old chapel we only saw once a year.

Did your parents ever use any aspect of religion to discipline you children?

Not really. Catholicism gives you enough guilt. My parents didn't want to reinforce that. We were brought up on the Dr. Spock model. We had the "punishment chair," or the "discipline chair," where we would have to sit for certain periods of time when we'd acted up.

Elena's life—an interweaving of family, school, music, dance, and religion—expanded to include politics in the fifties.

The post-dinner time in Cuba is called sobre mesa *(over the table). While the adults had coffee, the family talked. This was meant to be instruc-*

7. Elena's first commun-
ion, 1954.

*tive to the children. In Elena's family, her parents would talk about opera
and other things that interested them while the children listened and offered
their own comments.*

*As political tensions began to mount, more and more the conversation
turned to the political situation. I ask Elena how she would characterize her
family politically.*

Apolitical in many ways but of a good social democrat mold. Let me
give you some examples of where we stood.

Elections had been scheduled for November 1952, and Batista's military coup was on March 10. My mother says that the saddest day of her
life was to see what happened two or three days after Batista took over.
Batista was still at his farm, a big *finca*, on the outskirts of Havana. My

mom says ninety percent of Havana society went and prostrated them-selves in front of Batista, currying favor and supporting him. This was one of the things that made the American government recognize his government, because it appeared that he had the support of the people.[29]

My father's older sister Elena, her husband, and her children sup-ported Batista. Mom still talks about their going to the *finca*. Jorge Ledo, Elena's husband, was a diplomat. Evidently Jorge felt his career was go-ing to take off if he supported Batista, so he was one of the people who filed past. The day after, the newspapers published a long list of the people who had gone to Batista's.

My dad had never been too popular with Batista. My mother said that on two occasions Batista did things to thwart projects my father was working on. The first one had to do with the Havana woods. In the late thirties, in the center of Havana, in the upper Almendares River basin, there still remained one of the last stands of virgin woods. President Laredo Bru wanted to create a *bois*. He said every important city in the world has its *bois*, like the Bois de Bologne in Paris.

Let me add an aside here. President Laredo Bru was a relative of my mother's family. He would have been a second cousin of my grand-mother. My mother says he was one of the few really good elected presi-dents.[30] He was very cultured and well educated. He did a number of things in terms of sponsoring national contests about culture and things like that. As a matter of fact, Alejandro won a prize for composition. It wasn't nepotism; Laredo Bru had nothing to do with the jurying.

Now back to the *bois*. My dad was one of the pioneers of landscape architecture in Cuba; he loved plants and gardens. He had already begun working on the project that was going to be the *Havana Bois*. Batista and his cronies had their eye on the land for a development. When they took over politically, they bought the land cheap and then sold it to develop-ers for a suburban development for rich people. The vegetation and the woods were cut down. One of my dad's life projects was undone.

There was another thing even more blatant. There was a competition to design a monument to honor our national hero, José Martí. My dad won the first place with his design of a beautiful neoclassical library. He had worked with the well-known sculptor José Sicre.[31] Winning first place meant he should have received the commission for this, but Batista, though not in power officially, had enough political pull to rearrange the results so that the third runner-up, one of his cronies, received the commission.

The third-place winner created something that came to be called *La Raspadura.*[32] *Raspadura* is a purely Cuban term for one of the by-products of sugar; literally, it means "the scrapings." These scrapings are what is left in the vat after you've skimmed off the good part. The *raspadura* was turned into candy, which was shaped into these boxy shapes like truncated obelisks. Since that was coincidentally also the shape of the monument built from the third-place runner-up's design, the monument was immediately labeled *La Raspadura.* The Cuban sense of humor can be devastating.

I never saw my Dad's project; I don't know if he destroyed the drawings in disgust or kept them hidden away. I didn't know any of this until I was about seven. I overheard my first piano teacher talking to my mother about the ridiculous things Batista had done, building this unsightly monument when my father's design was so beautiful. This is when Mom told us the story.

As I'm putting the tape recorder in a bag, I ask Elena where she wants to start next time.

We'll follow history: after Batista comes Castro.[33]

Mrs. de la Maza and Cecilia's Flight to the United States; Together in Albuquerque, New Mexico

Just before Castro took over, elections were scheduled. Everyone was talking about the fact they would be rigged; we asked my parents who they were going to vote for. The Progressive Party candidate was a man named Márquez Sterling, who was a well-respected historian and lawyer. He had been one of my mother's university professors, and she and my father were looking forward to voting for him even though he didn't belong to one of the bigger parties.

Elections took place in October or November.[1] *Márquez Sterling was not one of the winners. None of the elected candidates was ever installed.*[2] *Castro was poised to take over, but he had to wait for Batista, whom he knew was on the way out, to leave. Arrangements had been made for him to exit safely. The next morning, New Year's Day 1959, when news of Batista's departure became public, Castro began his victory trip to Havana.*[3]

On January 7, 1959, we knew the parade route that Castro would use to march into Havana. We dressed in red and black, the revolutionary colors. We went to the home of one of our cousins who lived along the parade route and watched it from their second-story balcony. We waved and yelled with lots of other people in Havana. Castro was greeted with real relief and celebration. At last we were delivered from Batista.

The changes that Castro instituted were gradual, but his retaliation against Batista's people began quickly and continued for the next several months.[4] Some of the executions were televised. The *Morro* Castle stands over Havana. The back part, *La Cabaña*, has always been a prison. Prisoners were traditionally executed at the ancient stone walls, one of which is known as the *Paredón*, the big wall. This tradition continued in the early days of the Castro regime. The cry of the mobs throughout Havana in those days was "*Paredón! Paredón!*"

Some of the moderates in Castro's government protested that legal procedures were not being followed. Trials were held, but there was no pretense of trying to present a defense or to give the accused the right to refute any charges. These trials were televised, and Elena and Beatriz were glued to the television.[5] Beatriz told Elena that after she watched a press conference with Castro for almost four hours, she began to see what a manipulator he was.

About a month or two after he came to Havana, we met Castro. We always used to shop at one of two small stores. My Aunt Toya, who did the shopping, liked the Mini-Max, an American-style grocery store that was ten blocks from our house. The other place was a more old-fashioned *bodega*, a small grocery store in the Spanish tradition.

One day when I came home, Toya was excited, which was unusual. She said, "Guess who I just saw at the Mini Max? Fidel is down there. Do you want to go and see him?" Cecilia and I were the only ones around. We hopped in the car, and she took us down there. I shook Fidel Castro's hand. In those days we supported him. He made a great impression on me. He seemed very tall, very handsome.

He had the beard? The khaki fatigues?

Yes. I could have died of jealousy because Cecilia, being a cute little nine-year-old, was picked up by Castro! He gave her a big hug. All the reporters were taking photographs of this. That night Cecilia didn't want to wash her face because he had kissed her on the cheek. She was the star of the family for several weeks.

I give Elena a personal example of the impact Castro had in the United States, particularly on young people. In February 1959, I was at a gathering of folk singers on a farm outside Staunton, Virginia. On Saturday night after we had eaten, someone was playing a guitar and singing. Everyone was sitting on the floor quietly listening. Suddenly the front door burst open, and three young men came in. They were dressed in khaki fatigues and had the beginnings of short beards. There was a collective gasp; then the room be-

came quiet again. They turned out to be students from the University of Virginia in nearby Charlottesville. Finding this out did nothing to demystify them. Despite their posturing, to us these young men represented Castro and the new liberators of Cuba. They were the heroes of the weekend, and every young woman there wanted to sit beside them.

Elena smiles at my story.

Yes. He was our hero, too! Later as our opinions changed, we thought, "Oh, how could we ever have done that? How could we have let him touch us?"

Our opinions changed as the details of the Agrarian Reform became clear. We have already talked about the *latifundios*—the large tracts of land owned by a few people. The Cuban peasants were poor because they didn't own any land; one way to help them was to redistribute some of the land. Castro's government said that the enormous tracts of land owned either by Americans or by one or two Cubans families weren't producing; they were just being held. This was perceived to be vastly unfair, even by the middle class. As I've said, my family went along with this at first: we did need to redistribute the land to give some of the poor farmers a small plot of land so they wouldn't be tied to being tenant farmers. This was passed as law. All of the people who owned large tracts were gradually divested of it, but then the law was interpreted to apply to anyone who owned any land. This affected my family because my mother's father had inherited four small farms in Las Villas. As I told you earlier, my grandfather had always had tenants on it. Some of them had been living there their entire lives. The largest farm was ten or twenty acres, tiny plots. When we first heard of the *reforma agraria*, this land didn't qualify. Then my grandfather lost his lands, and my father lost his family's townhouse, where he had his architectural office as well as rental space for other offices. People began to get the drift: the state would take over all private property.[6]

You've told about how and why you, Beatriz, and Silvia left. Tell about your mother and Cecilia's leaving.

It came to a head after the Bay of Pigs. This invasion was anticipated and feared before it happened. Castro had spies everywhere. Mother tells me that on the day the invasion started, Castro rounded up more than thirty thousand people in Havana who were suspected of being sympathizers—nothing more concrete than that.[7] Many of them were professionals; some were women with children. They were detained in different areas in Havana. We lived on Fourteenth Street in Miramar. In Batista's times, the house on the corner of Fourteenth and Fifth Avenue had become a *cuartel* (military post) where Batista's police detained and probably tortured people. When Castro took it over, it was also used by the G-2, Castro's secret police.[8] It was packed with prisoners after the Bay of Pigs Invasion started. The other place they used in our neighborhood was a large movie theater called the *"Blanquita."* We would go there frequently because there was a *bodega* on the ground floor.

Mom very unobtrusively went by the theater to take in the scene. She wrote down her impressions in tiny writing on a piece of paper that she sewed inside the lining of a coat. She did not take it out until several months ago when she remembered it.

The following section is taken from Elena's translation of her mother's "The Caravan of the 'Blanquita'":

> The *"Blanquita"* is an immense theater, which a rich man from another era, who owned a newspaper besides, had ordered built. The Revolution changed its name, but everyone continues to call it by the one it originally had.
>
> Just as it changed names, it changed in purpose during the *"Week of Terror."* The *"Blanquita"* is an enormous prison where more than *3,800* persons of both sexes are trapped.
>
> Yesterday evening, when we got closer, from the interior of the theater came a deafening clamor; it was the prisoners screaming something that couldn't be made out. My little daughter [Cecilia], close to me, pointed to the shadows of women gesticulating at a window. They say that what is happening is that they have not given water to the prisoners. Night fell, enveloping the neighborhood in darkness. Absolute silence reigned then, more oppressive than the diurnal noises. Not a radio, nor laughter, nor the echo of conversation. It was like a mute protest that pressed down on the heart.

Mrs. Maza describes the next day at the "Blanquita":

> Among the women detained there were four in an advanced stage of pregnancy. One gave birth among the orchestra chairs. Another almost hemor-

rhaged to death; her companions mutinied so she might be given medical attention.

The multitude of relatives and friends that surround the building lived through real moments of panic the afternoon militiamen began to fire at the feet of the women [spectators] who, seeing a group of thirty-six priests being brought as prisoners, began to sing a Catholic hymn. A spectator described the scene, "The women ran as if crazed toward the other nearby streets: one lost her shoes; another dragged her children along." Many blocks away, the screams of terror could be heard.

There were prisoners such as [those] at the "Blanquita" everywhere in Havana; at the Morro Castle and La Cabaña as well as with the loathed G-2 [secret police], which advanced its tentacles like an octopus engulfing all the houses which surrounded it, turning family homes into prisons. There were also hundreds of prisoners at Sport City, and a veritable anthill of humanity spread throughout the Loma del Príncipe, which overflowed into the city jail. All together there were thirty thousand prisoners in the city of Havana.⁹ There is no news from the interior, but it is feared that everywhere it's been the same mass imprisonments.

And no one was informed where their relatives were taken; so the poor populace went from prison to prison, asking without receiving an answer.

This was an advantage at the "Blanquita," since the shouts launched from below rose up, and after repeating the question, after a while one could determine from which window the familiar or friend would appear, responding, "Yes, I'm here." And this, for those waiting undeterred, sufficed.

. . . The "Blanquita" . . . has become a symbol for Cuba. That there is our liberty, enchained, and that the whole country suffers for her and joins her in the painful moment. . . .

*. . . after the defeat of the Bay of Pigs Invasion, hopes lost, there was only one way towards freedom . . . exile.*¹⁰

Panic swept Havana. After what she had seen at the "Blanquita," Mom was so distraught that she went walking with no particular destination in mind. Her only thought was that she had to get out of Havana with my Dad and Cecilia and come to the U.S. and find us. She walked down Quinta Avenida (Fifth Avenue), which becomes Calzada when it crosses the Almendares River, down past Margot's School, until she was in front of the Argentine embassy.

We had had a classmate at Margot's School named Enid whose parents were diplomats from Argentina. Mother told me that when she saw the Argentine embassy she remembered that Enid's mother had said the previous year, "If you ever need any help, you can contact me; my husband will do whatever he can to help you." She went to the door of the embassy.

A guard opened the door and showed her in and said, "Lady, do you want asylum?" They were expecting people to be looking for asylum to get away from Castro.

My mother said, "No, I don't need asylum, but I need a favor. I want to write a letter to someone in Argentina, and I want it to go by diplomatic pouch." The guard agreed; he gave her some paper, and she wrote a letter to Enid's mother, begging her to pass on another letter she wrote to the former U.S. ambassador to Cuba, Philip Bonsal. My father had done the landscaping for the new American embassy that had been built in Havana in the fifties. When the garden had been dedicated, there was a big party where my mom and dad had met the ambassador.

In my mother's letter to Mr. Bonsal, she asked for three visas to be sent to the Argentine embassy. At that point you could only get visas through channels like these because the American embassy had closed. Most of the business was being transacted through the Swiss embassy. My mother wrote her letters, then walked back to the house wondering what would happen.

Amazingly, in a month or so the visas came. Then Mom had to go through the rounds of completing the paperwork to leave. She got on the list to get the airplane tickets, but when they came, there were only two airplane tickets. Pan American had one flight per day—it was probably regulated by the Cuban government to restrict the number leaving. A dilemma arose as to who would go. My grandparents wanted Dad to go with Mom and leave Cecilia with them. My mother said, "Absolutely not. I'm not leaving my youngest." Dad agreed. So they worked it out that she and Cecilia would leave and my father would join them later.

Mrs. de la Maza and Cecilia got two tickets for August 31. Mr. Maza was promised a ticket for September 21, only three weeks later. In the meantime, new procedures were set up by the Castro government to clamp down on those leaving. Another whole set of forms was required. This delayed Mr. de la Maza's leaving.

When Mrs. de la Maza and Cecilia left, the government let people leaving take only one bag. She was able to wear her wedding ring. The government wouldn't allow other jewelry to be taken out. Elena's father gave her a gold chain that had belonged to his mother who had died in 1960. It was a very long, solid gold chain that hung around her neck several times.

My father said, "If you need money when you get to the U.S., you'll have this." Being a clever seamstress, my mother sewed that in the lining of a very heavy wool coat. She was worried about the weight and tried to disguise it. She did such a beautiful job; you could never guess it was there. When she got to Albuquerque, she showed me the coat and took it out. She never touched the gold chain; she still has it.

I can't believe it now, but I don't remember the day my mother and Cecilia came. I'm sure it was exciting to see them at last, but I actually didn't get to go and live with them right away. Helen didn't want to let me go when my mother came. I guess they were concerned about her supporting four children. Mom had to go to battle. She spoke to a social worker and got her to talk to Helen. The social worker said it would be in my best interest to live with my family. I came to live with them the second or third week in December.

We lived on Roma Street. We had a little tiny house there, which we called the "chicken coop" because it was so small. The number was the same as the regular house in front, but "½" had been added to the number. In other words, we had half of a house. It was like an outbuilding, a little shed in back of a regular house. The house had no closets, just a few cupboards. Catholic Charities had outfitted the house. They got us pots and pans and some things so we could get started on our life there. Silvia and I shared a double bed on a porch that had been converted to a bedroom. There was just enough room to stand between the bed and the cupboard. Beatriz and Cecilia weren't much better off in a small bedroom in the back. My mother slept in the living room on a couch that opened up to become a very hard bed.[11] The little house and Saint Vincent's were near old downtown Albuquerque. Saint Vincent's was twelve blocks away.

8. 1405½ Roma Street, the de la Maza's first rental house in Albuquerque, New Mexico.

When you came to live with your mother, you had to change schools. How did that work out?

It was hard, especially in the middle of the year, just a couple of weeks before Christmas. I guess the only good thing about it was that I had no academic problems. Not knowing anybody in the school except my sisters was hard. And I was wearing my thick glasses!

I had to change uniforms. Saint Vincent's had a different one, which was a navy blue jumper. I've always been into shoes. At that point I had an old pair of tennis shoes that Helen had bought me. I decided that since the uniforms were so dull, I'd paint and decorate my tennis shoes; they didn't have any specific rule about shoes. Maybe I got this idea from the *Gidget* movie I've mentioned. I sewed a bit of lace on my tennis shoes and decorated them with ballpoint pen drawings. They were an icebreaker. The nuns would look down at my shoes and try not to remark about them. They did say something about how they didn't quite go with the uniform.

At that point I probably would have said, "Well, this is the only pair of shoes I have, and I can't change them." That sort of signaled my artistic bent. It helped me to make a few friends. I became good friends with Pat Duran and a native American, Regina, who was quiet and shy. Regina invited me once to go to her reservation. I was also shy in those days; I was worried about what I would say and do there. To this day I regret not having gone.

One time in English class we had to do a speech. Like most people I was terrified of speaking in front of people. If I stood up and spoke to more than two people, I got tongue-tied. As I said, Regina was shy too, but she was a drum majorette. She found a wonderful way to do this speech. She did a live demonstration of what she did as a drum major-ette. She used up her time very well, getting the whole class involved. She got an A.

I decided to do a speech on Cuban dances. I had talked Regina into being my partner for the demonstration. Unfortunately, we hadn't spent enough time practicing. My particular speech was not as successful as hers.

What was the dance?

The conga. It was fairly salacious, because when Cubans dance they wiggle everything—hips, breasts, shoulders. It shocked the nuns, but they were too nice to say anything. I was making all the mistakes of a kid who doesn't quite understand what's appropriate. I was trying. I did get points for that.

I ask Elena how her mother adjusted to being a mother of four again with the added career of teaching in an American school. Elena says she did well in her teaching. She was liked by all her students. The only problem was with her pay. She had gotten two weeks' advance pay. During the two-week Christmas break, she wasn't paid. She was getting just a little over two hun-dred dollars a month. Although Catholic Welfare paid the rent for the house at Roma Avenue for two months, their payment went for October and No-vember; they had thought Mrs. de la Maza was going to be arriving sooner. On December 1, the rent was due. Saint Vincent's had advanced her the two weeks, half of which went for the rent. This didn't leave much to live on for a month.

We ate pretty well for six dollars a week, as I remember it. Mom tells me that several days before Christmas she counted her money; she had $1.75. That very evening, Mom had an additional and unanticipated expense with the laundry. On Roma Avenue, to save money, we washed everything by hand. We had a little clothesline—the kind on a circular pole—outside to dry the clothes. Mom was shocked when she brought in the sheets and found them frozen. We put the clothes inside the house to dry them. We had gas heat, but it was not well distributed. There was one grille in the middle of the floor and all the hot air came out there. We hung the clothes by the grille between the dining room and the little living room.

This evening, when the clothes were drying in the house, the Garcías came to visit. You remember that they were the family that Beatriz and Silvia had lived with. When they came in, they commented that the dampness would make us sick. They said to my mother, "Let's go to a laundromat and use the dryer. Do you have forty cents for the two dryers?"

Mom was embarrassed to tell them how short she was of money, but she gave them forty cents and then had only $1.35 left. Her problem was how we would get through the next week. She didn't tell us any of this; she played it very cool. That evening she was very quiet and thoughtful. I had no idea what was going on.

Fortunately, we were invited out to Christmas dinner. Our first Christmas in the States was with the Durans, Pat's family, a Latino-Mexican family. We probably wouldn't have had much to eat otherwise. For Christmas dinner the Durans had ham and corn, a sort of New Mexican menu. It was wonderful. It wasn't a traditional Cuban Christmas meal, which would be roasted pork or stuffed turkey, but we wouldn't have eaten that well on my Mom's $1.35. We spent most of the day there. We had a good time. There were five or six children in their family. We felt very comfortable with them.

That year the only presents we could afford were ones we made. I made my mother a tiny coin purse. Later my mother told me how ironic it was that I made this for her when she was so short on cash. I used a little piece of felt and lace I'd found.

The day after Christmas my mother decided to check all the suitcases and see if there was any loose change there. She looked in one of the little side pockets in her suitcase and found twenty dollars that she'd forgotten she had. This had been given to her by a friend in Miami who was also living on welfare. She had insisted, "I know you'll need it. Just take it." Mom had salted it away in her suitcase. It literally saved our lives until she got paid again, when she was able to use the coin purse I made for her!

As we talk, Elena is working on a beaded heart that will become a pocket-book, to be shown as part of a Valentine's benefit. Her hands move with sureness as she talks. I ask her where she learned to sew. She looks up and says that sewing was something she learned from her mother. Her grandmother sewed a lot, and her mother had an aptitude for sewing and designing dresses for the sisters. Her grandmother and mother would move everything out into the dining room when they were making party dresses, which were sometimes finished at the last minute. Elena remembers that she and her sisters would be standing around, almost dressed, waiting for them to put on the final touches. Elena describes a dress/costume made to represent Valencia, which is in eastern Spain on the Mediterranean: a beautiful blue satin skirt, white blouse and shawl, and a lace apron that was embroidered with sequins. As they were leaving for the party, the sequins were still being sewn on the apron.

When I was eight or nine, I became interested in learning something about sewing. I asked my mom to teach me how to embroider; this seemed like good place to begin. She taught me the chain stitch and then the satin stitch, the one where you go over and over an area to fill it in. I remember stitching these roses on a handkerchief and giving it to my dad. This was not appropriate for a man—it was far too feminine—but I didn't know that.

She laughs, as she often does about memories of good times and also of her mistakes.

That's how I learned to embroider. When I was twelve or thirteen, Mom taught me to do hand sewing in my spare time. When I was at Helen's, I would hand sew clothes for the Barbie dolls we played with. They were very impressed that I could sew. I hadn't learned to sew on a machine, but I could hand sew.

My mother is such a darling lady; she makes friends wherever she goes. She met Mrs. Davies and through her the rest of the family; they were a lovely Greek family. The Davies had a daughter in Saint Vincent's too. They sort of took us under their wing. Mr. Davies was a piano tuner and restorer who was well known. He would travel as far as

California to tune pianos for symphony orchestras. Their daughter, Demetria, was a classmate of Silvia's. They invited us often to their house to play their beautiful Steinway. They were very, very nice.

After I left Helen's, I didn't have a piano except for the Davies'. They lived about six blocks away. We could walk there after school. They often asked us to stay for dinner. That helped with our tight budget. They gave my mother sewing once in a while to give her some extra money. They could see the hardships we were going through.

At Saint Vincent's occasionally we did small musical presentations. I remember Silvia sang. I played the piano. We were able to practice a little on the piano at the school, a beat-up old upright, but it wasn't as good a piano as the Davies'.

In March 1962, the U.S. Cuban Refugee Program, which was part of the U.S. Government's Department of Health, Education and Welfare, sent Elena's mother a form letter inquiring about her resettlement.

> *We are pleased to have been of service in your resettlement. We trust it will be so successful, through your efforts, that it will lead to many more sponsors and opportunities in your community for Cuban refugees.*
>
> *Where you are now located, you represent all Cubans who have fled from political oppression in your homeland. Your advancement in your work, among your acquaintances, in the community in general, will help you and all free Cubans—particularly those yet to be resettled.*
>
> *After you read this letter and think about these points, I hope you will write me about your experiences and your hopes for the future. . . . Please tell me about your job and the cooperation that has been extended to you.*[12]

After several weeks Mrs. de la Maza replied. She never sent her letter because she decided she didn't want to go on record as being so negative. It was only recently that she showed it to Elena. These are some excerpts from her letter:

> *I have tried in every moment to be worthy of your kind efforts to resettle me; worthy to represent the free Cubans, we political, exiled people, searching for a democratic country where our children could be raised in democratic codes of life, according with the principles that allow men, as un-*

alienable rights, the right to life, the right to liberty and the pursuit of happiness.

. . . You asked my first impression of my home and surroundings. Sir, the Catholic Welfare commissioned the lady in whose home my daughter had been living, to rent a house for me. It was the house I still live [in], but it hasn't seemed a home to me [for] any moment. It is a furnished back apartment, surrounded by earth with one bedroom only; the land-owner placed a bed on the porch to use as another bedroom; but the front [door], he locked. For this reason the only entrance is the back door by the kitchen sink. It makes me so uncomfortable when people come to visit the teacher [this refers to her position at Saint Vincent's] and find me washing dishes; there is no other door. The bathroom lacks a shower and a curtain. We Cubans are so fond of showers! Through its broken window glass the cold air filters and makes it chilly.

The only heating is in the center of the house, close to it you feel too warm but the rest is chilly! The floors are so crooked: the bathroom is like this [slanted line drawn], the porch-bedroom [another slanted line drawn in the opposite direction], the living room [a curved line drawn, indicating buckling]. My daughters sleep two in a bed, two in another and myself on the toughest sofa in the living room. For two weeks I slept without a pillow until a friend sent one my little daughter brought from Cuba. We have to walk ten-and-a-half blocks from the house to school. For it I had to pay eighty dollars the 21st of Dec., and sixteen dollars [for] gas heating . . . and $3.85 [for] electricity. . . . [This] left me broke for Christmas. My wages are $70.66 a week, but the 22nd of Dec. began the Christmas vacation and then I had no work and had no pay until the first Friday of January.

By the 21st [of] Jan. I tried to move to a better apartment, just two blocks from my work, only renting for seventy-five dollars, gas included and with two nice bedrooms, carpeted, with front and back doors, shower and bath, a good heating system. But one of my sponsors came here and prevented me, [saying] that if I persisted in moving I would make it "difficult for myself and for the rest of the Cubans here." So I had to remain here. She reminded me also I was here by her kind help, finding me a job, "because Cubans were not welcomed [sic] here." When she left, I cried and felt so sorry that I wished I had never come here where we were so unwelcomed [sic].

I don't know if it is because I have worked without any rest, day in, day out from 6:30 A.M. to 3 P.M. and sometimes have to wash all our clothes, sheets, and towels by hand, but I feel so tired, so discouraged![13]

Mrs. de la Maza concluded her letter by expressing the hope that they will move soon to another city when her husband gets work. Elena says this means that by the time she responded, her father was probably at Opa Locka. Mrs. de la Maza praised the staff at Saint Vincent's as being helpful and the students as smart. She wanted desperately to get her teaching credentials certified by the American system.

Elena shakes her head as she shows me her mother's letter.

I never knew how hard it was for her and how discouraged she became. She tried to have good spirits around us and pretended everything was normal or that it would get better soon. She wanted to make sure we didn't feel sorry for ourselves.

Mrs. de la Maza knew that she and the girls had to move from Roma Avenue. Besides the unstable floors in the house, the landlord was pressuring them to cut the grass on the 10' by 6' postage-stamp-size yard, but they had no experience in yardwork and had no tools to cut the grass.

In the end, the house was so unstable that it actually shifted on its foundation. After a big storm the floor began to tilt. At that point some friends—maybe it was the Durans, who had already helped us in so many ways—found us another *casita* (a term still used in the Southwest meaning little house) that was much bigger.

Once in a while we would get to make a call to Cuba. We'd call Cuba and the operator would say, "There is a two-hour delay"; or, "Today there is a five-hour delay." This was usual. Then we'd sit around—maybe all day—and wait for the operator to call us back. There were delays because the Cuban system was so primitive.

We got to talk to our parents several times on the phone after the month-long blackout following the Bay of Pigs Invasion. After my mother came, we didn't have a phone in Albuquerque; we couldn't afford one. If anyone called us, they would call someone whose number we'd given to them. We'd get the message and try to call back. We probably called from Mrs. Davies' house.

One of the things I always did was write letters; I had become a letter writer. Before my mother came, I wrote my aunts, my mother and father, and a few friends twice a week. Around April or May, we got a

9. Elena and Cecilia celebrating Independence Day of Cuba, May 20, 1962, in Albuquerque, New Mexico, with a Cuban flag made by Elena.

brownie camera. I took pictures of everything we saw and did. I would send these back to my father and aunts in Cuba. My mother has a few of them. The ones sent to Cuba were probably destroyed by Aunt Nina. She burned a tremendous number of letters and personal papers before she, Toya, and my grandfather left. We'll talk about their leaving later.

Elena pauses, then comments that it is strange what is remembered after years have passed.

My strongest memory of my first year at Saint Vincent's doesn't involve any of the subjects I was studying. It is the fund raising the school had after Christmas: selling candy. The school said the person who sold the most in each class would get a prize. I started my rounds, first in Old Town Albuquerque, but then I decided to do the southwest section, which was where the rich people lived. With the help of my sisters, Mrs. Davies, and her daughter, I ended up selling sixty-eight boxes, an amazing number, and I won first prize.

The nuns asked me what I wanted for a prize. I wanted to take the after-school art lessons that had to be paid for. Silvia was taking these classes, I guess as part of her regular schedule of classes or because the Garcías had paid for them. So my prize was twenty-five dollars, which was the fee for the classes. Of course, we didn't have that kind of extra money. It was so generous of my mother to let me spend the twenty-five dollars that way. Even though we could have used the money for many things, she insisted that it was my prize. She totally approved of my taking the art classes. Dad did, too. I've found a letter he wrote me about my winning the prize and some other matters when he was still in Cuba.

Elena went to find the letter, returned, and remained standing. The winter light from a window fell on the pages as she read his letter, translating it as she went.

Dearest Elena,

From a letter on Feb. 19 we know you had great a success with the Sweetheart Campaign at your school, having been the girl who sold the most: sixty-eight dollars in sales and donations. All this was with Mrs. Davies' help, her daughter, Demetria, and your younger sisters. I congratulate you, my dear, and I am very glad to see this example of togetherness from your sisters who helped you so that you would do even better. In the Friday call of the 23rd, I found that you are in the art class and that the Sisters saw drawings of Maria Elena of Switzerland.

I interrupt.
Who is Maria Elena?

This was my childhood project. My mother was able to bring it when she left Cuba. Maria Elena was my alter ego; she was my fantasy self as Heidi. I had started this project when I was about nine or ten, after I had found a calendar that had these wonderful pictures of Switzerland. When it was going to be thrown out, I asked if I could save it. These beautiful pictures inspired me to start a pictorial or drawing record, one drawing for every day of the year. The idea was that there would be 365 drawings of this fantasy as Maria Elena in Switzerland. I still have it. By the time I left Cuba, I had almost 110 drawings. They were all pencil drawings on 8½" x 11" paper; any new techniques I learned went into this project. This was a family project. Occasionally I would browbeat Beatriz into helping me. When she discovered some interesting ways of using colored pencils, I got her to show me those. Sometimes I would actually get her to do some of the drawings for me. At one time I got my dad to draw a castle that I was having trouble with.

Did you ever spread them all out and show them together?

No, I kept them filed by month. Many of the elements in the drawings reflected our lives in Cuba, but I would use my imagination to figure out what a Swiss girl would do. At other times I would try to be accurate. I had read a lot about Switzerland.

Silvia had taken my drawings of Maria Elena to the sister who taught the art class. The sister judged from my talent that I should be included in the class.

Was the Maria Elena project the first time you consciously did art?

No, I had art classes at Margot's school. That had always been my favorite class. I've mentioned that for the half year I was at Ruston, I was in an art class that was more formal or structured. The art class at Saint Vincent's was a continuation. There we had real art materials, not just colored pencils, which was all we had at home. It was great fun. I got to do some ceramics, a little tiny mosaic, and a large mural, which was a group project.

I was really interested in art and music, although I didn't have any problems in academics. I generally got between an A- and a B+.

Now, back to my father's letter. He says that someone has told him I am becoming a great cook and am increasing my culinary skills. My dad loved to eat good food.

I just returned from Pa's house [Elena's maternal grandfather] where I go every night to converse with the old folks and Nina and Toya. Here the latter is the cook and she is making us some really good, tasty things. To-night she made us croquettes. The roast chicken she makes is also very delicious. Other times she makes Ajiaco (a vegetable stew). Another time she made carne fría (a cold meat loaf).

This was another one of my aunt's specialties that she made for our parties. The thing I liked the best was the bread and the pumpkin pudding, which was based on my grandmother's recipe. There was also a kind of bread pudding that we used to help make. After the bread was soaked in the milk, we put the bread and the pumpkin through a sieve, then cooked it. It came out like hard custard.

My father's letter continues:

> *Tonight we are seeing something on TV you would like:* Le Médecin Malgré Lui *or* The Doctor in Spite of Himself *by Moliere.*[14] *The synopsis in three acts was very good. There is a scene at the end where the people beat each other with sticks where a charlatan is pretending to be a doctor. He has a string of funny malapropisms—lots of crazy stuff.*
>
> *Your Uncle Juan is much better. They are going to prescribe some eyeglasses for him. We still have to read to him. [He had just had a cataract operation.] At the moment I am reading him a mystery which occurs in a haunted house. It is called* The Man Who Couldn't Shudder; *on page forty-five there was already one murder.*[15]

He wrote only about things that he was sure the censors wouldn't cross out. He told me later that he mentioned the food to reassure us they were getting enough to eat.

I ask Elena to tell me more about her Uncle Juan.

Uncle Juan lived in the same house with us, but I didn't have much of an idea about him until I was an adult. I learned from my mother that he had studied law and that he had worked as a lawyer. When I was little, I just assumed he had reached the age when one retires. My mother tells me that in Cuba he would be called neurasthenic. He was high-strung with some emotional problems. My grandfather really pushed him when he was young to work at his law firm. He reached a point where he couldn't take the pressure and criticism from my grandfather anymore. He just stopped working very young.

The one thing that he and my dad liked to do together was weather watching. In the evening they would go out on the terrace or up on the second-floor roof terrace and look at the sky and make their predictions. It was almost a game to see who would be right. He always alerted us when a lunar eclipse would occur. We would go out and watch it.

Juan liked cats. My whole family, even my dad, were cat people. There were strays in the neighborhood. Juan felt sorry for them; he would find table scraps and put them out in the back alley. My mother didn't let any of the cats sleep with us. Uncle Juan was the only one who had cats in his room. There were a couple he had adopted as the inside cats, while most of them were the outside cats.

Elena is quiet for a minute. She smiles, raises her head, and we share an unstated conclusion that every family has its own charming eccentricities.

Did you see your sisters during the school day at Saint Vincent's?

Not generally. Most days we would bring our lunches from home, so we ate in the classroom. Beatriz and I were in the high school. Silvia was in the middle school, and Cecilia was in the elementary school. I would see Silvia in the art class. I didn't get to see my mom during the school day; she was in her own classes unless there was a problem.

It must have been comforting to know you were all in the same building.

Oh, yes, it was.

Elena describes how they walked to school and back home together. On a particular day when the temperature was close to zero, they were galloping, trying to get to school quickly. Their coats were the lightweight ones that Mrs. de la Maza had made them in Cuba. A man stopped and offered them a ride. Mrs. de la Maza hesitated. She had told her girls repeatedly, "You don't accept rides from strangers."

The man insisted, "It's real cold. I just want to help you."

There were other people who helped us out by driving us places. Occasionally we would get rides to church, which was near Saint Vincent's. One Sunday we were in the car with a woman who gave us rides. We were at a stoplight; the light turned green, and she started to go. A car on the other street didn't stop and kept going through the intersection and slammed into the car we were in. No one was injured, but we had to wait for the police. The lady whose car was hit—I can't remember her name—decided she was going to take the man who hit her to court. We were all witnesses. Our whole family ended up going to traffic court.

Did she win?

Of course! With all of us as witnesses, there was no denying that he had run the red light.

Do you remember if you had any sense that "the system works" or that "justice triumphs?" You have mentioned that your family had a strong sense of right and justice.

I guess we did get a sense of this country being a participatory democracy, but it was mostly the novelty. They didn't actually ask us anything. Traffic court is so mild. I was expecting and hoping for Perry Mason![16]

Now back to my family. When I first saw Cecilia, she seemed really spoiled. My grandparents, particularly my grandfather, who had adored her since she was the baby, had evidently spoiled her. Everything had to be her way. She turned eleven right after she and my mother came to Albuquerque. When she started school in Albuquerque, she began having problems. She complained that she didn't want to talk English, that she didn't want to socialize with the kids or follow directions in the class. My mother had several conferences with her teachers. My mother always blamed the teachers. "They are being mean to her; they don't understand what she is going through. She is having a difficult time adjusting. It's just her way of coping with it."

It's probably true that the teachers didn't understand. None of us quite understood the emotional trauma we were feeling; it was coming out in strange ways. It became clear to me that Beatriz, Silvia, and I were doing better than Cecilia.

For me the transformation involved adjusting myself rather than expecting the world to adjust to me. Cecilia, being younger, expected the world to accommodate her more, and she was less willing to adapt to the situation. Academically she was not doing as well as the rest of us. Socially she was not making friends. We had always been very sociable. Even though I was shy in front of strangers, I usually made friends wherever we went. I always had one or two good friends.

I was surprised that Cecilia didn't want to use English. She had gone to Margot's school, so she was bilingual, although she might not have had as much exposure as Beatriz and I to American history and culture. When we were there, we studied about the Indians and the Pilgrims; we had some sense of the U.S. and what went on here. Cecilia wasn't old enough to have gone through those courses. She probably didn't have the overview we had, and she wouldn't have had as much of the language; but, being younger, after a few months she should have been able to pick up English the way most children of immigrants do. She expressed this rebellion by refusing to speak English. This resistance was the beginning of emotional problems that would bother her all her life.

At home Cecilia tried to be helpful; she liked to experiment with cooking.
Although they had never kept house or cooked, the sisters were trying to learn

new things. Their grandmother hadn't allowed them to be in the kitchen, but seeing the burdens their mother had, they tried to help. Elena did some of the cooking, but it was Cecilia who staked out the kitchen as her territory. She experimented with cooking. One time she decided to put blue food coloring to spike up the dish natilla, *a custard made from eggs and milk that usually has a yellow color. Elena says it wasn't too bad, but the blue food coloring turned it green. Failure or success, Cecilia would say, "I'm just trying to help out."*

Do you think the deprivations that she and your mother went through in Miami registered with her more because she was younger?

I don't know. I remember having a conversation with her. I asked her what was it like after we left. She said, "I really liked it. I always wanted to be the center of attention." She was very spoiled. Beatriz and I have always wondered why my parents let her get away with so much. My mother would let her go on and on when she had a temper tantrum. After it was over, it was my mother who would apologize.

Do you think it was because she was the youngest and left behind when the rest of your sisters went to Florida?

Probably. My mother perceived Cecilia as being a little delicate. Silvia was big and was almost matched physically to me. We were always pushing ourselves to our limits, challenging each other physically. We played rough games, climbing trees and scaling fences, but my mother didn't like for us to play with the boys in our neighborhood because she thought they played too rough. Beatriz was a little more delicate and ladylike. She didn't participate in all our physical contests. Cecilia was much smaller. She was really petite. I think that contributed to my mother's feeling that she was defenseless.

In retrospect I can see that Cecilia was a bit of a manipulator. She understood that she wasn't going to win any physical contests, but that she could use negative emotions to manipulate people. She did this with my mother. This was a lifetime pattern. She would victimize herself so that my mother would stand up for her.

What was happening with your father? How long did he have to wait to get leave?

My dad had to wait longer than he expected. As I told you, he had agreed to let my mother and Cecilia use the two airplane tickets that came through.

Did he still believe that Castro would pass?

I think after the Bay of Pigs, he began to see the pattern very clearly. He knew he had to get out as soon as possible. The family sort of closed ranks. Small family squabbles were put aside.

At the time Elena and her sisters left, their father was working on a proj-ect that was to be a resort hotel at the Laguna del Tesoro, in the Matanzas province, a day's drive from the Mazas' house. Mr. de la Maza had become the head of the project. The engineer who had been heading it had disap-peared in the middle of the night. Castro had said this project was going to be a tourist resort for the people. A year or so before leaving, Elena asked her father to show her the drawings. Elena says she loved his renderings. She and her father were skeptical and wondered why Castro would build a resort in the middle of nowhere. It has since become his own private resort. Mr. de la Maza would see Castro once in a while. When he began to see the way things were going under Castro, he decided he would resign. He thought that if they couldn't get any work out of him, they would be more likely to let him go.

I ask if he was persecuted for this.

Not that I know of. He never mentioned it. Some years later he told me about being imprisoned on the Isle of Pines when he was young.[17] This was the worst prison in all of Cuba. He was set up by a neighbor in the thirties when he was student at the university. The university was a source of constant student agitation. Although he didn't have any strong political leanings, he was against the Machado dictatorship.[18] A group of students ran a little newspaper that spoke out against the government. My father had access to a mimeograph machine in the basement of someone's house, so he was asked to mimeograph the sheets of the pa-per. It was rather harmless; he wasn't in a conspiracy.

At the same time some neighbor of his, who probably didn't like him, decided to set him up. In those days foodstuffs were very scarce.[19] It was sort of like it is today; everyone was hungry. A neighbor lady told him there was someone who had a canned ham that she and her husband des-perately needed; but they lived far off—halfway around Havana Bay. Getting there was complicated by the fact the buses weren't very regu-lar. She kept pestering him, and he kept trying to put her off. He finally agreed to do it.

He got on the bus and went to this place where the lady's ham was supposed to be. The place was closed up tight. While he was standing there trying to figure how to find the people and get the ham, a policeman appeared. As soon as my dad said he was a student at the university, the policeman said, "Come with me." He was taken to a police station and accused of being a conspirator. He was in a place where he was alone, where he couldn't easily call friends or family. It looked suspicious that he was so far from home.

The police decided they were going to hold him without benefit of a trial. Then they asked his family to pay fifty dollars, which in those days was a small fortune. Today this would be equivalent to several thousand dollars. My grandfather could have scraped the money up, but my dad was really rankled. He felt he was being held for a ransom. He told his father, "You're not to pay it!"

The only incriminating thing he had on him when he went to jail was a list of the students who were very involved in the underground newspaper. He didn't want the police to get this list. For a few days he was at *La Cabaña*. When his sister Piedad visited, they cut the lining of her jacket, and she sneaked the list out. He didn't compromise the others.

Mr. de la Maza, then in his twenties, was sent to the Isle of Pines, where he stayed imprisoned for three months. He told his family that it got very cold because they didn't have enough warm clothes or covers. Elena says that from letters he wrote, his family realized it was bad and paid the fifty dollars.

I comment that this is a pattern in Cuba: of people being arrested and of having to pay their way out, like those who were taken prisoners after the failure of the Bay of Pigs.

In Cuba, Thomas describes the release price as being several tens of thousands of dollars, depending on the rank and importance of the prisoner.[20]

It's a pattern in the previous dictatorships because they were greedy. As long as you bribed them, you could get out. It's different these days.

Elena's voice is hard, her lips tight.

They still require bribery, but it's more than money; it is a matter of humiliation and a total capitulation of your principles.

In 1962, Mr. de la Maza resigned from the ministry and waited for his permits and plane ticket. At one point he was so desperate to leave that he contacted one of the people who made runs to Florida in a boat. He went to the dock to give the man the money, almost two thousand dollars. He normally didn't go there because of the distance from where he lived. It was at night, and very quiet. After being imprisoned once, Mr. de la Maza had learned to be circumspect. He was walking around and saw one of the milicianos *(one of Castro's soldiers). The* miliciano *asked who he was and to state his business. Mr. de la Maza said he liked to come there and walk by the water and think about things. Since he appeared to be a peaceful, respectable man, the* miliciano *didn't search him but said, "You might not want to be around here because we just arrested a man who was going to help a bunch of people sneak out."*

It was probably the man whose boat my father planned to escape in. If he had gone there a little sooner, he might have been arrested, so he decided he wasn't going to try that.

Dad finally got all the forms and was able to leave. By the time he left, people were able to take less and less—maybe just a carry-on. He was allowed three changes of clothes. It was one of the tactics to humiliate people and to give them less of an opportunity to smuggle things out. The bigger your bag, the more chance you'd have to hide things.[21]

The first time we were able to speak with my father by phone in this country was such a treat. It was near the end of April. For three months he was at Opa Locka, Florida, where Cuban men were processed.[22] By that time the regulations were much stricter. They were so overloaded with Cubans coming that new arrivals were not at liberty to leave the camp. It took them a long time to process everyone. Dad probably didn't start going out on job interviews right away. The Cuban Refugee Center got him a ticket to come to Arlington, Virginia, for an interview. They must have been pretty sure that he would be hired. He was offered the job as a draftsman for a construction company in the Washington, D.C., area.

He found an apartment with two other younger Cuban men. For the first months they shared a small apartment. By phone he and my mother figured out how we would all get together.

The amazing thing was that, as tight as things were, my mother had salted away five hundred dollars. I don't know how she managed this— paying rent, buying groceries, and everything. We began looking into how we would come across the country to join my father. Beatriz and I checked out the Greyhound and Trailways bus lines. We found that for five hundred and some dollars all five of us could get a bus to Washington.

Since we were with my mother, and my father was now in the country, for me the trip was not about resettlement but about adventure. We would see a lot of America in our cross-country trip. I wanted to see the great industrial part of America. This sounded so romantic to me. Beatriz and I found out that if we went by what was called the "northern route"—north from St. Louis—we could go through Pittsburgh. It wasn't any more expensive.

We left Albuquerque on July 31 or August 1, 1962. We arrived in Washington on August 4. We left in the late afternoon and drove through the mountains on Route 66. Beatriz and I made a little notebook about our trip. We listed every town we got close to or went through. Our first night we crossed the Texas panhandle. When we woke up the next day, we were driving through the cornfields of Oklahoma. We had our breakfast in Oklahoma City. We continued through Arkansas. I remember being very taken with the landscape of Arkansas. It was a wonderful change after the flatness of Oklahoma.

After Arkansas we went on up to St. Louis, where we were scheduled to stop for dinner. While we were out eating, our seats were occupied by a black family. The bus driver said that we couldn't get back on the bus. If we got on, the black family would be put off. The situation was difficult. The bus driver wanted to make sure that no one would cry "racism." Our bags were taken out from underneath the bus and we had to wait a couple of hours for the next bus.

Did you feel this treatment was unjust?

My memory is that we were glad we could stay in St. Louis a few more hours and maybe see a little more of it. We were assured we would arrive in Washington at the same time. It wasn't a big deal with us.

This was 1962. Three years before, the "sit-ins" at Woolworth's lunch counters began, eventually desegregating eating facilities across the country. The federal government had become involved in the slow battle for equal access that included interstate commerce, which was regulated by the federal government.[23]

You told me that it was important to you to see Pittsburgh because of the industry there. Where did that interest come from?

Most of my information about the U.S. and Switzerland came from an encyclopedia that my grandfather had bought. By the time I was about eleven, my grandfather felt the *Tesoro* was a little out-of-date. A door-to-door salesman came to our house, selling the *World Book Encyclopedia*.[24] My grandfather thought the terms were right and that it would help us in our studies. I read that encyclopedia from front to back. It had this black-and-white photograph of the area in Pittsburgh where the three rivers come together: there were a lot of bridges, smokestacks, and a huge railroad station. There wasn't any thing like this in Havana. It seemed very romantic. I thought at that time I might study engineering. I had gotten interested in how things got built. I felt I had to see a big industrial city like Pittsburgh. My sisters and mother went along with this.

So what was Pittsburgh like?

What I remember was that once we left St. Louis, crossed the Mississippi, and went through Illinois, Indiana, and across Ohio, it was very foggy, very gray. By the time we got to Pittsburgh the next afternoon it was still gray, not as colorful or romantic as I had hoped. It was rather quick. We didn't get to stop and look around. We never saw the big railroad station. I did get to see the bridges. I was satisfied with that, but a little disillusioned about the glamour of industry.

Then we came on down through Pennsylvania to western Maryland. The weather began clearing. By the time we drove through Baltimore it was seven at night and almost dark. My main recollection is that all of a sudden all the buildings had become red brick. That was unusual. In Albuquerque everything was adobe or modern suburban, ranch-style houses. In Cuba, at least in our neighborhood, houses were made out of stuccoed concrete that gave them a colonial look. The older houses were built of stone, then stuccoed. All I could see in Baltimore were apartment buildings and row houses made of brick. There were a lot of trees, too, a lusher vegetation than in Albuquerque.

Even though my grandfather went to medical school there, Mom had never seen Baltimore. We thought it was a little run-down. This was long before the Inner Harbor and the other improvements. We never got near the downtown area, where the medical school at the University of Maryland is located.

I can't remember seeing my dad for the first time, but I'm sure we all jumped on him and hugged and cried. Then we gathered up all our bags and took a taxi or rode in the car of one of my father's friends. We went to the apartment he had rented in Lee Gardens in Arlington. The apartment was on the third floor, but because the ground dropped away in the back, it was more like the fourth floor. We were on the top floor of the building. There was a great panoramic view. I remember the first time that night that I looked out.

Elena pauses.

After all we'd been through, after almost a year and half, here we all were. It seemed much longer to me. At the same time, leaving Cuba, going to Kendall, then Albuquerque seemed like a long dream of only one night. So much in my life had changed. I looked out the window of our apartment into the darkness. In a strange way it seemed comforting and reassuring because I knew when I turned back around my family would be there. We were free—and we were together.

Starting Again in Arlington, Virginia

My father started to work as a draftsman with a construction company. Later he changed companies to work for the Cafritz Construction Company. At the time my father worked there, Mr. Cafritz was still building up his large real estate holdings.[1]

You've told me earlier that you thought Cafritz liked your father because he was from the "Old World," by way of Cuba, of course.

It was a mutual respect. My father liked Mr. Cafritz and felt he was well treated by him. I think Mr. Cafritz, as a self-made man, understood my father's situation. He knew my dad had had a successful practice in Cuba. Mr. Cafritz thought my dad was very knowledgeable, but he wasn't able to use him as an architect because he wasn't familiar enough with the American codes. For this reason my father never took the exam here to become an architect.

How did your father feel about what had happened to him? He had been successful and renowned in Cuba as an architect and a landscape designer. Was it hard for him?

I know it was hard, but he never talked about it. He was grateful that Mr. Cafritz had given him this opportunity. He was very loyal to the firm.

My mother really wanted to teach again. It was good money, and it was her field. But she didn't have her certificate or the papers stating she had a degree from Havana University. In Albuquerque the requirement that she have a teaching certificate had been waived. In Arlington she needed to have employment as a teacher or a commitment from a school to get her certificate. It was a catch-22: she had to have one to have the other. So she had to give up on that. One of the first jobs she took was just down the street. I think they paid her two dollars an hour or whatever the minimum wage was to stuff envelopes for four to six hours a day.

For Beatriz, Silvia, Cecilia, and me, after getting settled, our first priority was school. My mom and dad inquired about the location of the nearest parish. Ten blocks down, just on the other side of Clarendon, was our nearest Catholic church, Saint Charles. Since Silvia and Cecilia were still in elementary school, they were going to be attending the parish school there. It was small but nice. We found out that Bishop O'Connell was the corresponding high school for Beatriz and me, but this was way out, close to Falls Church. It was quite a bus ride.

It was a huge expense for my parents at that time. We did get the usual break: the tuition is half for the second child. I think my parents asked for some kind of terms so they could pay an amount every month. I remember at the time I was aware that this was a tremendous amount of money for my parents to pay.

Did you consider going to public school?

It was suggested, but my mother was very much against it. Although we'd been to private, secular schools in Cuba, my parents had been told Catholic schools would provide a better education than the public ones in this country. O'Connell in those days was a relatively new school. They had had two or three graduating classes before us. Eight different parishes sent their students there; they had pooled together to build it. It was supposed to be one of the best in the area.

What I found so interesting about it was that there were boys and girls, but it wasn't really co-ed. The girls had their wing, and the boys had theirs. We were only together in the lunchroom, on the bus, and in the carport, where we usually waited ten or fifteen minutes for the buses. The cafeteria was L-shaped; we had separate wings of the "L" to eat in. After you finished, you could socialize. Most of our school years had been spent in single-sex classes, so this change was very important to us. It was exciting and novel.

And you had uniforms?

The boys wore ties and navy blue jackets. The girls had navy wool vests and skirts and white blouses. Again this was an expense for my parents. Beatriz and I ended up buying second-hand uniforms from a store that carried the uniforms. We got new blouses, of course.

I liked O'Connell, but I was intimidated. I didn't know anyone in the school. I was coming in as a sophomore, and Beatriz was a senior. I had great luck on the first day when I was wondering who to sit with in the cafeteria. A lot of people were already sitting down with friends. I was standing, looking lost, I'm sure. I saw another girl who looked like she was in the same boat. We turned around to each other and said, "Why don't we sit together?" We sat down and started talking. Her name was Pat. We started a friendship that lasted through that whole first year. She was almost my only friend until I joined the chorus. She was an army brat and had just moved to the area and didn't know anyone either. That helped ease me into the school.

Just as Elena was getting settled in her classes, the Cuban Missile Crisis occurred. In the fall of 1962, United States reconnaissance flights detected that the Soviet Union had installed missiles and missile-launching sites in Cuba.[2] Cuba had been suspended from the Organization of American States. Because Castro feared another invasion, he sent his brother Raúl Castro to Russia to ask for more military presence in the form of troops and missiles. In Cuba: The Pursuit of Freedom, *Hugh Thomas speculates that Kruschchev, the Russian president, probably saw this as a way of exerting diplomatic pressure on President Kennedy and the U.S. government. After the missiles were installed, President Kennedy imposed a "quarantine"—a naval blockade—to prevent any more offensive weapons from arriving in Cuba The quarantine was to be enforced by destroyers, cruisers, an antisubmarine aircraft carrier, and other ships arranged in an arc from Florida to beyond Puerto Rico. A tense stand-off followed, during which many feared nuclear war was imminent. After behind-the-scenes negotiations, the United States agreed to withdraw its missiles in Turkey, and the Russians withdrew theirs from Cuba.[3]*

I ask Elena if her family was successful in communicating with her grandfather and aunts in Cuba at that time. She doesn't remember if they attempted to. As time went on, phoning became even more difficult. They would call on Sunday morning—as did probably all the other Cuban exiles in the United States. An operator would put them on a list and tell them how long the wait would be; usually it was five or six hours. The families had to be very circumspect about what was discussed. Since all the calls went through an operator, the government could easily listen in randomly.

When the Missile Crisis happened, I felt we were close to a nuclear disaster. We were all together in Arlington. I thought we'd be blown up—all of us as well as my aunts and grandfather in Cuba. I thought Washington would be ground zero.[4] I was talking to another Cuban classmate on the bus one morning during this time. When we said good-bye, we had the solemn air of people who felt they would not live to see another day. Miraculously, the crisis passed and our lives resumed.

Mrs. de la Maza had applied to the State Department to become a translator. She brought home occasional jobs, translating things from Spanish into English or vice versa. The sisters helped her with some of this work. Beatriz, Silvia, and Elena were given a batch of children's letters written to the astronauts in Spanish by children in Latin America. The children asked for every detail of the launch and for plans for the rocket. The letters had to be translated, typed up neatly, and given back to the State Department. The girls' mother gave them her pay for doing this.

Sometime during our first year in Arlington, the Garcías' son, who was here on business, stopped to see us in Arlington. They were the family that Beatriz and Silvia had lived with in Albuquerque. He was pleased to see that we were all together and doing well. He made some cryptic remarks about the fact that during the resettlement of Cuban children with foster families, each family got $170 per child per month from Catholic Welfare. He said with a wink that some people were paying off their mortgages that way.

Elena is more charitable to Helen's family than is Mr. García; she feels that it was important to Helen to be a participant in the program since she helped to administer it.

Not that it wasn't kind of them to offer us their homes, but it wasn't exactly the sacrifice I had believed for all those years.

I ask her if she has kept up with Helen and her family.

While we were in Albuquerque, I did in a remote sort of way. My mother suggested I call John on Father's Day and wish him well, but they had moved to another state soon after we left. We didn't have each other's new addresses, so we lost touch.

There were a number of after-school activities at O'Connell; chorus was particularly important to Beatriz and Elena. The chorus was supervised by a nun, Sister Cecilia. In addition to the regular chorus, Sister Cecilia had a group called the Choraleers, which gave special programs at Christmas and Easter. Being a part of this group required an audition. Beatriz and Elena were selected for the group. They felt their being able to sing in harmony helped them in the audition. Practice was for two hours after school twice a week and gave them another opportunity to make friends. The chorus was made up of girls; the boys had a corresponding group. Occasionally they did concert pieces together.

Pat had tried out too and was selected. Mary Ann, who lived in Pat's neighborhood, was also in the group plus another girl who was in the next parish from us. We would end up riding the same public bus after practice. In those days the students could get on the bus for fifteen cents.

What special performances did you have?

The Christmas show was really wonderful, but the highlight of our first year in the chorus was when we found out the school always put on a musical production. This year it was going to be *Brigadoon*.[5]

Beatriz describes this in her "Memoirs":

Almost eighty girls and twenty-some boys had signed up for the audition. Most of the boys got in, but the girls had to go through a long process of elimination. We started learning some songs in October, went through four try-outs, and every time, the morning after, I felt frozen as I looked at the list of those who had survived the latest round. Both my sister Elena and I made it through all four try-outs. We did not get any "lead" parts; she [Elena] became one of the accompanists, and I was in the chorus; but just being part of it was more than enough. Saturday nights, Sunday afternoons, through rain, snow and all else, the whole cast really came together. We imbibed the spirit of the play and its message: *Brigadoon* was about a miracle, faith and the power of true love. Our director, Mr. Hagy, who, so I was told, had had Broadway experience, made it a point to make us all feel important. From the lead to the dancers, the singers and stage hands, he made us all feel and think like "theater people."[6]

Elena continues the story.

As Beatriz said, we were part of the chorus. I think it was because of our

10. Elena in her costume for the production of *Brigadoon* at O'Connell High School, Falls Church, Virginia, 1963.

sense of pitch. We tended to be the anchor wherever we were placed. We could hold our pitch until everyone who was sitting around us could adjust their pitch to match ours. During the auditions they found out that I could play the piano. Several weeks into the rehearsals they switched me to being the accompanist. Sister Cecilia helped me learn the music. There were three pianists.

The final production of Brigadoon *played two nights, Friday and Saturday, to a full capacity gym with extra bleachers. Sunday there was almost a full house. Beatriz writes, "Emotions were running so high that on opening night, Archie Beaton, the school hunk and Romeo, wept copiously as the body of his 'son, Harry,' was brought out in the second act."*[7]

The date of the opening night was March 29. This was an incredible coincidence: it was two years to the date of our arrival in the U.S. We were involved in a play with the themes, as Beatriz said in her "Memoirs," of a miracle, faith, and the power of true love. A miracle and faith were so much what our life had been about the last year.

When they were rehearsing for Brigadoon, *Elena needed to practice the piano music. Someone in their parish arranged for her to get an old upright piano and helped move it up to their third-floor apartment. She was having to practice several hours a day. This began to cause problems with one of the neighbors, who wanted her "peace and quiet." This woman was expecting when the Maza family moved in. After she had the baby, the piano playing kept the baby awake.*

We didn't even know about their complaints until they wrote the landlord. What bothered us the most was these neighbors had written that "Cubans are very loud." We thought this was most unfair.

Beatriz was playing, too. My mother had found a piano teacher for Beatriz and me. We had a class once a week on Saturday. The teacher wasn't too inspiring. What made studying with her difficult was that she had Beatriz and me playing Bartok. This was pretty advanced. Bartok struck me as very odd harmonically; I could never get his rhythms. I was working on some of Bartok's dances. Apparently this was what really bothered our neighbors. They actually recorded my practicing the Bartok dances, and then one night they blasted us out playing these back to us. Eventually they griped so much, we had to move at the end of June 1963. We had been in Lee Gardens almost a year.

We found a little house that was only a block away on Eleventh Street in Arlington. We moved to this bungalow. It's still there. It doesn't appear to have changed at all.

After finishing *Brigadoon*, I was sort of floundering and was on the point of giving up the piano. I told my mother, "This piano teacher doesn't do anything for me. I want to play Chopin and not Bartok!" I looked for every excuse not to go to class.

In the meantime, Silvia had gotten to know another lady who taught music who lived only two blocks away from the other teacher. Mrs. de la Maza went to this teacher, Mrs. May, to see if something could be worked out for Elena to study with her. Elena wonders how her parents were finding the

11. De la Maza family in front of their house in Arlington, Virginia, 1966. *Left to right:* Elena, Silvia, Cecilia, Mr. de la Maza, and Beatriz.

*money for all this, but somehow they were squeezing the money for tuition
and lessons out of their budget.*

As soon as I met Mrs. May, we hit it off. She was wonderful, a dear, dear person.

Did Beatriz continue with the other teacher?

No. She had graduated and had received a full scholarship to Dumbarton College in Washington, so she didn't have time to take music lessons. At that point I was very focused on my playing. I had developed a great deal of manual dexterity because I had been playing so much. Silvia and I began group lessons with Mrs. May.

She began to encourage me to perform. She could see I enjoyed playing and loved the classics; she told me this is where I should concentrate. When I worked on several Haydn sonatas, she thought my playing was a little heavy. She said Haydn should be light and sprightly. She and I particularly shared a love of Brahms. I worked on a lot of his rhapsodies and a few of Chopin's etudes. She thought they were a little too difficult for me, so she got me into the preludes, which were a little simpler in technique. She was an all-around inspiring teacher.

*Mrs. May was a graduate of the University of Michigan. Her husband
was a mathematician. They had a very small house with two grand pianos in
the living room where they played duets. The couple was childless, and Mrs.
May's students and other music connections were important to her.*

We used to play musical games with her. When we came in she would tap out a rhythm and ask Silvia and me to imitate it on the piano. She could then check on how much we were learning. One day she tested me for pitch; she would play a note, and I was to name it. She played a whole bunch of notes, then asked what they were. She was pleased with my answers and said, "Elena, you have perfect pitch."

In our Saturday classes we had to learn to take down musical notation. Then I remembered something that had happened when I was in Cuba. In one of my classes we also had to take down musical notation. Usually I did well, especially on the notes, but one year I did poorly; I couldn't understand why all my notations were wrong, as if I had suddenly lost the knack. When I went back and checked my answers, I saw they were all off by a half step. The piano in that room was different from the one I was used to, but since I was only ten, I was too self-conscious to try to explain this to my teacher. When Mrs. May told me I had perfect pitch, it made perfect sense: the piano in Cuba was not tuned to concert pitch, but no one noticed but me.

I had learned the solfeggio system. When you are learning to read music, you are supposed to beat out the rhythm. If it is 4/4, you would beat out 1, 2, 3, 4. If it is 3/4, then 1, 2, 3. While you are counting out the beat or measure, you are also saying the names of the notes. When we learned this, the first year we would just say the name of the note. As we moved along, then we sang the note. It's supposed to be in pitch. We learned this at the conservatory we studied at in Havana. Even today, when I hear a note, it sings its name to me.

During her junior year, Elena had her first taste of demonstrating for a political stance. In spring of 1964, the Organization of American States (OAS) was going to pass sanctions against Cuba in response to the Cuban Missile Crisis two years before.[8] A group of Cuban exiles got a permit to demonstrate on the Mall. The purpose of their march was to let the OAS know that the exiles wanted specific sanctions imposed against Cuba, especially since Cuba was still a member of the OAS. Everyone had been impressed with the orderliness of the 1963 civil rights march, and the Cuban group wanted do the same thing. People came by buses from Miami and New Jersey. Elena estimates that between seven or eight thousand attended the march.

My parents wanted us to participate. The whole family went down. I was curious because I had heard, of course, about the 1963 march on Washington. I wanted to go and see what a protest march was like.

There were speeches and it was pretty orderly until the actual march started. We found the permit didn't include permission to march in front of the OAS building at the corner of Seventeenth and Constitution. This upset the march leaders, who thought we should be on the sidewalk in front of the OAS building, holding our placards. The fact that we couldn't march on the OAS side of Constitution Avenue didn't seem to me to make a big difference. The march itself was symbolic enough; the march was the staged media event whether anyone inside the OAS saw us or not. Some of the leaders of the march began agitating and urged the marchers to cross the street and storm the gates of the OAS.

There was a police line right in the middle of Constitution Avenue to make sure we didn't cross the street. There were also park police on horseback to help maintain order. One group in the march decided they would storm the police line, so they moved from the sidewalk into the street. I remember shouting for people to stay calm and not run into the street. The park police moved into the crowd, their nightsticks flying. I was right where they moved in; I was afraid I was going to be pulled under one of the horses. Some of the marchers had tried to overpower the police, but later they just tried to get away. I ran back onto the Mall; I was separated from my family. As things staring clearing out, I wondered what I was going to do, how I was going to get home if I didn't find my family. I didn't know the bus routes from that part of the city. Finally I found my parents.

The entire Maza family was very disappointed that the Cubans couldn't stick to a plan and continue to be orderly. If the event had been orderly, it would have been more impressive and made the Cubans look like a unified community.

That was the beginning of my idea that you can't get three Cubans in a room to agree to anything.

Is that true?

In many ways. With Cubans, I have found out we have too many chiefs and not enough Indians. Everyone has his or her own ideas and wants to lead. Many times the Cubans are overcome by their emotions. This demonstration was an example.

Elena and I talk a few minutes about the fact that Cuba has often experienced change as a result of some type of overt, even violent activity. When the demonstration in front of the OAS took place, Castro had been in power for five years; no one had thought that he could possibly last that long. The frustration level was building every year. Elena thinks that part of the problem is that Cubans have never had a parliamentary tradition.[9] The Spanish model for government was based on a monarchy. There was no tradition of two opposing parties such as exists in Britain and in the United States. Elena thinks this is probably what makes democracy work as well as it does. In Cuba there had never been the tradition of sitting in a parliament and hearing someone espousing a completely opposite point of view in a very orderly fashion. There were always a few people like her grandfather who tried to maintain decorum, but they were often drowned out. When an opposing view was presented, there would be heckling and noise to interrupt the speaker. Then it became a free-for-all. She sees this as what happened at the Mall demonstration, but on a smaller scale.

I could see this was the problem we were going to have in getting any political power: we do not have a unified voice and seem unable to do what is necessary to create one.

Elena returns to her discussion of O'Connell.

When Silvia started there, my parents really started feeling a pinch. Even though Beatriz had a scholarship, there were still expenses. My mother was trying to find a better job. She had signed up to take a course at Georgetown University; she was still trying to get her teacher's certificate. My parents must have talked to the school, because in my senior year they gave me a job as a cafeteria server.

I ask Elena if it had been psychologically hard to have to work at such a job. With no hesitation, she answers that it wasn't. Elena was given the job of selling ice cream in the cafeteria line. She would go in and eat lunch quickly, then get behind the counter and sell the ice cream and keep track of the money. She says the only thing she missed was the fifteen or twenty minutes at the end of lunch to hang out.

I didn't feel it was a hardship; I was actually kind of proud of what I did. I even got to go to the meetings for all the cafeteria workers.

My mother was now working at Kahn's Department Store that was located in the Ballston area. She worked in the alterations department. They thought very highly of her. She was there three or four years.

How did she feel about having to do that instead of a professional job, for which she was educated?

She never really complained. I think at that point she and Dad felt that any job was a good job, that there was a certain kind of dignity in just being able to work.

I guess they had seen the handwriting on the wall that things could have been worse for the family if you'd stayed in Cuba.

That's true. I found out later how close to the edge we were by the time we started leaving Cuba. Mom has told me, "We really didn't have anything." There was no money. My father's private practice had been closed. He only got a small salary from his job at the Ministry of Public Works. If they hadn't been able to live with his parents, things could have been tough. There wasn't much for them to lose by leaving. Most of their life savings had been invested in a small lot they bought a year or two before Castro came in. My parents had wanted their own house in

12. Portraits of the Maza sisters used for their residency application in 1964. *Top row, left to right:* Beatriz and Cecilia; *bottom row:* Silvia and Elena.

the same neighborhood as my grandfather's house. That had cost 17,000 pesos, which was a lot of money. After Castro outlawed all private property, the government claimed the lot.

I didn't get to take art classes again until my senior year in high school because I was trying to get all my requirements out of the way. The first two years I didn't have space for any electives. My last year at O'Connell, I finally had room in my schedule to take art. In my junior year I became friends with another student, Joanie. She was very talented, very focused. She already knew art was what she wanted to do. When I took art in my senior year, Joanie and I were in the same art class. Our art teacher was one of the younger nuns, so we identified with her. She was very simpatico. I lived for that class!

In the art class they were exposed to a number of techniques new to Elena, including silk screen, using acrylic paints, airbrushing, and drawing from models—using fully clothed classmates. O'Connell prided itself on being progressive and having a state-of-the art educational facility. They invested a lot in materials.

My friendship with Joanie really developed. She was an only child. Her father had died. Her mother's brother and his two children lived in the house with Joanie and her mother. She invited me to her house a lot to spend the night. She had a studio in the basement. We'd stay up all night yacking away. Occasionally I invited Joanie to spend the night with me even though we had no room, and we had to sleep on the floor.

We both loved Georgetown; it was so picturesque. When I invited her over, we'd walk over to Georgetown. We were much closer to Key Bridge. Rosslyn, Virginia, in those days was a conglomerate of pawnshops and run-down gas stations and clubs. So on the way to Georgetown we'd look in the pawnshops. As a matter of fact, I bought a guitar in a pawnshop. It was a cheesy guitar, absolutely awful.

I had learned to play the guitar with the help of a Cuban friend, one of our neighbors in Lee Gardens who played the guitar beautifully. She was from one of the first three or four Cuban families who lived in that area. She had an amazing repertoire of old songs, the kind we had learned in the conservatory in Cuba. She loved to sing these songs, and we would sing along. Silvia and I performed in a couple of talent shows in the school, singing and playing a couple of American and Cuban folk songs.

Joanie also tried to learn to play the guitar. We were already reading about the beatniks and Greenwich Village. We had formed these notions of how artists lived. We got involved in trying to learn folk songs and music. Joanie had a tin ear. After a while we had to tell her, "Just mouth the words; don't sing."

Joanie told Elena about Sophocles Pappas's guitar shop. Although she wanted to take lessons from him, Elena knew there was no way her family could afford the fee of forty dollars per class.

We had developed this style for wearing our scarves that became part of our fashion statement. Instead of tying them under our chins, we tied them in the back. Silvia began to wear hers like that too. They stood up on our head like a triangle. I did my self-portrait in pastels, showing the scarf standing up.

Before graduation they had an art contest at O'Connell. I entered my self-portrait and was extremely surprised that I won the first prize. At the last minute they decided to give a prize for music, which I also won. I ended up getting one hundred dollars as the combined prizes for art and music.

Being so enamored of the guitar, I decided that what I wanted was a nice acoustic guitar. I found a beautiful guitar at Sophocles Pappas's store, a floor model, that was $110. I took my hundred-dollar prize money and some baby-sitting money and bought it.

In her senior year, Elena met Jessye Norman when she was just about to graduate from Howard University, before she was well known.[10] *Mrs. May invited her to do a small recital at her house. The living room had one wall with glass doors. Elena says it seemed as if those doors might shatter because she had such a great, powerful voice. Paul Hume, the music critic for the* Washington Post, *was there. Besides having connections like Mr. Hume, Mrs. May was involved with the Friday Morning Music Club.*[11]

Mrs. May encouraged Elena to try out for this group. She became one of the youngest members and performed twice for them—once to audition and once in a small concert in the spring. Silvia also tried out, but as she was younger, they told her to wait a few years and audition again.

At the concert, I did very well. I played a Haydn sonata as my opening piece, then a Brahms nocturne. I've forgotten the rest of the program. I probably included a piece by Lecuona, a famous Cuban composer.[12]

Was he a contemporary of your cousin's?

Yes, he was, but he lived much longer than Alejandro so he is much better known. He was both a classical and popular composer. Lecuona had a fabulous mind for melodic invention. He was one of these people who gets memorable melodies out of the blue, each one distinct. Many of his songs have become popular in Cuba. One, "Siboney," has become a standard. Everyone loves Lecuona, including my parents. His work was perfect to round out the program.

Mrs. May felt that I had the talent to become a concert pianist. She taught Ann Schein, who is still a well-known touring concert pianist. She thought that with some more training, I, too, could become a concert pianist. My mother was just delighted, because this was a sort of fulfillment of a lot of family traditions. My dad was thrilled, too, but I was still wondering how I would make a living.

Elena is laughing.

What would I do for the how many years until I began touring? At the same time I was thinking about this, I was reading different college catalogues. It was very important to me to go away to school and live in a college dorm. That seemed to be every kid's dream at that age. Most of my friends in high school were doing that or planning to. There was never any question that we were going to college. I never took typing or shorthand in high school.

Was O'Connell a school for the college-bound?

Primarily. I would say two-thirds of the girls went to college; the other one-third became secretaries.

I really wanted to major in art, but I had read enough about artists' lives to know how difficult it would be to make a living this way. If we had been in Cuba, I would have gone to San Alejandro Academy, which was the big traditional beaux-arts school in Havana. And I would have griped and complained until my grandparents had paid for at least one trip to Paris, so I could have seen that art world. If I had never married, I could have lived with my parents and done my art without having to support myself. But in this country, without a dime, I didn't want to be a burden on my parents. My early experiences pointed me to the fact I needed to be self-supporting. Already my parents were spending a lot of money on my education. Their living expenses were high. I wanted to be able to contribute as soon as possible.

When I was applying to college, my mother even asked me if I really wanted to major in music instead of art. She was excited by what Mrs. May had said about the possibility of my becoming a concert pianist, but she always thought that art was my first talent. I told her that I could do art on my own, that I wanted to major in music so I could make a living.

I chose James Madison College in Harrisonburg, Virginia, because they had a music program and Mrs. May knew some of the faculty there. I had good grades, so I was accepted.

Did you have to audition?

I think that my work with the Friday Morning Music Club, maybe the concert I gave with them, counted as that.

The Maza family had met Mrs. Patterson, a Canadian whose husband worked for the World Bank. Mr. Patterson was out of the country a lot, and Mrs. Patterson didn't have any children or even many friends. In an informal way she adopted the Maza sisters and took them many places. When the Pattersons finally adopted a little baby girl, she needed babysitters. They asked Silvia to come with them when they rented a house on the outskirts of Bethany Beach, on the Chesapeake Bay in Delaware. Elena wanted to go to the beach, so she volunteered to help with the babysitting. Beatriz also took a turn.

That's how we got to the local beaches. Bethany was so wonderful. I realized how much I'd missed the sea, which was a block away from our house in Miramar in Cuba.

When I graduated from high school, my parents didn't have a lot of money. Maybe, I got a cheap watch; some girls got cars. What I wanted was for us to take a vacation. We talked to Mrs. Patterson about the place she rented, an old farmhouse about half a mile from the beach. Silvia and I talked Dad into renting it for a week or two. My dad could only come on the weekend. Since we didn't have a car, we had to go on the bus. We talked our parents into letting Joanie and me go ahead. We were there for two days on our own before our parents and my sisters came. That was very exciting.

Surfing had just started to get big on the East Coast. We met a couple of guys who were learning. They gave us rides and tried to teach us how to surf. We never got anywhere with it, but we hung out with them. So by the time my parents came, we had adopted these two young handsome guys who'd been sleeping under the boardwalk. They hadn't eaten very much, so we'd say, "Oh, come on over; we'll make you some sandwiches." It was very innocent, but we were actively looking for boyfriends at that point. One night we had an all-night party and got up the next morning to see the sun rise. My parents would have been horrified if anything had happened. Nothing did, except that the guys drank some beers and got sleepy.

A couple of days later, I was surfing on this inflatable raft. A big wave caught me and dumped me right at the feet of a tall handsome young man. By the way, the same thing happened to Beatriz, but she got knocked down hard enough to break her rib, and she had to be taken to the hospital. I knocked this guy over. I apologized. He said, "Don't think anything about it. It can happen to anyone." So we got to talking.

He told me later he had been watching me for some time and was trying to figure out a way to meet me. So he had actually thought that if he got in my path, I might run into him! We started going out. He invited me to several beach parties. Then we went back to town, and his family stayed longer. We decided that even though we'd both be going away to school, we'd stay in touch.

In the fall I entered Madison as an instrumental music major with a specialty in piano. I liked my dorm; I was on the third floor. I had two roommates. One was from California and was rather cosmopolitan. The other was—well, she was one of these southern belles from a small town. It was my first encounter with a Southerner.

My next question came from my own memories of growing up in the South. Did she think of you as a foreigner?

Oh, yes. I had not encountered that kind of prejudice before. By this time, I guess, I had developed my own prejudice against people who have very southern attitudes. She seemed so vulgar to me, at some level. She had friends who had attended the same girls' boarding school in Richmond. They discussed guys in rather graphic, indelicate ways. I was totally naive. I had never heard women talk this way. I couldn't keep up with her. She eventually changed rooms. We got another roommate who was more in our style.

In those days Madison was primarily a girls' school. The girls came from all over; one roommate, as I've said, was from California, and the new one was from New Jersey. The males were all local. I think they didn't have any dorms for them. The faculty was about evenly male and female.

In the music department the faculty was primarily male. My piano teacher was disappointing to me because I had had such a super relationship with Mrs. May, who had been my friend and mentor. My piano teacher at Madison was distant. He had me start on Bach, who struck me as so cerebral, so mathematical. It was difficult for me to handle. As I've told you, I liked the more romantic composers. My teacher also made me aware that I had some severe technical problems: fingering and how I used my muscles.

Was he too harsh?

No. I don't think so. He wanted to be encouraging, but I was at the age when I thought I knew it all. I had overcome so many problems to get where I was.

And you had been accepted and played with professionals.

That's right. Here I was being put back to doing unmelodic finger exercises. And then to discover that my first year I was going to be concentrating on a musician with whom I felt no affinity. I appreciated Bach, but he wasn't the kind of musician I wanted to spend a year with. I did work on a Liszt sonata; it was one of the few pieces that I liked in my piano studies.

Do you think it was your teacher who had the affinity with Bach?

Probably. He might have felt this composer would provide the discipline I needed. It was just one of those things. I had gone from a very intense and personal relationship with a teacher; then that wasn't there any more. I had thought that my studies at Madison would be a continuation of what I had had with Mrs. May.

Another thing that was almost traumatic was the group recital that all students were expected to do second semester. I only had to do two pieces. My performance was terrible. It was one of the few times in my life that I've blanked out. I was playing one of those pieces that repeats, then has a different bridge. I got stuck in the bridge, and I wasn't sure I could find the transition to go to the next section. It was probably the worst performance of my life. People in the audience said, "Oh, it was fine," but I felt very disappointed in myself.

When you wrote home from Madison, how much of your life could you share with your parents?

Some of it. But I didn't share with them the reservations I was developing about becoming a musician; I couldn't share my doubts about myself. For Mom, it was so important that I be able to accomplish this. I really didn't want to disappoint them. They would have been understanding, but I felt that to admit my doubts would have been letting them down. I couldn't bear to do that.

When I was at Madison, I also began a private debate about religion. For the first few months I continued to go to Mass; there was a church I walked to in town. I never felt much of a connection with that church or the people in it the way I did with Saint Charles in Arlington, where we had been in the choir and my parents were very involved in the parish activities.

I had read *1984* after my junior year in high school.[13] It was one of the summer readings. The following year I read *Brave New World;* these were considered companion pieces.[14] They had a great deal of influence on me. Orwell's *1984,* particularly, made me question a lot of the Catholic beliefs that it had never occurred to me to question before. That summer I began thinking about all of this, and I didn't know how to come to grips with it. Even though I began to see there were certain things in Catholicism I wanted to question, I just put it all aside because it wasn't the right time. As long as I was at home, I wanted to be part of that life; I didn't want my questions to cause a lot of disruption. It was when I went away to college that I began to focus on thinking about and questioning my religion.

At Madison, Elena was exposed to people of a lot of different faiths. Before this her primary associations had been with other Catholics, her schoolmates, and friends from church. For the first time she made friends with people who were Jewish, Methodist, and people who claimed to be agnostics or atheists. She was trying to forge her own philosophy. She was bothered by the Catholics' attitude about women and by the disparity between what was expected of women and what was expected of men. After going through this crisis of conscience during the first half of her first year at Madison, she decided to stop going to Mass. Elena's family was unaware of this change, but Elena says that it was her own decision and that she didn't want to involve them.

At that point another aspect of the college scene was beginning to interest me more. I met this other young woman—let's just call her J.—who was also a music student. She was a tuba major!

It seems so improbable, we both laugh. I comment that I didn't know anyone ever majored in tuba.

She had been in her marching band in high school. She was from one of those very small southern towns where she had been the oddball. She liked to write poetry and sing folk songs. She was very much into the bohemian life. One of the fun things I remember was her introducing my roommate and me to the San Francisco beat poets. So we would have these poetry readings in our room late at night. We read Ferlinghetti and Ginsberg.[15] It seemed so cutting-edge to me.

Let's pin this down in time.

It was 1965. I never had experiences like this in high school. J. and I became friends during the first couple of months of my first year. One of the courses we had to take was an orchestra course where we had to learn to play all the instruments. We spent about three weeks on each instrument; we were supposed to get a sense of what the technical requirements were to play it. I found out that I was a string-oriented person. When I went from the violin to the bass, I had no problem. My minor became the cello. The cello teacher was very impressed. Although I couldn't bow, I could get a very good pitch from the fingers. With wind instruments, I was a total failure. I couldn't make a sound with even the mouthpiece of any brass instrument. The reeds weren't much different. What a contrast. J.'s strength was in the brass wind instruments; in the string instruments, she was at a total loss.

I think J. selected me to fulfill a fantasy of hers. Of course, I didn't see it at the time.

What was the fantasy?

I think she had this fantasy that I was a Latin lover. She had probably already fixed sexually on girls as opposed to boys. She told me about one bad experience with a boy; he had not been gentle or shown any finesse. I guess in these days we would call it date rape. She felt that she had been used. This had turned her off, so she didn't want to have anything to do with men.

She had all these other fantasies of escaping her small town. She was different from so many people there. She looked to me as a foreign, exotic person and a way into new experiences.

I ate in the cafeteria with girls from my dorm, and J. would always eat with us even though she lived in another dorm. One day some of the girls we ate with decided to play a joke on us. This was in the winter. When we came out after lunch, my coat had been put on the floor; it was on top of J.'s.

They said, "Well, we thought you were so in love with each other." They were joking, but I didn't get the joke. J. wanted to put her arm around me. I thought of it in a sisterly way; my sisters and I did that a lot.

I corresponded with my boyfriend from the beach first semester. Over the Christmas vacation we became lovers. He let it drop at the end of the vacation that I wasn't his first, that he'd had one girl before. That disappointed me, so at that point my feelings for him began to wane. In the early spring he did come to visit me at Madison for the weekend. He brought a friend, whom I got a date with J. I was still not totally aware of how she felt about men and about me. The weather was nice, so we went on a long hike. We were walking and walking, and soon it was going to be dark. The guys waited until it was pitch dark and then said, "We're lost; we can't find the car."

J. and I were panicking. We knew we had to get back to the college, that they might send out the campus police to look for us. It turned out the guys knew that the car was fifty yards down the path. J. and I eventually stumbled on it; losing the car seemed very staged. I was ticked off at my boyfriend and wanted to break up with him then and there. The next morning J. and I had to figure out how we were going to ditch them. When my boyfriend came to the door, I told the other girls to say I wasn't there. That was the end of my first romance.

At the end of the year, J. told Elena how she felt. Elena says that she was so naive she never knew what had been going on. When J. told her, she went to the library and got out the only book generally available at that time about this kind of situation—The Well of Loneliness.[16] *The book didn't help Elena very much; she felt it confused her even more. J. threatened suicide and began to play psychological games if Elena didn't accept her and her feelings. Elena had never encountered anyone before who was so compulsive and manipulative.*

I didn't understand that this was what we now call emotional blackmail.

How did this affect your college work?

It was getting harder and harder to concentrate. The first semester it didn't interfere. I was on the dean's list. In spite of the fact that I was not thrilled with my piano teacher, I was doing the work and doing well at it.

J. and I continued our friendship. We came to Arlington to spend the weekend with my parents. When we were going back on the bus, we missed our bus connection and ended up getting to Harrisonburg too late to make it to the dorm. I thought that maybe we should try to go in late and explain, but J. said, "No. Let's just stay out here." We spent the night on someone's porch, then walked to school the next morning. Some of the girls, who were starting to suspect there was something between us, saw us. They worked up a Student Council hearing. I began to feel under attack. We had to appear before this board. The implication was that we were lovers and had stayed out all night. We went through the hearing, and I thought maybe we could just roll with the punches. Then things looked bad. I told J., "I want out of here. Let's run away." She agreed with me. It was a week before final exams.

I nod at Elena's situation. Well, what you and J. did was really in the spirit of the times.

Oh, definitely. My roommate from California said, "You guys should go to San Francisco." We thought that was a great idea. Although we only had $3.75, we decided to hitchhike out to San Francisco!

It was a story that was played out in at least a hundred places with hundreds of college students at this time. J. and Elena had already had one hitchhiking experience, and this had emboldened them. They knew they could hitch rides with the trucks that went up and down the Shenandoah Valley. They left town at dusk with backpacks containing two changes of clothes. They started north, then headed west through West Virginia. After being on the road two days, all of their restraint was released and they became lovers.

By Wheeling, Ohio, we were getting really hungry. Someone had bought us a burger, but we really hadn't had much to eat. J. had an aunt who lived in Wheeling. We decided to stop and see if she could help us out. She was very nice. She fed us, and then she told us, "You shouldn't be doing this. You need to call your parents. They're probably worried sick about you." She was the voice of reason. At that point I was starting to feel pretty bad about everything. I thought our parents might even think we'd been kidnapped.

So first J.'s parents were called, then my parents. Both parents agreed that the only thing was to put us back on a plane to Washington. My parents would pick us up. That was the end of the escapade.

I talked to my parents, who were sympathetic up to a point. They negotiated with Madison, arranging for me to withdraw and for Madison to expunge the record.

Did the lesbian aspect bother your parents, or were they even aware of it?

Years later my mother told me she had never liked J. and that she had suspected what had happened. She felt I had fallen under J.'s influence. She knew I would never have done all this on my own.

I moved back home. Mom got me a job at Kahn's Department Store. She was still working there as a seamstress. I loved to shop there. Of course, I couldn't afford very much. This was my first formal job. When I went in for my first day, I found out that I wasn't going to be working with the nice clothes that I liked but was assigned to the drapery department. I knew nothing about this. They were having a sale, and the store was very busy. It was just awful. When I got home, I told my mother, "I hate this job. I have to get out of it." She wanted me to stay, of course. She said, "You have to have a job. Maybe they'll reassign you."

I didn't see it that way. I called up J. and said, "I can't stand it. I've got to get away from home." I told my parents I had to get away to think it all out. So I went to visit J. in Virginia. I took my paint set with me. The first week at her house I did a gray "romance of industry" painting, which I still have somewhere in the basement.

During the second week, her father began urging us, "You girls can't just sit around here." So we looked for work in an adjacent town. The only job we could find was waitressing. With both of us working and sharing expenses, we realized we could get our own apartment. We found a place in a large old house that had been converted into four apartments. Ours had a nice front and back porch.

It was kind of fun. We used to earn twelve dollars a week plus tips. The tips weren't bad. We did have to pool them. We worked the evening shift from 7 P.M. to 2 A.M. Since it was so late, the owner or manager would give rides home to all the help. There was no public transportation that late. We were an odd assortment of people. There was one old waitress who used to come in with black eyes, really out of it. The other workers would pour coffee with Tabasco into her to try to sober her up. There were a couple of black guys. The staff changed a lot. The turnover was amazing. We stayed there almost a year.

With our great earnings, we bought a car. We made the down payment with J.'s saving and some help from her parents. We bought a new Renault, which had some strange kind of automatic transmission. We picked it out and waited for delivery. When it came, J. had to teach me how to drive it.

I made my very first art sale during this time. I had done a portrait of J. in an English riding habit. The woman in the downstairs apartment liked it so much that she traded us some good wooden bookcases for it.

We'd begun to talk about what to do next. We knew there was no future in waitressing. I wanted to go back to school, to give it another try. I realized that maybe I wasn't cut out to be a music major. I needed to think about that. We'd found a job advertised in the paper for a photo assistant. At that point I convinced J. to apply for it. She liked doing that sort of thing. The job was near a resort in the mountains of Virginia. Her application was accepted.

In March I went with J. to her new job. I couldn't find any work in town so I ended up being the lifeguard at the resort. It was an easy job: open the pool, make sure the towels were out, and then just hang around looking out and, I guess, looking good!

There were very few unmarried young people in the town. People tend to marry young in small towns. By this time, I was interested in dating males again. I didn't meet anyone. I told J. that I was going to come back to Washington when the school year stated. She had decided to stay there. My going back to school was my way of breaking off the relationship.

All during this time I had had a kind of distant relationship with my parents. I don't know if my father disapproved so much of what I was doing that he thought it best not to stay in close contact. He probably thought I had made a dreadful mistake and that it was going to be hard to come back from it. I did always feel that ultimately they supported me. I know they were pleased when I decided to go back to school.

I thought about architecture as a profession. I had recently read *The Fountainhead*.[17] I knew I could go into this field. My father was an architect. I applied to Catholic University in Washington, D.C., and managed to account for the year at Madison. Catholic University accepted me.

Introduction to Art;
the Hippies' Life of the Sixties

Besides architecture, Elena shared another interest with her father: plants and landscaping. All the houses in her neighborhood in Sandy Spring, Maryland, are large, many with lots over two acres. Some sit on rather imposingly manicured lawns that appear to have been designed for symmetry and order, lawns that reflect nothing, or everything, about the owners. Elena's house is inviting; the porch across the front of the house has a bench, a wicker chair, and, in warm weather, many potted plants. These create an informal and inviting entrance, but it is her yard that states even more clearly that this is a place where a gardener lives.

The landscaping in her yard appears random, even haphazard, but when Elena talks about the plantings, her personal design with its own intuitive arrangements is revealed. The plants are positioned for sun and for growth, and particular groupings are made also for color, texture, and seasonal blooms. The whole plan is linked with the family tradition of landscaping, which began with Elena's father and continues with her, her mother, one of her sisters, and a nephew. Once one makes the connection with this family tradition, the design of Elena's yard becomes a metaphor for the lives of her and her family: no matter how disjointed or disparate the elements appear, underlying all is the strong, unifying taproot of family.

A slate walk comes from the driveway to the front porch. A cut-leaf Japanese maple is in a circle in the walk. Small Japanese-inspired lanternlike lights line the walk. Two pear trees out in the yard came with the house,

Elena tells me, and the builder supplied the small bushes. The miniature hollies, rhododendrons, azaleas, and junipers were planted by a landscaper who was hired the first year Herb and Elena lived here. Continuing the landscaping has become a personal project that Elena does when there is time after her painting, working as a draftsman, teaching tai chi classes, leading or attending various meetings, and planning cultural events for the Cuban community.

It is spring when we stand on the porch. Elena identifies the plants in the front yard.

In front of us you can see a weeping cherry tree, but the weeping part of the graft never took.

Pink azaleas grow underneath it. To the left in a little circle is a Japanese snowbell tree. A little farther away are a blue Colorado spruce, a golden juniper, and pink peonies given to her by her mother from her yard in Falls Church. Also in the same bed are aster frikarti. Out by the road is an oakleaf hydrangea.

Elena points to a plot close to the porch.

The purple flowers are lavender. I have several other herbs: a pot of rosemary on the porch and French tarragon in the back, which I like for seasoning. There are also pots of geraniums and several different kinds of begonia.

I ask about the plant in a pot on the porch that looks like a small mimosa.

Actually it's a flamboyant. I'll show you what one looks like.

She goes into the house and is back in minutes with a book, Flowering Trees of the Caribbean.[1] *She turns to the page with the flamboyant. It has flaming red flowers with five petals; four are bright orange-red, and one is white with red stripes.*

These trees are all over the tropics. They're native to Madagascar. The colonists brought them over, and they spread all over the Caribbean. You can see them in Miami, too. There was a flamboyant next to our yard in Havana. When I was eight or nine my dad bought a copy of this book, which unfortunately had to be left in Cuba. The one I'm holding is another copy that I was able to get through a book search. This was one of my favorite books as a girl. It was like recovering a little piece of my childhood to get this copy, which you can see is even autographed by the author.

Since he was a landscape architect, my father bought his copy by subscription. He shared his love of plants with us when we were small. He'd

13. Elena and Herb's house in Sandy Spring, Maryland.

sit us on his lap and read to us and show us the illustrations. This was my father's idea of entertaining us—not by reading "Snow White and the Seven Dwarfs."

She turns a few more pages.

In this book are many of the other trees that were in our yard.

She points to the illustration of a roble blanco.

This is a cross between an orchid and a lily—the petals extend like an orchid but the extra-long stem makes it like a lily. It breaks off easily and has a very sticky sap, but it does have these beautiful white blossoms. It is all over parts of Florida, especially the Keys.

She unfolds a piece of paper that she keeps in the book. It is a drawing of a roble blanco, *based on the one in the book and inscribed, "For my dear daughter Elena: All love from her dad on her birthday, Sept. 29, 1957."*

Elena looks longingly at the drawing.

Our *roble blanco* was in the back yard by the pond with the water lilies. It bloomed around Silvia's birthday in June.[2]

Elena returns to the plant on the porch that I had mistaken for a mimosa.

Herb and I went to Barbados in 1982. We had never had a honeymoon. When his mother died, we decided to use part of his inheritance to treat ourselves to the honeymoon we had missed. It was in April, and a lot of the flowering trees were coming out. To see them all made me feel like I was in Cuba again. I collected seeds, not realizing that they would be taken away from me; customs said I couldn't bring any of them back. I had forgotten that I had tucked the seeds from the flamboyant in my suitcase. I found them when we got back and threw them in a pot, thinking they were probably too dry and too old to do anything. Nothing happened for a year. Then this plant came up. So I have sort of a bonsai flamboyant. No blossoms, just the leaves.

She continues pointing out the plants in the yard. Near the driveway are three blue junipers, a pink dogwood, azaleas, and a miniature Alberta spruce. There are four rose bushes, two of which are from cuttings from her mother's yard; two forsythias, a golden honey locust, and a blue hydrangea are also from her mother's yard. The plantings in the front yard are completed with a Japanese maple and dogwoods that were put in when the walk was landscaped.

Elena points out the horse pasture next door that backs up to the right side of the yard. The horses are out running and prancing; they are mesmerizing. The backyard slopes from a deck to an open area the size of the front yard, then on to an acre of new-growth woods. In the yard there are dogwoods that Elena has planted.

There are ornamental grasses and heather by the driveway. Every time I come to Elena's, new perennials have appeared beside and among the plants and bushes. Seasons can be clocked by what is in bloom.

Elena's father never got to see the landscaping she has done around the house. He died in 1979, and they moved to this house in 1986; however, Elena is sure her father knew of her love of plants and landscaping.

In the mid-seventies when everyone was into houseplants, I went through a phase where I loved to read gardening books, especially right before bedtime. I called it my "plant mantra." When Herb and I were living in a tiny apartment in Hyattsville—and we knew we wouldn't be there long—my only decoration was plants. I had a sort of indoor greenhouse. What I noticed when I was reading these gardening books was that the Latin names of the plants would stick with me. My Dad had an excellent memory for plant names. After several years when I was talking to another botanical buff, I realized I had a vocabulary of hundreds of plant names in Latin.

Back inside we settle into our usual places on the Chippendale couch.

At the same time I was trying to get my life together, things had begun to get strange with Cecilia. I have to back up to when I came back from Madison for the Christmas vacation. I was amazed at how Cecilia had changed. She had transformed herself. She had become sophisticated and good-looking. She was fixing herself up, using make-up.

Is the photograph you showed me of her for that period?

Yes.

She had become really glamorous.

She had, and she was only thirteen, maybe just fourteen, but, as you can see, she looks seventeen or eighteen. All of a sudden she had really slimmed down. For three or four years before that she had always complained, "Oh, I can't lose weight. I want to diet. Will you help me?" Silvia and I would get on her case. We had been going on drastic diets from time to time. The week before we went to Bethany, we starved ourselves for a whole week just to lose five pounds.

Cecilia would tell us she was going to diet; then the next thing we knew she was eating two or three pieces of toast with jelly. We would tell her to put it aside, and she would cry, "Oh, I'm so hungry. I have to have this." She never stuck to her diet. Later she would come back to us, saying, "I don't have any willpower. Why don't you help me?" We would say, "We tried! We tried!"

When I got home from college, as I said, there had been this transformation in Cecilia. Cecilia confided in me that she was having an affair. It was such a coincidence, because this was the Christmas vacation when B. and I became lovers too. But Cecilia was very girl-like in her emotional maturity. I was very curious about how her affair had happened. She told me she had walked all the way down to Parkington to shop for Christmas presents for the family. That was quite a walk. Since we didn't own a car, we relied on public transportation or our feet. By the time she came back, it had turned bitter cold and started snowing. A guy stopped and offered her a ride. He really charmed her and quickly made a date. He seduced her on either the first or second date. They became secret lovers. She fell head over heels in love with him, even though he was twenty-six.

I felt there was something not quite right; he was much too old for her. She made me promise not to tell Mom and Dad anything. That was part of our code and bond, that we didn't tell on each other. I asked her,

"Are you sure you even know his real name? He could be married and have a family."

She said, "Oh, no, he thinks I'm so wonderful and beautiful."

He told her she was the most wonderful person in the world, that he loved her. He played her like this for a year. They kept meeting, but it was just to go to an apartment for trysts. He was blond and blue-eyed, her physical opposite. Cecilia had this strange idea from early childhood that her life would have been so much better if she had looked liked my mother, who was blond, instead of my father, who had dark hair and eyes. Cecilia was the darkest one of us. She had always wanted to be the opposite.

My parents knew nothing about her affair; they were both busy working. To them Cecilia was still a little girl. I kept my promise to her not to tell. In our family the joke was that Silvia couldn't keep a secret if you confided in her. I always prided myself that I could keep secrets. At that time, I was having my own troubles. I had dropped out of Madison and had moved away with J.

Later Mom told me what happened. One night Cecilia didn't come home. Mom called the police to report her missing. The police told her they couldn't do anything until she had been missing longer, that this was not unusual for a teen-age girl. This was 1966, and a lot of teenagers were running away. The next morning my mother was looking out the window and saw Cecilia getting out of a car. As soon as she saw her, she knew something was wrong. Immediately she memorized the license plate number of the car. When Cecilia came inside and got close enough for Mom to see her face, she knew something really bad had taken place.

Little by little, Cecilia told my mother what had happened. Her male friend had met her in the usual place, and then he had taken her to an apartment where she had never been before. There were three or four men there who proceeded to rape her, one after the other. When they finished, they debated about what to do with her. Right in front of her, a couple of them discussed whether they should kill her. She begged for her life and told them she would swear on anything they considered sacred that she would never tell the police or press any charges if they would just let her go back home. She convinced them to let her go, and one of them brought her back. Cecilia insisted that the police could not be called.

My mother did call the police immediately and reported what had happened, but Cecilia would not submit to any kind of medical examination. Nothing more was ever heard about the men who raped her. I don't know if the police really did anything.

Cecilia went into a dreadful depression and attempted suicide—I'm not sure how—within a day or two. My parents were very worried and took her to a psychiatrist. She was emphatic that she didn't want to keep seeing a psychiatrist, so they left her alone.

Shortly after that Cecilia took up with another man who was a known child molester and seducer of young girls. The police caught the two of them in the park in some stage of undress, about to have sex. They arrested the man; Cecilia was under sixteen, still a minor. The police asked her to testify against this man, telling her that she wasn't the first he had seduced.

She said, "Oh, no, he didn't seduce me. It was mutual."

The police pressed her, "It's still statutory rape. We'll make you a deal—all you have to do is testify against him."

Cecilia was rebellious; she did not want to cooperate. When she came up before the judge, the judge tried to talk to her. He told her that she was going to have to begin controlling her behavior, and that her parents were going to have to control her more, too. She told the judge that her parents couldn't control her, that she was going to do whatever she pleased. This did not sit well with the judge. He said, "If that's the case, we are going to have to put you in a juvenile home where you can be controlled."

She was sent to a juvenile home in Virginia. There she found a really rough bunch of girls. She felt it was a dreadful place. She began to cry on the shoulders of the authorities and begged for another hearing, promising she would be a good girl this time. Another hearing was set up. By this time I was at Catholic University. My parents called me and asked me if I could be at the hearing. They thought that maybe I could be a steadying influence on her. We were in court waiting for the hearing to begin. Cecilia had gotten permission to go the ladies' room to smoke a cigarette. The matron appeared suddenly and said Cecilia had tried to set her clothing on fire. It was acting out, but the judge was impressed enough to call off the hearing and sent Cecilia for observation at a local hospital.

She was there a week to ten days. I went to see her once. I began to see that she had become different from the way she had been as a young girl. They had given her a truth drug to try to get her to tell her story. I presume it was sodium pentothal. She had not liked the effects of the drug. She was released with the condition that she seek out psychiatric treatment.

By this time she had lost the entire school year. She didn't want to go back to O'Connell; she wanted to go to public school. I really feel the traumatic experiences she had been through changed her whole life orientation. Instead of wanting to go to college, she decided she wanted to go to secretarial school and not be involved in academics. So when she graduated, she went to secretarial school. After that she got a job in a local branch of a bank. Part of what happened after the rape was that a psychiatrist told my parents that Cecilia needed to be regressed and babied to help her heal from this. For a time my parents were bending over backward to please her. In a way she began controlling my parents. It gave her a different way of using power that set a pattern that she later used with my mother for the rest of her life.

Mom told me that the first psychiatrist Cecilia went to was a Freudian. She went to the number of sessions required by the court except for the very last session. She refused to go to the last session, saying that she didn't like this woman psychiatrist; Cecilia said the psychiatrist didn't understand her. My mother didn't insist that she go.

With hindsight, it seems to me now that this first experience with a psychiatrist set up a pattern that would continue with Cecilia. I don't know what it was she did not want to face about herself, but when a psychiatrist would lead Cecilia to the point of insight of, perhaps, her own complicity in what had happened to her, she couldn't face it. Then she would decide this doctor was no good, that she had to find a new psychiatrist. The new psychiatrist would be more understanding until it got to that point again of her having to face up to herself.

And who was paying for these sessions with a psychiatrist?

At first, I think it was social services, then much later it was Cecilia herself who paid for it. That made no sense to me—why would you pay for treatment and then not listen to what was suggested?

Elena pauses, purses her lips, and says that Cecilia's story is not finished, but for now she wants to talk about going to Catholic University.

I began in the fall of 1967; it was an exciting year. Everything in the Architectural School had been turned upside down. Doug Michaels, a young hot-shot architect who had graduated from Yale, was revamping the whole program. He was working with another teacher for whom I still have tremendous respect and affection, George Hartman. They were our two design teachers. The third teacher for the first-year students was an architectural historian.

Those three guys were amazing in terms of the freshness of their approach. This was when the Archigram concept from England was big. In order to bring modern plumbing to older buildings in London, an architect would build modules and plug them into the side of the buildings.[3] The main idea was to bring disparate elements together. We discussed new radical concepts like this and tried to apply them to our work. The first few projects we had to do in class were unusual. For example, we were supposed to use a cube and explore the cubeness of the cube! It was a riot. Everyone came up with incredible things.

The architectural historian loved art. He may have been an influence on my developing into a painter. Although he showed us many slides and photographs of buildings, some days he would just show us paintings. We were supposed to be studying Greek temples, and he'd be showing us Renaissance paintings.

I was sharing a suite with three other girls. These suites were small apartments just across from Michigan Avenue, owned by the university. I was able to save a little money because I could cook my own meals. We had a pretty good time there. One roommate was another architecture student who was very much an activist. She was always our spokesperson with the teachers. I wanted to model myself after her. She was the only female in the fourth-year class. In my class there were three or four women, but by the end of the year, I was the only one left.

Elena and I compare notes on what it was like to be a woman in an architectural school. I had taken a painting course at the North Carolina State College School of Design in the late fifties, a time when there were almost no women in this school. I found that a woman had to be tough to be taken seri-

ously and to deflect the constant sexual innuendoes and banter, often by the instructors.

Did you find the work difficult?

Not the first semester. What was difficult was that a lot of the guys in the class had done construction work. They had a slightly better sense of how things are put together. They had this advantage and loved to lord this over me. There was a lot of gender rivalry. I loved it; I flirted with all the guys and played it for all it was worth—just for fun.

I had one bad experience about being Latino. The first day of class we were sitting around, waiting to be assigned a schedule. I had just discovered another female Cuban in the first-year group who was from a different part of Cuba. There was another Latino guy there, talking with us. It was natural that we would speak Spanish. When the teacher called our names, he found out there were three Latinos sitting together. He called us down to his desk, saying, "I don't want you to form the Spanish ghetto back there. I want you to sit in different places."

A couple of weeks later I found out that the year before there had been sixteen Latinos in the first-year group; this was half of the class. They had caused a bit of a problem, because the American students who didn't speak Spanish resented them always yacking back and forth in Spanish. The administration wanted to make sure they didn't have a repeat of the problem. It made me so self-conscious that for the rest of the time I was at Catholic University, I didn't associate with the Latinos in any of the classes. A friend who majored in economics at Catholic University still teases me about this: "Elena, you wouldn't speak to any of us."

One of my roommates was working at the Washington Gallery of Modern Art. Through her I made contacts there and met the curator, Walter Hopps. I began gallery sitting on the weekend and painting the walls before exhibitions for a little extra money. It was really exciting for me; it got me going into galleries.

The Washington Gallery of Modern Art (WGMA) was a small museum in a townhouse in the Dupont Circle area. Its avant-garde programming hit staid Washington, D.C., like a small bomb. Elena and I probably passed each other there, maybe even spoke. I was there a lot with students and other artists. I met Doug Michaels; he and another recent Yale graduate spoke to a group of my high school students about a show they'd organized that was built around the funky aesthetics of the suburban strip. The museum was the most exciting place for art in Washington at that time.

One exhibit I remember was the Ed Keinholtz exhibit.[4]

I nod vigorously. The stunning, often grotesque installations of the California artist had never been shown in Washington before.

The fourth-year students helped install that exhibit. I was along peripherally. One of the guys helping even locked me in the installation that was supposed to be a jail cell or room in an insane asylum. The main figure had a fishbowl for a head. At first I was afraid he wouldn't let me out. After I got good and scared, he let me out. We got to go to the reception and meet Keinholtz.

Elena and I continue talking about the WGMA and Walter Hopps and the impact he had on the city. It was a very exciting time in Washington to be involved in art. Suddenly a cover of Time *magazine was devoted to a show Hopps curated: Tony Smith's large sculpture* Smoke, *which filled the atrium at the Corcoran Gallery.[5]*

I had seen *Smoke* at the Corcoran. I was so excited by it. We had been given an assignment to design a museum for an artist. I wanted to design an entire museum for Tony Smith. I designed this complex structure that tried to echo his sculpture. One of the teachers came by and tore my design to pieces. He felt that my complicated design wasn't suitable. He suggested that I should make something that was completely different from Tony Smith's, maybe a simple, round building. When he told me to think of curves instead of angles, I was crushed. I left the classroom almost in tears. I was able to hold them until I got to the ladies' room. I felt unequipped to deal with Tony Smith. I picked another artist who has turned out to be so unmemorable I can't even recall his name.

In retrospect I realize how fortunate I was to have been part of the art scene at this time. Things at Catholic University were beginning to get bumpy. By the second semester the administration was very unhappy with the way the program was being run. They fired Doug Michaels. He ended up forming an architectural firm, the Ant Farm, that did a number of very avant-garde projects. George Hartman still has his own firm, Hartman and Cox.

I acknowledge that this is a well-known architectural firm in the metropolitan area. Elena smiles.

Recently when I was working for an engineer, I had to survey the building of the Maryland National Park and Planning Commission. I noticed that Hartman and Cox had done the addition, which is the only interesting part of the building. I felt a connection to my old teacher. Here I was doing retrofit work, as it's called in the industry, on his design.

The Architectural School at Catholic University decided that all the revamping that had been done was not going to work, that they had to go back to a more academic environment. But that first year opened my eyes to lots of creative ideas and helped me realize the potential I have.

The first semester I had a number of personal problems that dealt mainly with my relationship with J. When she worked at the resort, she had paid our expenses so I could save money for school. She was sending me some money to help with daily expenses, so in a way I was still financially dependent on her. But after coming to Catholic University and immersing myself in that milieu, I wanted to untangle myself from the relationship with her. I didn't quite know how to do it. In the spring, I started dating a young graduate student and fell in love with him.

It was hard to break to J. She was still in Virginia, working full-time. I did see her from time to time. I knew she was lonely. At first she accused me of betraying her. At that point she had begun to understand I was not as easily manipulated as I had been when we lived together. During a weekend when she was visiting, it became obvious to my CU roommates what my relationship with her had been. They made a big stink about it as if it were an ongoing thing. They didn't want a lesbian in the suite. I tried to explain to them it was over as far as I was concerned. My roommates weren't totally satisfied with what I said; they went to the administration. The dean of women called me in and suggested that I was interested in architecture because I wanted to be a man.

This was even more extreme than Madison.

Yes, but there weren't any grounds for any kind of suspension. I sort of acted out my disgust with the attitude of my roommates. On an "Open Sunday," we were entertaining some guys. This was the time we were allowed to have males in the dorm. I got wild and tried to set a bead of rubber cement on fire. I had done the same stunt outside the architectural building. I had not realized how dangerous it was. When I lit the rubber cement, I was just playing around. My roommates thought I was going to set the suite on fire. It was near the end of the school year. It was good thing we were going to be going our separate ways.

In the spring of 1968, my first year at Catholic University, my parents moved to their own house in Falls Church.

I comment on what a success her father had made of his life in the United States: he had been in this country six to seven years, supported a wife and, for some of that time, four daughters, and was able to buy a house. We remind each other that you could buy a house back then for thirty thousand dollars. Elena agrees and says that her father and mother's house cost around thirty-seven thousand—still, not an insignificant amount of money at the time.

My parents had become citizens in 1967. Because of their age, Silvia and Cecilia were included in their application, but Beatriz and I were on our own. Since I was living near Catholic University, I had put in for my citizenship papers in the District. My interview was scheduled for early April of 1968. It turned out to be the day after the riots following Martin Luther King's assassination. Downtown Washington was like an armed camp.[6]

Everyone who lived or worked in Washington at this time has clear memories of where they were when the riots started in April 1968. Elena tells about her experiences on that day.

We were in the architecture building. We were waiting for our teachers, who were all late. We heard on the radio about the riot. We went on the roof to see what was happening. I thought, "After leaving Cuba, is this the revolution that I will be in?" We didn't know what to do. I was still in the campus suite. The guys offered to come to the dorm and arm themselves with sticks, T-squares, whatever and defend us. After an hour someone came from the administration and told us to leave, that spring vacation was staring early. I got a ride home with the son of Mr. Borges, a very famous Cuban architect who lived in Falls Church.

Two or three days later I went downtown with the guy I was dating. There were so many troops, it looked like an armed camp. All of Washington looked like a war zone from the damage the riots had done. I began to think that maybe I shouldn't apply for citizenship in America, that maybe there would be a revolution here. For several days I thought about going to Canada.

When the next year started—that's the 1968–69 school year—I was a little disillusioned with the program at Catholic University. I began to have academic problems. I flunked Design II for the first semester. This was the main architectural course, with six to nine credit hours. I was outraged. The faculty said the entire class was in the middle of sophomore slump. A lot of the students were weirding out on drugs. The entire faculty decided to take everybody down one letter grade, which put me into the F range. I did work harder, but I was very distracted by a relationship I was having with an older man.

Men and women were letting their hair grow long. I had started smoking marijuana. Many of my classmates got involved with harder drugs. One guy in my class was so into drugs his hair turned white overnight. One time someone gave me a lid of marijuana. I made the Alice B. Toklas brownies with it and brought them to class and passed them around. A couple of hours later everyone was giggling their heads off, and the professor couldn't figure out what was going on. Some of my classmates got heavily into amphetamines. I tried them once or twice. We stayed up and studied all night. I was so wired I was shaking; I realized I didn't need that.

J. had found an apartment near CU. Since I had, more or less, been kicked out of the student housing, we moved in together. I didn't have anyone else to help me financially. I wanted to be independent from my parents. J. began frequenting the gay bars that had just opened in Southwest Washington. She met a young girl there.

That helped me finally break it off. But I had one hundred dollars a month rent to pay, and I didn't have any extra money. I had just turned twenty-one that fall, so I began to wait on tables. I got a job at the Silver Dollar in Georgetown. The club is not there any longer, but the building is.

What made the Silver Dollar famous was it had one of the loudest local bands known to history in its day—The Cherry People. This band had a little vogue in Washington in its day. They were off the dial; it's a wonder to me that I don't have more hearing loss. The lead guitar player was named Punky. It was fun for me to hang out with them. They were all rail-thin; I found out they were doing speed. I never wanted to get into their drugs. They had actually jammed with Jimi Hendrix, which impressed me. They claimed to have a whole suitcase of tapes they had made with him.

I would work Friday, Saturday, and Sunday night 7 P.M. to 2 A.M. I was still in school. The hard part was switching back to the daytime schedule on Mondays. I never made my Monday morning classes. I was amazed at how much money I could make on tips, even in a beer joint! On a good Saturday night, I would make sixty to eighty dollars, a small fortune for me in those days.

This is where I met Herb. During spring break, I worked the whole week to make as much money as possible. On a quiet Sunday night Herb was there with his buddy Sam, who was on leave from flying body bags from Vietnam. They came in for a couple of beers. Herb struck up a conversation with me by mentioning that he had an antique silver lighter that he had lost or left there on a previous visit. He asked me to look in the lost-and-found to see if it might be there. There was nothing like that in lost-and-found, but it gave us an excuse to start talking. There was something about Herb I liked. He chatted me up for a while and asked me if I would like a ride home after the bar closed. Usually I took a cab; there was no way I would ride the buses at two in the morning. Because it was spring vacation, I was staying at my parents' house.

I decided to take a big chance and accept Herb's offer of a ride home. I called up Silvia and explained what a cute guy Herb was. I asked her to wait up for me to make sure I got home. Herb gave me a ride home with his friend Sam fast asleep in the back seat. Herb wanted to talk, so we sat in front of my parents' house and talked until 4 A.M. Silvia was about ready to call the police when Herb delivered me very politely to the door.

He called me in a couple of days. On our first date we went to the movies and saw *I am Curious Yellow*.

Quite a movie to see on the first date!

Herb says I fell asleep soon after the movie started. I was just exhausted from changing from a day to a night schedule. What I remember—the parts I saw—was that the sex looked really staged. It just wasn't believable that they were having intercourse in these ridiculous positions.

But seeing it on a big screen in a "legitimate" theater at the Biograph made those sex scenes shocking, staged or not, to a lot of people who saw the movie. I remember the theater was very quiet during those parts. People were kind of holding their breath.[7]

Elena shakes her head in disagreement.

I had gone many times to see Pennebaker's movie about Bob Dylan's tour of England.[8] They were saying outrageous things. *I Am Curious Yellow* didn't seem very far out.

I was still at CU for the rest of the year. One of the other students told me about another female student who needed a place to live, so I took her in. Herb and I were dating. We fixed up Herb's roommate and mine, and they hit it off. Herb and his roommate were sharing a small house in Bethesda. Soon we were all were spending a lot of time there. At the end of the school year my roommate thought we should move in. I didn't want to. Although we were sleeping with the guys, I wanted to keep up appearances. I knew my parents would be upset if I moved in with Herb. I was outvoted, so in June we moved in.

Their house was on Ridge Road near the Y on Old Georgetown Road. It was a small cottage that still had well water. The pump broke down over the summer, and for three days we didn't have any water.

The guys had a band. Everyone had the band fantasy in those days. Herb pretended to play lead because it was a bit easier to play one line; he was just learning to play the guitar. His roommate had a little more experience, so he played rhythm guitar. The living room was their bandstand. They had an orange parachute, draped from the dining room light fixtures. It looked like one of those houses in the Beatles' movies.[9]

Herb and I must have seen *Monterey Pop* about seven times; that just reinforced the fantasy.[10] Our house was rife with pot; everyone was smoking. The younger kids in the neighborhood would come over when they heard the band playing. They were there so much that their parents starting calling us up to make sure they were with us.

I bought an electric bass so I could be part of the band. After a day, I realized there was no way I could play it. The strings were just too thick. A neighborhood kid came in, picked up the bass and started playing it, so I gave it to him.

Herb, his roommate, and another friend wanted to have a rock show. It was going to be called the "Illegitimate Theater" and would include a light show. We were aiming for what Jefferson Airplane did.[11] We thought we were going to make tons of money. We had a friend who put up some of the advance money. I made the posters that we distributed all over, and we had radio ads. Of all the places, our backer booked it at the American Legion Hall near Maryland University.

Anyone who had grown up in America, of all places, should have known that these guys were not going to go for a bunch of drug-smoking hippies! We did get to start the show. There was a local band, Claude Jones, whom we'd booked to be on the program too. They had a small local following that we'd counted on to draw a crowd. My roommate had worked up a comedy skit with some of her friends. Herb and his band were the warm-up act. In those days, of course, the bigger your amps, the better the band. Halfway through the first song, we lost the electrical power. The American Legion guys were at the back, drinking at the bar. When the music got too loud for them, they cut the power. This went on for a while. Claude Jones did play, but the small audience was getting tired of the power being off and on, and many left.

Our backer ended up losing money on the concert. He came to us the next day furious; he blamed us, saying that we hadn't promoted it enough. He couldn't seem to understand that it had been in the wrong place.

While all this was happening, Herb's dad was very ill. "Borky," as everyone called him, was from Springfield, Massachusetts. He had gone to Harvard and had come to Washington during the New Deal to work with the Roosevelt administration. He had worked in the Justice Department, then stayed and set up a private practice with Mr. Bergson, who was the grandson of Henri Bergson, the French philosopher.[12] Borky and Bergson were two unusual people. They had a very successful practice working with anti-trust laws. This firm grew and was the one who was involved with the early litigation to break up AT&T's monopoly in the phone business.[13]

I never got to meet Borky. Herb and I had only been dating a month when the doctors discovered he had lung cancer. It was too advanced for him to come home from the hospital. Herb went every day to see him. I offered to go, but Herb said he didn't want me to see him so sick and wasted. He ended up dying two days before Woodstock.

We had been making plans to go to Woodstock all summer. After Herb and I saw Jimi Hendrix in Baltimore, we decided we had to go to Woodstock: it was going to be the *one*. We had read about it in *Rolling*

Stone magazine.[14] That was kind of our Bible. We read every issue, cover to cover. Also there were a zillion underground publications; they were everywhere. There were underground comics. I still have some downstairs in my time capsule.

What's your time capsule?

When Herb and I would see something that we felt was important to save, that might become a collector's item, we would carefully wrap it in plastic. Most of it was print material, but there were some LPs—The Ultimate Spinach, and groups with unusual names or music like that. Unfortunately some of these things were stolen at the parties we gave, where people we didn't know would come in with friends, or strangers would just wander in with everyone else.

Elena and I discuss several local alternative press magazines that were popular at the time.

All the magazines were modeled on this one from San Francisco called the *Oracle*. This magazine was quasi-religious and had overtones of Indian mysticism. The magazine grew out of people gathering in San Francisco to expound on ideas influenced by eastern thought. This is when Richard Alpert became Babba Ram Dass. The *Oracle* called these gatherings the "Holy Man Jams." All the hippies would turn out for them.

Now back to Woodstock. As I said, we'd been planning for it all summer. We had a tent and had bought groceries. Then Herb's father died, and he had to go to the funeral instead. Herb took me aside and told me very seriously, "We made this plan. Just because I can't go, doesn't mean you can't go. I want you to go."

I went to Woodstock with a young kid from the neighborhood and one of Herb's buddies, who drove us there in his new car. We had gone up there thinking it was going to be the beautiful experience of *Monterey Pop*. Woodstock was a piece of work. We got up there on Thursday afternoon. We wanted to get a decent tent site, which we did. There was a beautiful little lake; people were swimming. We got out of the car and rolled up our jeans and went in. When we came out of the lake, we discovered the keys to the car had been lost in the lake.

Then we had to figure how to break into his car, so we could get the tent and everything. We used the spiral from someone's notebook. We had to do this by flashlight. We managed to set up the tent. The next day we realized we had come much better prepared than most people. We had a tent and groceries. A lot of people had come to that festival with only the clothes they wore—nothing to eat or drink. We shared all of our things with a few kids from New York City who had come totally unprepared.

A young couple in this group got terrified when a cow started mooing at them. They had never seen a cow up close. They were surprised that it was so big. They were from the Bronx. They even thought the trees were big.

My immediate concern was how we were going to get home. The car was one of the newer models where the steering locked. I seemed to be the only person really concerned about it. The driver had this idea of calling his roommate in Washington. He had the serial number of the key, which we could use to have one made. We hitchhiked into town and got the key made, but it didn't work. I thought that maybe we had gotten the wrong serial number or that maybe the locksmith didn't make the right cut. By this time, the first night of music had started.

I hadn't even bought a ticket for the concert. We had been trying to pay for our tickets when everyone behind us pushed forward and tore down the barriers. Then Woodstock became a free concert. The first night was really good. They had the folk acts. Joan Baez sang.[15] There still weren't too many people in the audience.

The next morning I hitchhiked back into town. It was good because I picked up some money Herb had wired me and got some more water and supplies.

By Saturday morning when everyone started pouring in, it became obvious that it was going to be something very different from *Monterey Pop*. People were dropping acid and freaking out. Herb and I had been experimenting with acid that summer, but we were of the moderate school: we'd split a tab. The announcement kept coming over the public address system that people who were having bad trips should come to a certain tent. This insistent announcement took away from the music.

There were some wired people at Woodstock. You had to wonder what kind of drugs they were on. That afternoon there was some guy hawking "sunshine acid," which was supposed to be the best. For five dollars I bought a tab from him. It turned out it wasn't "sunshine acid." I can only think that it must have been PCP, which people got into later. I couldn't see straight. It was very strange. I couldn't believe anyone would take it for fun. I didn't go to the festival on Saturday afternoon. I just stayed out by our tent until I was feeling more normal.

I came back on Saturday night. You couldn't walk without stepping on people. I ended up sitting with some young girls from New York City. They said they were trapped in this place and had been there for ten hours. They thought the festival was so wonderful that they didn't want to leave it even to go to the bathroom.

I can't even remember the acts. The main event was the audience for me. The audience got enormously hostile when there wasn't any music on. The promoters were trying to rush act after act on. People kept trying to climb onstage or up the metal amp towers. It was a miracle that no one was hurt.

Was it drugs or was it just that crowded?

It was both. There were people who were drugged out. I've never been in a crowd that was so unruly. Physically they were very uncomfortable because they were jammed together.

After Woodstock I could see why these concerts could turn violent. Six months later in Altamont someone was stabbed at the Rolling Stones concert.[16] There were a lot of people with trigger nerves, caused by drugs and being pressed together.

At Woodstock there were basically good vibes and a spirit of sharing among a lot of the people. There wasn't any outrageous stuff, but I would feel angry when I saw these people climbing the towers. The concert would have to stop. Then an announcement would come on that the concert wasn't going to resume until they came down, and they wouldn't move. By ten or eleven that night I felt I had had enough. I went back to the tent to sleep. Sunday was when the thunderstorms came, then the mudslides.

When I came back from town the second time, that key hadn't worked either; we were in a predicament. I had developed a terrible cold. I felt that it wasn't worth staying. There were other people leaving. I told the guys that the best thing for me to do was hitchhike back to Washington so I could get them a key that worked. I'd figure out how to get it to them.

For a few minutes Elena and I nostalgically discuss hitchhiking. It was very much a part of that time, and it was mostly safe.

Coming from a festival, everyone was in the same boat, so it was easy to get a ride. I rode to New York with some people from the city; they dropped me off at one of tunnels leading to New Jersey. There was a policeman standing there, eyeing me. I was praying I wouldn't get arrested. I was just trying to get home. I got a ride from someone from New Jersey who let me out at a rest stop. I went around looking for cars in the parking lot with Maryland license plates, and I found a family that was more than willing to give me a ride. It was one in the morning, so they were concerned about a young woman traveling at night by herself. They gave me a ride back to D.C. I got home Monday morning, around 6 A.M. I was so beat that I slept until noon; then I called the driver's roommate to see what I could do about the key. He said, "He just called me; they are on their way back to Maryland. He tried the first key again and it worked; it was just tight."

Do you have any memories of the high—excuse the pun—points of the music?

I don't. There was just too much going on the periphery. When I saw the movie, I realized that the concert peaked with Jimi Hendrix's playing "The Star-Spangled Banner" at dawn.[17] It looked like a battlefield with all the mud and the sleeping bodies. I had left by then, but anyone who was there must have felt like they had survived a battle.

We discuss the movie Monterey Pop *in relation to* Woodstock. *Elena comments that the crowd in California was so much smaller, easier to control. I observe that even the name had such a feel-good quality.*[18]

All the acts at Woodstock were well known. The performances tended to be overblown and not outstanding. There didn't seem too much artistic inspiration in what was being done. I think the drugs made it sound good to a lot of people. So much of the myth of Woodstock was just the crowd vibes.

To many people it was a beginning; to me it more like an ending. The concert at Altamont kind of proves my point. I'm sure when the promoters planned Woodstock, they couldn't know that a quarter of a million people were going to show up. There were just too many people for the site.

Herb has said that at that time there was a kind of telepathy going on, that young people were getting into the same kinds of things. You were reading Aldous Huxley, and then you talked to total strangers, and they were into the same things.[19] Both groups would then share their wonder at the coincidence of discovery.

I think when you first discover cultural synchronicity, it almost seems divinely inspired; then you begin to realize that things do happen at the same time.

A sort of cultural impulse.

Things come together at the same time. The farther you are from the actual event or events, the more you can see how separate things came together to create something new that was shared and built on independently by many.

Woodstock was one of these things.

Discovery of Tai Chi; Grandfather and Aunts Leave Cuba; Other Family Events

After Woodstock, Herb and I were trying to figure out what to do with our lives. I was in a state of mental explosion. I told Herb that I didn't have any interest in or money for going back to school.

I was still working at the Silver Dollar on the weekends, but I needed to find a full-time job. When I met Herb, he had just been fired from a job at Channel 9, the local CBS station, where he had been an assistant director. This was his first job after graduating from the University of Virginia.

Herb had worked at Channel 9 as a teenager; he was the MC for a show called "Teens Ask," which won an Emmy award. When he applied at Channel 9 after college, the station hired him, but after a year, when the station's management changed, everyone but the union people were fired. When Elena met Herb, he was out of work; then he found a job at Channel 20 as a film editor.[1]

I nod in total agreement when Elena says that this was a real comedown, since Channel 9 and CBS were both kings in those days.

But Herb had access to some interesting things at Channel 20. He was in the right place, in one way. He got to watch four movies a day; the bad part was that he had to edit them. He was always complaining about having to cut out the best parts.

Channel 20 used to put on the *Barry Richards Show*; he was a local DJ. We knew him; he was a piece of work. We teased him; he was considerably older than us but was always trying to be "hipper than thou." This show brought in nationally known musicians; they were interviewed and played their music live. Alice Cooper was on the show, as was Buddy Miles.[2] Sometimes they would go to Walt Whitman High School and dig up a few teens for the audience. Herb called me one day and said, "We're getting ready to tape this singer you might really enjoy; her name is Linda Ronstadt. Can you come over and be part of the studio audience?"

That fall both of us were working. I had landed my first job at Cohen and Haft's architectural office. Although we were working in the day, our hours off were something else. We had developed a strange relationship with a group of people; two of them were the two people who had gone to Woodstock with me. We got into a pattern of experimenting with acid on the weekends. We became an "acid family"—like the Manson family, but we were harmless.[3]

Under the influence of acid, you can become very vulnerable. You have nowhere to hide who you really are. Herb and I both came from stable families. We had absorbed both stability and caring from our families, so that when we began dropping acid with friends, we dealt with it in a familial way. We imitated our parents. We looked out for everyone and made sure they didn't get too far-out.

Acid trips are dependent on the dosage, Elena says. She and Herb usually split a tab because they knew taking acid could be dangerous. They had also read what Timothy Leary and Aldous Huxley had written about it to prepare themselves.[4] They found out that the setting was very important: the more pleasurable the setting, the better the trip. A quiet place was also important so there wouldn't be sensory overload.

On our first trip we split a tab. We were never sure when the acid took over. I saw a flickering of tiny lights around my peripheral vision. We weren't even sure we were really tripping. We ended up making love, and that was fine. The next morning we realized that maybe that had all been a mild trip.

A very common experience in using acid is that all the things normally projected by your mind are intensified so much that you can forget it's your mind that is projecting them.

Give an example of what happens.

Everyone would look at their faces in a mirror while they were tripping. You were feeling all the stuff in your brain, so you'd want to see what your face looked like. On one acid trip I saw spiders growing out of one of my eyes. As I was looking, I realized that the spiders were from my imagination.

I comment that there would almost be a dual track in your mind: what would be happening and then seeing the "happening."

That's right. I realized that if I was projecting this, I could control it. Almost immediately my face went back to normal. My pupils were a little dilated, but I wasn't growing spiders. This is the danger some people have when tripping—the barriers they normally have in place suddenly disappear. They lose control, and all kinds of buried stuff comes out.

Sometimes trips became a little hyper because of what had been added to the acid, speed, and other things. We'd usually drop acid at night, and then by morning we'd be coming down. We'd go out at dawn for a walk to kind of clean out our heads. Herb used to say that it wasn't that we were coming down—it was that the pavement was rising up to meet us! One morning when we were out on a walk, I jumped up on the railing to a bridge over Sligo Creek. Herb grabbed me by the hand. I never missed a step; I did the whole length. I go by there now and then and am still amazed; I was up so high. I could have fallen so easily. At the time I felt no risk or danger.

We don't seem to have any scars from taking acid. I think part of it was that our growing up hadn't left us with major psychological scars. We were just experimenting. In other words, we weren't using acid to run away from problems. We tried to be reasonable in using it and not use it in unsafe places or situations.

Herb really looked out for me. He had been in a big drinking fraternity at the University of Virginia, and he had been the one who cleaned up and put everyone to bed at the end of the parties. He said the more he drank, the more sober he became.

At this time Elena's life resembled a kaleidoscope, the kind that mirrors one small part of the immediate environment, reflects and repeats it into eight or ten sectional images in a dizzying continuum. She continued working as a draftsperson and experimenting with drugs. Part of the detail in the mirrored, repeated design belongs to Elena's discovery of tai chi. She also began to paint, something she says she had kept doing "on the side" since her

childhood "Maria Elena" project. In this complex composite of self-discov-
ery, Elena's family, ever present, was sometimes the dominant facet.

Herb and Elena were living in an area in Silver Spring, Maryland, where
drugs were sold and where there was some violence.

It was almost like we were living with a golden cocoon around us;
none of the violence ever touched us.

Influenced by Aldous Huxley's Doors of Perception, *Elena and Herb*
had approached hallucinogenic drugs as a way to gain personal and spiritual
insight. At that time they were exploring eastern religions; as Elena says,
they were looking for englightenment. Eventually, though, they decided to
stop using hallucinogenic drugs.

After several paranoid episodes, we made a pact—no more psyche-
delics. Some of the drugs were making me too strange. After experimenting for a year on the weekends, we both felt that we had gotten all
the insights we were going to get out of it. We saw that the kind of insight you got out of it was limited by the kind of person you were to
begin with. If you were intelligent, even an intellectual, you had more
complex trips. If you weren't, the trips could be almost primitive. The
intensity of the drugs was tremendous. After a while we could see that
our bodies could take just so much of this. We had friends who continued to use acid; after ten years, their minds were almost gone. These
people often had creative promise but ended up in a slow-motion suicide.

In the fall of 1972, we were still interested in all kinds of mind/body
extrasensory experiences. Herb had read about tai chi, and it sounded
very mysterious. In addition to LSD, we had done psi experiments and
even took the Silva mind course, in which they tried to convince us that
we could function as psychics after a three-day workshop.[5]

The Silva courses focused on a lot of the telekinetic and psychic experi-
ments that were being done in the Soviet Union. Kirlian photography was
mentioned. Since then Elena has discovered that a lot of these experiments
were faked. None of the data could be checked because the experiments were
being done behind the Iron Curtain, but some people in the scientific commu-
nity here accepted the research.

Elena adds that Kirlian photography is real, that this was an extremely
important discovery and is quite legitimate.

In the middle of all this, we found out that Robert Smith, who lived down the street from us, taught tai chi at the Y in Bethesda. Bob had been in various Asian countries and had gotten interested in the martial arts. He had been stationed in Taiwan and became fluent in Chinese. He had first studied judo and jujitsu. He had met a lot of the martial artists already there, and he had begun writing about them. He and Herb really got along since Herb was a writer, too.

Herb was working for Universal Data Systems (UDS), a computer software firm. Bob told Herb that if he could get a group together, Bob would teach it. We didn't want to get up early enough to go the classes at the Y. UDS had an office on Montgomery Lane in Bethesda, and the owner agreed that we could have evening classes there. All the employees and their spouses signed up.

After six weeks, most people had dropped out except for a couple of friends, Herb, and me. We needed more people. Bob found some space at the Bethesda Ballet and opened the class to others. He went on to build these classes little by little, so that eventually he and his wife were teaching every night of the week.

Bob's approach was based on Professor Cheng Man-Ch'ing's system. Professor Cheng is still considered the most outstanding master of tai chi that the century has produced.[6] What we really liked about Bob was that he never pretended to have great abilities himself. He would say simply that he could teach you the form, but you'd have to work on it for a long time. After the class, we would go out for coffee or tea and be regaled with stories about the professor and other martial artists from the time Bob had been in Taiwan in the sixties. He also had some wonderful 16-mm movies of Professor Cheng.

This was over twenty years ago. Tai chi was barely known on the East Coast.

That's right, but the first David Carradine *Kung Fu* show on TV had just come out.[7] Bob didn't like much about that show. He said, "Even the title is wrong. *Kung Fu* in Chinese does not mean martial arts; it means an art that you spend a long time developing."

Bob rented the auditorium at Bethesda–Chevy Chase High School and showed his films. They had no music or sound, but Bob would do a running narrative. Some of the martial artists had unbelievable ability with the incredible mind-body control at which the Chinese seem to be so adept.

Since Herb had worked as a film editor, he helped Bob patch some of the films together and put others on newer stock. Herb's reward was getting a copy of a 15-minute film. The film shows Professor Cheng doing the form, then doing "push hands." His ability is obvious. Four or five students try to pull him off his feet, and they can't budge him. At another point, a man who is an expert in "iron shirt qi gung" is standing there taking all these punches.

Bob had brought an impressive student of Professor Cheng's from New York.

Elena explains that one the skills of this student was in doing "push hands," which is a game with which tai chi players test their skills and sensitivity. A person takes the four movements from the form: the ward off, the pull down, the roll back, and the push sequence. While one person is pushing, the other person is countering with the ward off. When they push, the other counters by rolling back. Then the process changes, with the first person warding off. It can look like a mirror sequence.

The one regret I have is that I didn't take Bob up on his offer to go to New York and meet Professor Cheng. I didn't have a dime, and I didn't want to have to borrow the money. I thought that I'd go the next year. It was just before the professor went back to Taiwan for a visit. While he was there, he died.

After about a year and half, Herb got tired of tai chi and stopped the classes. Then we started having serious financial problems, and I had to drop out. I was disappointed; we had been practicing for a good long time, and I still had never felt or experienced *chi.*

How would you define chi?

Chi is nothing but the bioenergy that everyone has. Few people are aware of it because they haven't taken the time to investigate how they can feel it. I have an entire library of tai chi books.[8]

From 1975 to 1987, I didn't do tai chi. I tried to practice, but I began skipping days. Then I began to forget part of the form.

Even before beginning tai chi, I had started to paint. When we moved to Quebec Terrace, we had a spare bedroom that became my studio. Jimi Hendrix had just died, and I was painting a tribute to him. The painting was 8' by 4'. When we moved, I pitched it out; I could never get it to come out the right way.

Elena was experimenting with different techniques. She still has one painting from that time whose theme was a lunar eclipse. Titled Phases of the Moon, *it was made with broken mirrors and paint. The broken mirror came from a party where Elena and Herb had showed the movie* Les Enfants du Paradis.[9] *During the party, a friend of a friend broke the mirror of an old dresser. Elena told him that she had wanted the mirror to break, that he'd just given her some wonderful materials.*

Most of my paintings were abstract in those days. I was using organic forms and experimenting with different techniques. I silk-screened the Quebec Terrace Liberation Front T-shirts. I had the screen set up; everyone was invited to bring whatever shirt they wanted screened. The logo was a teddy bear carrying a bomb, and there was a two-color marijuana plant with eyes!

At one point someone gave us a giant zucchini. It was just too big to cook. Instead, Herb and I came up with the idea of spoofing the current craze for performance art. Among my junk collection—all artists collect junk—I had a long narrow box salvaged from an architectural model. Our friend T. took photographs as I squeezed inside with the big zucchini lying on the Plexiglas lid of the box.

Another collaborative thing Herb and I did was to combine the visual and the verbal in a box that we called *The Vible*. There were acetate layers with Herb's cryptic writings on them, inside a balsa wood box. If we had had the resources, I would have put the writings on Plexiglas. It was intended to be a sculpture or wall piece.

In addition to Huxley and others, Elena and Herb were reading the existential philosophers Sartre and Merleau-Ponty.[10] A lot of what was in The Vible *was quotes or Herb's responses to what they were reading. Herb would get into what they called his* Borkspeak, *a McLuhanesque term (referring to Marshall McLuhan) they had invented.[11]*

Our friends were always saying, "Herb, do your *Borkspeak*."

The conversation changes to focus on the political scene of the period. I ask how Elena and Herb felt about the Vietnam War, if they had joined any of the peace demonstrations.

I was at Catholic University when the Pentagon was stormed in 1967.[12] I didn't really know a whole lot about what was going on. I had been away for a year and was just getting settled at school.

My family supported the Vietnam War. At first I did too. There were some parallels with Cuba. I felt communism was a sufficient threat. The

Unites States government presented the case that North Vietnam had given sufficient provocation for us to become involved. I supported the war until the late sixties, when I became aware of the corruption of the South Vietnamese government.

Our government said we were fighting a limited war, but it seemed to me like it was just a place for American young men to go to die. Now we've found out that the Gulf of Tonkin incident may have been staged.[13] I had some arguments with my father about this, but my parents continued to support the U.S. involvement in the war.

By the spring of 1970, I was living with Herb. We were following all news about the war. Cambodia was invaded, and students were shot to death when National Guardsmen overreacted to an antiwar demonstration at Kent State.[14] A protest march here in Washington was planned. Herb and I debated about going. Things sounded a little unsafe. It was being portrayed that we were losing the war because of the hippies and the antiwar demonstrations. We thought if they can shoot innocent people at Kent State, they could do it in Washington.

We decided to go but didn't know whether we should tell Herb's mother. We thought someone should know in case something happened to us. We ended up not telling her; we didn't want our parents to worry about our safety.

The White House was ringed with D.C. Transit (as the bus company was called then) buses to keep the demonstrators away.[15] It was reported that Nixon sat in the White House watching a football game, completely uninterested in the demonstration; however, an official record was made of a lot of the people participating. At the end of the march, near where the Vietnam Memorial Wall is now, there were police cadets with cameras on tripods, photographing the marchers at regular intervals, this writer among them. Hundreds of photographs were taken.

When we got there, we found out that our fears were unfounded. It was a rather peaceful march. Some of the people in the march got disgusted that there was no confrontation and went into the small pool next to the reflecting pool. They took off their clothes and went in as a protest—a sort of Woodstock revisited. Herb and I joined them. It was so typical of the times. A black guy, a complete stranger, also nude, came over to me and hugged me and said, "You're beautiful." It was very innocent—like *Hair.*[16] We were all brothers and sisters.

On July 4 of the same year, the first "smoke-in" to legalize marijuana was held at the Mall. We spent most of the day there. It was like a mini-Woodstock, with people just smoking peacefully, sitting on blankets, playing guitars. In the evening, the traditional Fourth of July concert was being held; Kate Smith was singing.

There was a police line to separate those at the smoke-in from the concertgoers. There were so many policemen or National Guardsmen that we thought something might have happened. We had been down there all day and hadn't heard any news. We went up to one of the National Guardsmen, a young guy, and asked him why there were so many policemen. At first he looked at us like, "You dirty hippies." We talked more, and he began to see we were kids like him, just dressed differently.

Then we saw the police had begun massing, like they might rush in with billy clubs or whatever. We moved away; we didn't want to be in the middle of that. They began using tear gas. We left, but not before being blinded by it.[17]

Tear gas was new to most Americans. But it began to be used regularly as a crowd control method in the antiwar demonstrations. When there was a large demonstration on the campus of American University, in upper northwest Washington, D.C., in 1970, the police used tear gas.[18] This interrupted the normal afternoon rush of suburban commuters down Massachusetts Avenue. The commuters were outraged and suddenly found themselves on the same side of an issue as the dreaded longhaired, college-student, pot-smoking hippies!

In 1971 or 1972, Herb decided he wanted to be a writer. It was fine with me. I would work, and he would stay home and write. I was still working as a draftsman. I went from Cohen and Haft to another firm that ended up going bankrupt. We were becoming more involved in the arts. Even when we were involved with the band, it was obvious to us we weren't really band material. We helped pay for the band; we were working and had a little bit of money. We would rent space for recording sessions.

Elena and Herb were finding other ways to integrate their arts and their politics. Elena shows me two Christmas cards that she and Herb staged, photographed by a friend.

This was our card for 1973. We went behind a restaurant in Bethesda and used their dumpster and trash cans as the setting. David Bowie was

14. Elena and Herb's Christmas card, 1973. Courtesy of Tom Green.

popular at the time.[19] We had just moved from Quebec Terrace. We were in a kind of tearing-down mood.

First, we tore the David Bowie album. The hat in the foreground says, "Impeach Nixon." The Watergate hearings were underway. Nixon ended up resigning in August 1974. During those last months of 1973, general disgust with the government and with the materialistic, mainstream culture, too, peaked. Herb wore a black velvet cape and a dog collar. We had bought matching dog collars—the Alice Cooper sort of thing. I wore Herb's white dinner jacket and stuck a cigar in my mouth.

15. Elena and
Herb's Christmas
card, 1974.
Courtesy of
Tom Green.

season's
dreamings...

The idea was that we had switched roles. This started our sending these Christmas cards.

This photograph is our 1974 card. It was taken outside a club on Georgia Avenue near Missouri Avenue; they had the palm tree painted on their outside wall. It was November, very cold. I had borrowed the very thin dress I'm wearing from one of my sisters. Here I'm honoring my Cuban roots. This was the flip side of our 1973 card.

The summer of 1972 we decided to move out of Quebec Terrace in Silver Spring. We had been living there a year; the neighborhood was overrun with drugs and lots of other funky stuff. We had gotten fed up with the whole hippie scene.

I had applied to go back to school, as had another friend. We were both going to try to get our architectural degrees from the University of Maryland. We couldn't apply directly. We had to take general studies for a year and then apply.

At the end of 1973, we had moved to a really nice apartment in Bethesda in the Four Seasons. I had just left a very good job I had had with an architectural firm in Virginia. Herb had gone back to work as marketing director for a company that was producing computer software. The owner thought he was going to make millions of dollars. It was all a pipe dream. His programs didn't work the way they were supposed to. Within nine months, the company went under. In fact, Herb didn't even get paid for the last four months.

Suddenly we were struggling to make ends meet. Added to this was my finding out several months later, in the spring of 1974, that I wasn't going to be accepted by the Architectural School. I had missed by several hundredths of a point. I felt that they just hadn't wanted to give me the chance. I've talked to other people, mostly males, with lower scores than mine, who talked themselves over this hurdle.

In all our conversations, this is the only time I have ever heard Elena express even the slightest bitterness. I remember my experience of the Design School at North Carolina State College as a totally male enclave.

Herb's job had disappeared as the computer company went under. We had to move. We owed several months' rent. We didn't have any place to go. We were almost living on the street. I had had a part-time job in an architect's office. I got so much flak about being a woman, I had to quit. For the first time in my life, I couldn't take it.

We were crashing with different friends for a night or two. A friend from Quebec Terrace who had just graduated from Maryland had a pretty nice house in Silver Spring; he offered us his basement. His sister played the flute. The only entertainment we could afford that summer was to sit around and sing and play.

The hippies, to me, were antiquarians. They all had a sense of wanting to return to the past. Of course, it wasn't just the hippies who wanted to go back to simpler, purer times. Many other groups had tried to find a utopian way of life. So when we were sitting around playing music, we were consciously tapping into what we saw as the purity of folk music. I tried to represent that innocence and purity in a painting I called *The Flutist.*

All during the time you had the band and were getting involved with painting, what was your involvement with your family?

I was in regular contact with them.

And they tolerated this hippie lifestyle?

My parents knew there was nothing they could do to dissuade me. They seemed to know that there was a time of generational madness. I never mentioned the drugs, but I'm sure they suspected it. Since we didn't flaunt it, they didn't bring it up.

As we have changed the conversation to her family, I ask about her relatives in Cuba. Elena tells me about the increasing bleakness they were experiencing there and how Toya got arrested.

I have to back up several years and fill you in on what had happened to my family in Cuba since the Cuban Missile Crisis. In the mid-sixties, Uncle Juan died suddenly of a massive stroke. Then my grandmother died in 1968. She suffered from asthma. For her last four or five years she had been an invalid. I even remember when we were still there, Toya slept in the same large bed with her, so she could get my grandmother's medication if she had trouble breathing. My grandfather slept in another room so he wouldn't be bothered by all this. After we left, although food was rationed, they still got milk and a few other things because of my grandparents. The government felt the old people shouldn't suffer.[20]

I ask if Castro felt an obligation to honor the old people in Cuba. Elena hesitates as if she doesn't want to give Castro credit for any special humanitarian outreach.

At least they wanted to keep up a veneer of looking out for the elderly. To have not done this would have been too great a failing of compassion and tradition.

Elena's aunts were lucky, because her grandfather had had the vision to plant a lot of fruit trees. Sarah got to be an expert chicken farmer with two chickens Elena had had as a child. Those chickens bred, so they got both eggs and a chicken now and then.

She told me how careful she had to be. When the little chicks would hatch, people would come and try to steal them. When they had a chicken for a meal, they would even bury the bones because they didn't want any neighbors to know they had been eating nonrationed chicken. Some of the neighbors might go through their trash and report them to the authorities. Can you imagine a country where people go through your trash to see if you ate better than they did?

Several times a young boy had jumped over the fence and beat the lime tree to get some limes. He was beating it so badly that he was hurting the tree. Elena's two aunts lay in wait for him and caught him in the act. They took him to the Head of the Committee for the Defense of the Revolution, which was really the neighborhood spy committee.[21] Elena says every neighborhood had this, that it was really a spy network. Castro wanted to know everything that was going on. Counterrevolutionaries—that was Castro's term, of course—would be reported.

Aunt Sarah had always tried to remain on good terms with the woman on this committee in their neighborhood. So this boy was brought to this woman and reprimanded. The kid took it to heart. He staked out my aunts for retaliation. About a year later, Toya was waiting in line to get her groceries. She was the one in the family who took care of the house and shopped for the groceries. The person in front of her forgot part of their order and left the part she had already gotten on the counter. The kid who had been caught beating the lime tree stepped forward and said Toya had been trying to steal the other person's order.

Stealing rationed food was a great crime. The storeowner came over; the kid kept saying that she had tried to steal this food. Nothing Toya said could convince the owner that she hadn't. She was taken to the police station, which was some distance from the store. She had no way of letting my grandfather or Aunt Sarah know what had happened. About four hours later, someone from the neighborhood who knew what had happened came to the house.

In those days, many times people were taken from the police station directly to work camps in the interior. Beatriz's husband, Sergio, who is from Cuba, told me that he was forced to go into the cane-cutting brigade. They were given one glass of sugar water at noon. They were supposed to cut cane all day.[22]

Sarah was afraid that they might send Toya to the fields without due process, which had disappeared from Cuba since the revolution. Sarah went back to the neighborhood woman on the Committee for the Defense of the Revolution. By this time Sarah knew the accuser had been the same boy who stole the limes. Sarah pointed this out to the committee woman, who then offered to go to the police station with Sarah as a kind of character witness. Almost twelve hours had elapsed.

The police believed Sarah, especially when it came out what the accuser had done. They released Toya. Sarah didn't tell my grandfather until it was all over. She didn't want to upset him. He was blind and very old—eighty-eight years—at the time. When Toya got home, the three of them decided that they had to leave. This kind of thing could keep happening.

Sarah spent the next four years getting all the forms filled out for the visas. She would wait for hours in a line, then would find out she needed one more document from another office. Sarah told me that when she finally was close to the head of the last line, she made friends with the family in front of her; they had some friends in common. When they were called in, Sarah went in with them. She was afraid they might close the office after they went in. That's how she finally managed to get the visas.

In the meantime, my mother was calling every congressman and public official she could think of to see if they could help her get her father and sisters out.

After you had all the necessary forms to leave, someone from a government agency came and did an inventory of your house and the contents. Since you could take almost nothing with you, everything became the property of the government.[23] If there was anything that you didn't want the government to get, you gave it away. Sarah had been giving away a lot of things to neighbors, including a lot of linens and other things.

I ask Elena how they got out all the photographs out. In the course of our interviews, she has showed me a number from their life in Cuba. Elena says the photographs were sent in letters before they left; but the mother-of-pearl fans, the beautiful teacups that had belonged to her grandmother—these were sold or given away. Her aunts wanted to leave as little as possible for the government.

I remember one time in the late sixties, Sarah was trying to get some of the family effects out of Cuba. She was bold and brave in her own way. She found someone at the Mexican embassy who could sneak small things like jewelry or personal effects through in diplomatic pouches. You had to go through all these channels; nothing was direct.

She sent a number of small things—rings, bracelets, jewelry we had as children. She had to pay dearly to do this. She had developed a code in her letters to alert us that things were being sent. She would say, "Cousin so and so is doing well," something like that. We knew that the mail going out of the country was being read. Our letters going in were of course read. Often the censors would cross out almost half of what we wrote.

Their final trip out of Cuba was difficult, especially for my grandfather, who, by this time, was almost ninety-two. The main airport was no longer used for these exits. They had to get on a bus and go to Varadero. There they had to wait in one large room through the night for almost half a day. There weren't enough chairs to go around. Most people had to stand. After a long wait, they were able to get a chair for my grandfather. They weren't able to call us, so we didn't know when they left. After they landed in Miami, they called.

They arrived here in March 1972. When Elena's mother called her to let her know they were in this country, she didn't believe it. She'd heard so many times that they might come. The entire family went to the airport to meet them. Beatriz was engaged to Sergio; Silvia was back from William and Mary; Cecilia was still living at home—so they were all in town. There was a big tearful welcome at the airport.

Your grandfather was ninety-two. That's incredible! Did he ever say anything about what it meant to leave his country?

He only lived four or five weeks after coming here. He had already been diagnosed with cancer. It was a slow-growing type; he had decided not to have anything done in Cuba. His voice had been robust when he was younger; now it was just a whisper. He was very weak. He had a severe heart attack in April.

Nothing seemed to matter except that he had been reunited with his family. He fulfilled his last wish of seeing all of them again. Maybe, having achieved that, he felt that he could finally give up.

The death of Elena's grandfather was a seminal event for the Maza family. While it was the ending of one generation, it was the beginning of a new life for Toya and Sarah. They drew on the same personal resources and ingenuity that they had used to get out of Cuba.

At first the changes in them were gradual, almost superficial. All Sarah wanted to do was go shopping. When I took her to a drug store, she was thrilled with the abundance. "Look at these nylons. I want to buy them all!" It was the beginning of her and Toya's realizing that they had done the right thing to leave Cuba.

They stayed with my parents. It was quite crowded for a while. Silvia, Beatriz, and Cecilia had to double up. When my grandfather died, Toya took it very hard. It was only four or five years since her mother had died. It was as if the main focus of her life had died. She had never married. Toya was not sociable like Sarah; she liked to stay at home and care for people. When we were little, she helped raise us—making us special cookies and little treats. When we grew up, first her mother, then her father, became like a child to her. Sarah took it better. She helped with the funeral arrangements and picking out a plot. But it was Toya who thought that they should get their own apartment. She knew that Sarah, who was still very critical, had difficulty getting along with my mother. They got an apartment a mile or two away. They enrolled in English classes. They had been practicing English before they came.

Toya had a huge fibroma that must have been painful. When I saw her get off the airplane, I thought for a minute she has gotten fat, because her belly was so large. My mother explained what it was. After my grandfather died, she had surgery to remove it. She was so impressed with how clean the hospital was. She told me, "You can't imagine how wonderful it is to be in a real hospital which is clean and where you know you'll get your medicine." She had had no confidence in the Cuban doctors or hospitals.

When she recovered from her surgery, she and Sarah both got jobs. Sarah was sixty-two and Toya was fifty-six. They still looked young. On their job applications they took ten years off their age. Sarah, who had already worked for twenty years in Cuba, found a job at the Navy Credit Union doing clerical work. Toya got a job as a receptionist in the office of a Cuban doctor, a dermatologist, whom we had gotten to know when we first moved to Arlington. The job wasn't challenging for her, but it was comfortable. A few celebrities came to the office. Toya saved all the skin-care samples from the office for us.

A car was a necessity. Sergio helped Sarah find this beautiful Mustang, which she bought for five hundred dollars. When I was in high school, this was the very same car I had wanted. Sarah got her driver's license and once again became the family chauffeur. She kept that Mustang until five or six years ago. People would stop her on the street and offer to buy it, because it was so well kept.

Later Toya became a translator for the CIA. She said that she worked for the FBI. She tried to keep it a secret, but I found out. I was doing a building survey for phone lines that were to be put in by a company I was working for. I had security clearance and found out the building where she worked had something to do with the CIA.

When we were cleaning her apartment before she went into a nursing home, I found a retirement certificate of appreciation from the Central Intelligence Agency. She had worked there until she was seventy-seven. Her goal was to be able to retire with maximum benefits. She wasn't too active at the end. She was getting deaf; but she had saved a lot of leave, and she used it.

When Toya's and Sarah's health began to fail, Elena's mother did what she could to help look after them. After Sarah had a fall, arrangements were made for her to go into a nursing home.

We thought it might be temporary. My mother was trying to take care of Toya, and it became apparent that she couldn't keep doing that. Silvia and I decided that Toya and Sarah should both be in the nursing home together. They had always been together. It was not quite a year later that Sarah passed. You remember that morning you came here, and we had been up all night? Before she died, Sarah had purchased a lot adjacent to where my grandfather is buried. My mother also purchased a lot, so we ended up with a kind of family plot.

Toya is doing fine, Elena says. She is very deaf but is in good spirits. She had never wanted to discuss death or funeral arrangements. She wasn't told about Sarah's death, but apparently she found out anyway.

One Sunday when we came to visit, we found Toya very teary. She said, "Oh, my sister is dead." A priest usually comes to say Mass on Sundays, so he might have said something to her without realizing we hadn't told her.

Toya is totally focused on her body these days. She's almost like a four- or five-year-old. She goes over her entire litany of aches and pains when we see her no matter how small they may be.[24]

Your mother is in incredibly good health.

She is, although I worry about her. She fell recently hanging out her wash. She has a dryer, but she likes to hang her wash on the line in her backyard. She couldn't get up. Fortunately a neighbor, who was moving, came to say good-bye. He was able to help her. Her mind is clear as a bell, but I don't know about her body.

I remember at the opening of your show in Dover, Delaware, she had made a pastry. I was impressed that she had done it that very morning. They were delicious—so good that I had to distance myself from the table.

Those were *cangrejitos*, a Cuban pastry. That had been my special request. She also made them for the opening of my show at the Parish Gallery. It was something that I remember from childhood. When we were little, Toya usually made them.

Nineteen seventy-two was also a significant year for the rest of the Maza family: it began a cycle of marriages and births as well as deaths that continued for over ten years. By the time Elena's aunts and grandfather arrived from Cuba, Beatriz was getting ready to get married. She had graduated from Dumbarton College, then decided to go on for her master's. She had dated a Cuban for a number of years, and he had waited for her. When she told him that she wanted to get her master's degree, and that it would be another two years before she would be interested in marriage, he took umbrage.

Maybe they weren't made for each other. We Maza girls tend to be independent. We don't like to be told what to do or what is expected of us. We do all things in our own time, what we feel is right for us. She broke off with him and went to the University of Maryland to get her master's in math. She supported herself as a teaching assistant. Then she met Sergio, who, as I've mentioned, is also Cuban.

Was it important for Beatriz to marry someone who is Cuban?

I think it was. I think Beatriz never felt comfortable with American men. There's so much we take for granted—a gesture, a phrase. There's a lot to learn in a new culture. You don't realize it until you are in the middle of it. You have to reeducate yourself as to what is expected, and you have to educate your mate in what you expect. She never dated American guys like Silvia or I did; there were enough Cuban guys in the Washington area for her to date.

Sergio's family came to the U.S. in installments. First his sister, Oilda, had come; she had already finished her architectural studies in Cuba. She

16. Beatriz and Sergio del Castillo's wedding in 1972. *Left to right:* Mr. de la Maza; Cecilia; Mrs. de la Maza; Beatriz and Sergio; Silvia; and Elena.

had been in the first wave of Cubans. Then she brought her mother. Their father decided not to come.

Sergio came here around 1966. He had done a lot of work for the Cuban Tourist Bureau. He got to travel a lot through Cuba; he did architectural work for the government agency involving hotels and resorts. Fidel wanted to keep the tourists coming as source of income for the state. This would have been after the Missile Crisis. There was huge influx of Russian tourists and others from eastern European countries.

In August, Beatriz and Sergio had a relatively modest wedding at St. James, our parish church in Arlington. The reception was in the community room of the parish hall. The whole church was full with Cuban friends of both families. Oilda, Sergio's sister, Silvia, Cecilia, and I were the bridesmaids. Friends of Sergio's were the ushers.

They went to Spain for their honeymoon, and Beatriz came back pregnant. Samuel was born the following June. Mom and Dad were ecstatic: the first grandchild and a boy, after a whole generation of girls.

Samuel was a good baby, which was just as well since he got passed around a lot. Their next child, Sofia, was born in February. Sergio was in school finishing up his architectural degree. For the next few years, my mom's and dad's lives revolved around the grandchildren. Beatriz had six children.

Herb and I got married in 1975, the day after Thanksgiving. His mother, Margaret, had Thanksgiving dinner with us. Before that we had always had it at her house, and she did the whole feast. That year she wasn't feeling up to it, so we thought it would be nice to invite her to our place. At that time Herb and I had been vegetarians for two years. So we broke our vegetarianism for Thanksgiving, and then we decided to give it up.

Margaret had been having some health problems, and we wanted to give her some news that could cheer her up. We told her that we were getting married the next day, but we made it clear that we wanted to do it by ourselves. It seemed to us that we had been living together so long—seven years—that there was no reason to make a big thing out of it. We got married by a justice of the peace at the courthouse in Rockville, Maryland. I told my family the day after. My parents were very pleased.

I was getting quite concerned about my citizenship. You'll remember that the first interview for my citizenship was in April 1968, the day riots started in Washington.[25] I didn't decide to reapply until I moved in with Herb. We were living in Maryland, and I had to deal with an office in Baltimore. When I submitted all my papers, part of what I had to send was my Cuban passport. I waited for about two years.

In 1972, I called Immigration and Naturalization. They didn't have any record of me. I had sent everything that proved who I was, when and why I came. My file was lost. I went to Catholic Welfare to see if they could help me get any kind of legal form that stated who I was and when I came. They weren't able to help, and I had no legal recourse in the matter.

In 1974, I worked for an engineering firm that had some government contracts. They wanted to see my citizenship papers. Herb and I thought that if we got married he could claim me and give some kind of legal status. I knew that because of changes in the law, I couldn't automatically become a citizen, but I thought this would give me more of a legal identity. At the end of 1975, I was laid off by the engineering firm. When I went for unemployment, I was worried I wouldn't get it. As I had a Social Security card, it didn't come up.

In the fall of 1977, Immigration got in touch with me. They told me that someone had retired, and that when his desk had been cleaned out, they had found my file in the back. So they gave me the interview immediately. On March 3, 1978, I was to become a citizen at a swearing-in ceremony in Baltimore. When we woke up on that day, there was a blizzard in progress; already four or five inches of snow were on the ground. I thought, "Come hell or high water, I'm going to get to Baltimore and become a citizen."

We called Herb's mother and explained to her that we needed to use her car; she wanted to come with us anyway to see the ceremony. We got a cab to her house, and the rates were tripled because the roads were so bad. We drove to Baltimore in her big Buick. There were a lot of accidents—a huge tractor-trailer had jack-knifed on Interstate 95. We just kept going. One hundred and twenty people had been scheduled to be sworn in, and believe it or not, only eight people didn't show up. No one was going to take "no" for an answer from the weather. When it was over there were eight inches of snow on the ground—and I was a citizen!

Silvia worked for a year, then attended William and Mary for two years. Her scholarship wasn't enough to cover her expenses, so she came home to finish in math at Northern Virginia Community College.

When she was in college, Bill was one of a number of boyfriends she had. She met Bill in high school; he'd gone at St. Albans.[26] She finally decided that Bill was the one. The fact that Bill was a doctor was probably part of the final attraction, since Silvia had wanted to major in medicine originally.

My dad loved Bill from the start. They shared a love of opera. Bill learned Spanish and addressed my father as "Papi," our name for him.

Bill wanted a church wedding. Their wedding was in May 1976 at the St. Albans parish church. It was an elaborate affair with fancy matching outfits for the bridesmaids. Actually it was very beautiful. Beatriz was eight months pregnant with Pilar.

In the summer of 1976, Elena had her first show of her paintings. This was an important event because it brought together her art and her family as well as an old friend from Cuba.

In addition to my family, Zenaida and her family came to the show. She was the young girl who had come to work for my mother as a nanny when she was seventeen years old and I was seventeen days old. She had stayed with our family until I was about nine.

When she left Cuba in the early sixties with her family, they went to Connecticut and have lived there ever since. They had come down to visit my family, and so were here when I had my show in August. It was wonderful to have her there with my family.

Cecilia fainted at the opening. As it was hot, no one thought much about it. I ask Elena about her family's reaction to her show.

They have always been supportive. They thought it was wonderful. Everyone kept saying how talented I was.

In September for my birthday, my mom had us all to her house. She included Herb's mom. Margaret had met my family, but this was a sort of formal recognition of our marriage, of the fact that our families were joined.

Beatriz had had three children by now. Everyone was very taken with Pilar, the third child. She cooed and smiled. It was becoming obvious that the grandchildren were going to get all the attention and that those who produced the children were becoming the main focus in the family. I was becoming a little jealous, and I imagine that Cecilia was too. Cecilia came in; she had on a thin, loose dress. When she turned sideways, it was very obvious that she was pregnant, and that she was trying to hide it with the dress. All the women noticed, but no one said anything.

Did I miss that? Was Cecilia part of the flurry of Maza marriages?

No. She wasn't married.

Elena pauses and almost bites her lip.

And she was still having some serious psychological problems.

Cecilia's Dilemma

The next day I called my Mom and asked if she knew that Cecilia was pregnant. She said that she had noticed, but that Cecilia hadn't said anything about it until that morning, when she had told my mother the whole story and had been emphatic that she wanted to keep the baby.

My mother went to talk to the father, who worked with Cecilia at Bolling Air Force Base. Cecilia had told him about her pregnancy and had wanted to get married, but he didn't, and they had had a falling out. At this point they weren't even seeing each other. My mother's talk with Cecilia's boyfriend didn't change anything. He was firm that he didn't want to marry her.

Cecilia had had her own apartment since the time Silvia was married. She had begun the affair there that led to her pregnancy. She had come to see Elena when she lived in Hyattsville and told Elena about her boyfriend, complaining that he wanted her to use birth control. When Elena pressed her about whether she was using birth control, she got angry and spoke about how unfair it was that women had to take care of this. Elena tried to convince her that it was easy to take the pill, but she expressed anger about women having to bear the burden of birth control.

I think Cecilia really wanted to get pregnant to force this boyfriend to marry her. When she got pregnant, she had been in the Air Force for three years. When she first went in after basic training, she had this idea that she could get the training to become a meteorologist. Her orders to go for further training never came through, and she was sent back to

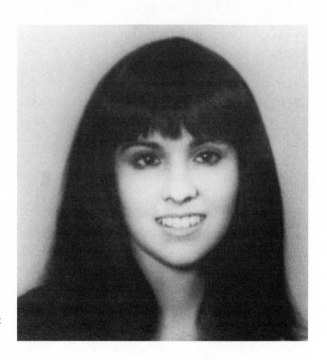

17. Portrait of Cecilia at thirteen.

Washington. I wonder if some of the counselors or people she saw in the Air Force realized that she had serious psychological problems.

Before she joined the service, in the early seventies, she decided she wanted to go to California—like other young people. She bought an antique Oldsmobile, a 1940-something, and she drove this car across the country. She made it out to the California desert. Then the car died. She left it with a farmer, who promised to take care of it until she could come and get it.

Cecilia hitchhiked into Los Angeles, got a job as a secretary in a car dealership, and stayed for six months. She was courted by a Chicano, but she broke up with him and came back to the East after six months. When she got back, she told her family she had stopped menstruating for three months.

We were sure she was pregnant, but she wasn't. We never knew what caused this—maybe it was emotional. As soon as she came back home, everything normalized.

Despite of her great desire for independence, Cecilia was dependent; she really needed her family to keep her on an even keel. After she told Mom about her pregnancy, Cecilia moved back home. She was still on duty when she went into labor. She hadn't gone on maternity leave yet; her baby was several weeks early. Cecilia named the baby David.

Was there any special reason she chose that name?

I think she may have chosen that name because of the biblical implications. David was symbolically going to be the little guy who was going to slay Goliath, his father, so he would marry Cecilia. Maybe I'm projecting too much of myself, my ideas, but I know that she was very interested in the effect David would have on her relationship with his father.

Cecilia was given thirty days maternity leave before she had to go back to work. All of her medical expenses were taken care of at the base hospital. The baby's father had asked for a transfer out of the area before the birth. When her maternity leave was up, Cecilia went back on active duty. Her mother, Olga, was the one who got up in the night for feedings and took care of David through the day. The Air Force offered her an honorable discharge after she had been back at work for several months.

David was born in 1977. Around this time, Dad began having a series of small strokes. Mom took him to a lot of geriatric specialists. There wasn't much they could do but give him blood thinners. When David started walking, Dad was still able to take him for a walk around the block. Over the next couple of years he gradually began to lose his balance.

Herb and I were living on my salary, which had not kept up with inflation. We had been living in an apartment in Hyattsville that wasn't air-conditioned. Herb said that when he was a kid, he had thought it would be so romantic to live in an apartment where there would be a big neon sign outside the window, something he'd seen in the movies. In Hyattsville we had the sign: there was a funeral home across the street that had a sign that was on all night. It wasn't as big as the one in the movies, and we found out that it wasn't romantic; it kept us awake half the night.

At that point all our former hippie friends were in Austin and San Antonio, Texas. We went out there for a vacation in 1978 and decided that Austin was the place to be. We thought we had been in Washington too long.

We were getting ready to move. Herb was going first with all of our things. Margaret, Herb's mother, hadn't been feeling well and then needed to go into the hospital for some tests. She had a very large blood clot that needed to be removed. When she came back from the operation, she wasn't strong enough to stay by herself. One thing led to another, and we moved in with her. She was glad to have us in the house. We thought we'd be there a couple of months and then could move to Austin.

She began to have small strokes. She had had an ulcer that everyone thought had healed, but apparently it had come back. She could barely even keep medicine down. I think she must have thought she had cancer and just didn't want to know what was wrong with her. She was enduring a lot of pain that she never really told anyone about until one night when it got so bad that Herb had to take her to the hospital. During some exploratory surgery, they found out she had a perforated ulcer.

When she regained consciousness, it became obvious that she had had another stroke. She needed specialized nursing. Herb's half-brother, Lonny, had remarried. His new wife was a nurse with a specialty in geriatrics. They wanted to move Margaret to Kansas City where they were living. Margaret didn't want to leave the house where she had lived for thirty-five years, but she accepted it. She died six months later.

One ironic thing. Lonny had a career in the Air Force. We saw him fairly frequently because he came to the Pentagon to do business. This is when we were going to the war protest marches. Herb and Lonny were on opposite sides of the issue, but they still got along.

Let's back up a minute. Did you mind living with your mother-in-law?

No. I really liked her. She had had such an interesting life. She was a native Washingtonian, the only daughter of a prominent lawyer. A color photograph of Margaret had appeared in one of the newspapers when she was a debutante. It was the first color printing the paper had ever done, and she was a beauty.

The Washington Bliss's were very wealthy through their real estate holdings. When he was courting Margaret, Alonzo Bliss would drive along Sixteenth Street in a Stutz Bearcat and shoot pearl-handled revolvers in the air. When the policemen would stop him, because he was Mr. Bliss's son, they would only say, "Young man, you shouldn't do that." Then they would let him go.

When she was seventeen, Margaret married Alonzo. When they were married, it was a great social event. This was in 1923, the height of the roaring twenties. His family owned about half of Miami, so Alonzo and Margaret lived there about half the season and would come up here in the summer. They gave and went to all the big parties. Margaret's parents moved to Miami permanently.

Elena describes the two children they had. Barbara, the first child, was raised by a nanny as her parents continued their active social life. When the second child, Lonny, was born, Margaret was ready to settle down.

Alonzo was jealous of the affection she gave her son, so he and Lonny never got along. When Lonny was six, his parents separated. After the divorce, friends of Margaret tried to set her up with Herb Borkland. They kept telling her he was perfect for her, but she said she wasn't ready for any more relationships. A friend of hers was giving a dinner party and called her at the last minute, saying one of the women had had to cancel and could she please come. In those days you had to have an equal number of men and women. She went and there she met Borky.

Was it set up for them to meet that way?

It may have been, but right away they hit it off. He said, "Oh, you are the Margaret I've heard so much about."

They did fall in love, as her friends had predicted, and were married. Lonny said Borky was his real father, the one who raised him. Herb was born three months before Armistice in 1945.

By the time Margaret died, the allure of Austin had passed. Things were not looking so good in that area. There had been a mini-depression there. We decided to sell Margaret's house and stay in the Washington area.

In 1979, my father had a stroke and didn't come out of it. He was going into a coma. When we gathered at Mom's, we decided he shouldn't be sent to the hospital. There wasn't anything they could do for him. Mom felt like she could manage, but it was difficult. David was two. He was tearing up the house. He was strong; he could pick up floor lamps. He wanted and needed attention, the way most two-year-olds do. We took turns going over to help Mom. Herb took David for a walk one day and put him on his shoulders. That was a big thrill for him because Herb is so tall. My father had never been able to do anything like that.

My father lived for one week after the last stroke. The afternoon he died, Silvia and I were negotiating with Arlington County to get a nurse to come once a day to spell my mother. A neighbor who was a nurse came over and verified that he had quietly died in his sleep.

Did you have any prescient sense that your father had died before your

mother called you? I'm asking because you and Herb had experimented with
ESP and related extrasensory phenomena.

The hour before he died, I was thinking about him. I felt very much his soul's struggling. I wanted to tell him to let go, that it would be all right to let go this time. At one point I did feel his struggle had ended.[1]

I had been working for Kenneth Cobb, an engineering firm. Their office in Silver Spring was only one-and-a-half miles from Margaret's house, which was in the Shepherd Park area of D.C. I could almost walk to work. In 1980, Cobb moved to Rockville. It seemed like the time for us to move to Montgomery County. We found a small town house off Randolph Road and bought that. I wanted a place that would be my own. As soon as we moved in, we realized it was too small, but we knew we had to stay for a while.

I never finished telling you everything that happened to Cecilia. I think I stopped when she got an honorable early discharge. David was six to eight months old. Cecilia had been in the Air Force for three-and-a-half years. She found temporary work with the Inter-American Bank and stayed until a full-time job opened there. She worked as one of the secretaries in the office of protocol. The bank had very good benefits.

David wasn't baptized immediately after being born. My mother talked Cecilia into having him baptized, so then he needed a godmother. The lady who was Cecilia's supervisor at the bank became David's godmother. She was very maternal with Cecilia, empathizing with her about her recurring feelings of being victimized.

By the time David was four, Cecilia had stopped taking her medicine. She was having paranoid delusions and was sure my mother was trying to kill David and her. She was also having a terrible time dealing with David. She felt she had to get David out of the house. She wanted to put him up for adoption. She called an agency to see how you put a child up for adoption. The adoption agency had certain procedures that took a long time. Cecilia didn't want to wait; she wanted it to be immediate. She found another agency that would do a speedy adoption.

She took off with David in her car, heading for Baltimore or some place. She was so confused that she ended up in Annapolis, Maryland. She went to a police station and just left David there. She didn't leave her name or anything. The police had no idea what to do with him, so they got in touch with a social worker, who arranged for him to stay some-where overnight.

When Cecilia came home without David, she wouldn't tell my mother what had happened to him. Mom was frantic but couldn't get anything out of Cecilia. The next day Cecilia was calmer, and she told my mother where David was. My mother called Silvia to go with her to get David.

They had to go to court to get David back. The judge could see that anyone who would abandon her child was having serious problems. The judge said Cecilia was too unstable to have custody of David; and he didn't want to give David to my mother because of Cecilia's ravings about my mother's trying to kill her and David. The judge had to weigh whether her accusations that my mother was a dangerous person were true.

Silvia spoke up and said she would take custody of him. Silvia kept David for a couple of weeks. David was going through a terribly defiant stage; he wouldn't show any respect to Bill, Silvia's husband. David had fixed on him as the bad guy because Bill had tried to discipline him. Bill tried to set some reasonable standards of behavior for David, but he only succeeded in becoming the focus of David's anger. It became clear that David wasn't going fit in their family.

Beatriz then stepped in to take him, because Sergio was David's godfa-ther, but they didn't have room for him. They already had four children at the time, and Beatriz became pregnant again soon after. David was going to require a lot of attention; he would become the main focus of the family. The family thought that Beatriz's other kids might become jealous because David would be center stage for a while. Herb was reluctant to take him because he was a problem child. It was very obvious that whoever took him would have to spend a long time working with him. There would be a real investment of time and emotional resources.

These problems about where he was going to live and who would be foster parents or have custody were resolved when the family went back to court for another hearing and Cecilia regained custody. David went back to live with Cecilia and Mrs. Maza. The family felt that Cecilia needed David, that having her child with her anchored her to reality.

After this incident of leaving David at the police station, Cecilia committed herself for resident therapy and treatment. She had done this once before. The week after my father died, she began to have paranoid hallucinations. She accused my mother of switching my father's medication and of giving him poison to kill him. This became an obsessive fantasy. Later she said our mother was going to kill her or harm her. I guess it went back to the betrayal by her first lover. She transferred her anger about that to the person closest to her—my mother.

Elena relates the problems that David was having in preschool: he had become so disruptive that his teacher suggested that he be tested. These tests confirmed that David was emotionally disturbed, and therapy was recommended. Mrs. Maza went too, because she was in the position of being the "enabler." Elena says her mother has never been able to understand this concept. She had never set realistic limits on Cecilia's behavior; she felt she was just showing maternal love.

After Cecilia went into the residency program for therapy, she would straighten out for weeks, even months; then she would become depressed and resentful and disconnected from reality. My mother would try to find things to distract her, to reinvolve her, and she tried to get the rest of us involved in trying to help Cecilia. She'd say things like, "Maybe we should have a big family dinner. Ask her over and make sure she knows that David is welcome." We would conspire among ourselves to find activities she could do, often with one of us. We wanted to try to distract her from her problems.

Did that work?

Yes, it was a good ruse to get her to short-circuit the cycle, to interrupt the downward spiral she was about to begin. I know it was difficult for her, but for me it was like living on top of a volcano that could explode at any moment. It seemed like each time there was an explosion, it was worse than what we had expected.

When Cecilia was going into one of her depressed times, she would start gaining weight. She had had a weight problem all her life. She would begin to focus on food too much, on cooking. She liked to cook. Sometimes she would see that she had crossed the line; she would pull herself back, start losing weight and fixing herself up. Then there would be a bad turn of events, and she would start the downward spiral again.

Soon after David was tested, Elena went to Texas to visit a friend who had just had a baby.

Herb and I had been trying to have a baby without any success. My friend's child became my surrogate child. I was there a couple of weeks. We had a lot of time to talk. She told me more of the details of her own family life, and I was bringing her up to date about my family. We talked about Cecilia. Of course I was worried about her and shared my concerns. I told her I wasn't sure if Cecilia could ever break the cycle of depression. I said Cecilia seemed stuck, that she needed to move on, move away from this behavior. I said that Cecilia might try to kill herself to break the cycle. This was in March 1983.

A few months later, on Mother's Day, we had a celebration at Beatriz's house. Nina [Sarah] was still driving and brought over Mom, Toya, and David. Cecilia wouldn't come. At one point Mom called her house to see if everything was OK. Cecilia sounded calm, so we didn't worry.

The Monday after Mother's Day, Cecilia had taken the day off from work. Mid-morning she told our mother that she was going to get her prescriptions filled. She was on several medications. She went to a shopping center that had a drug store where she usually got her prescriptions filled. At some point she doused herself with gasoline and then set herself on fire.

Elena looks away. It is the first time she has averted her eyes in this conversation about Cecilia's suicide. She's still looking out the window when she speaks again.

She must have been thinking about this for a while.

Did you have any sense that she might kill herself?

I think that I did. Looking back, I see it was very much on my mind when I was in Texas in March.

I comment that there wasn't much a person could do in that situation. Elena had already found out how difficult it was to get her sister involuntarily committed. Elena agrees reluctantly and says that the fact Cecilia kept changing psychiatrists added to her problems.

She just couldn't face her problems, so she decided not to deal with them anymore.

Elena's face is covered with tears.

Several weeks later, Elena talks about the terrible last hours of Cecilia's life.

Cecilia was taken to Fairfax Hospital. She was in such serious condition that they flew her to Washington Hospital Center, where they had the best burn unit. Someone called my mother and told her what had happened. Then she called Silvia. In turn Silvia called her husband, Bill, who was an anesthesiologist at the Hospital Center. Silvia asked him to find out what was going on; then she called Beatriz and me.

My mother had been waiting for David to get home from school. As soon as he got off the bus, Mom got a cab to the hospital. I called Herb and we went together. Cecilia was unconscious in the intensive care unit. Mom and my sisters could only go in one at a time, for fifteen minutes every hour. David was not allowed to go in; he was left in a playroom. By the time I got to the hospital, they were trying to keep everyone out. I never got to see Cecilia.

Sarah had retired and was at home. I called her. She was too upset to drive. We decided not to call Toya, who was still at work. I went to get them, and I took David with me. I thought he needed to get out of the hospital; he'd been there five or six hours. In the car after we picked up my aunts, I tried to tell them what had happened without letting David know. He was six, a very impressionable age.

When we got back to the hospital, the doctor told us that there wasn't much hope for any kind of recovery for Cecilia. She was on a respirator; we agreed among ourselves that we didn't want anything else done. The doctor said it would only be a few more hours.

Elena decided to take David to her house for supper. She fed him and put him to bed.

He was very scared and looked so lost in our big queen-size bed. We didn't have any toys, but I found this elf that had been part of our Christmas decorations. I made up a story about the Christmas elf and hoped he would fall asleep. Just as I was ready to turn out the light, the phone rang. It was my mother calling from the hospital. Herb stayed with David while I took the call. Cecilia had just died.

I told my mother to come to our house and spend the night. David was so scared that I thought it would be better if he woke up with Mom here to provide a little continuity. He had never spent the night with Herb and me. He had spent only afternoons or evenings at our house and always with his mother or grandmother.

The big question was how to break this terrible news to David. I had no idea. How do you tell a six-year-old that his mother has just died, especially when that's the only parent he's got? I wondered if he could even comprehend that she had died by her own hand. It wasn't like a random accident had happened; she had deliberately taken her own life.

The next morning Mrs. Maza reminded Elena that David had one of his regular appointments with his therapist that afternoon. They decided to wait and let the therapist tell him. Unfortunately, she chose to tell David by reading him the article about Cecilia's suicide that had appeared that day in the Washington Post.[2] *According to the article, when the police interviewed one of the sisters in the hospital, she told them that Cecilia had had a lot of serious problems, that no foul play was involved, and that it was a suicide.*

After the therapist read him the article, all David knew and heard was that his mom was gone. He was so angry that he kicked the therapist. When Mom and David left the therapist, they came to our house. Mom was devastated by the session.

Meanwhile we had been trying to make the funeral arrangements. My concern then became whether we should take David to the funeral. It was going to be a closed casket, but I didn't know if this would help David or upset him even more. I knew we shouldn't take him to the cemetery. In our family the children didn't go to the cemetery until they were old enough to have some comprehension of life and death. The therapist had suggested that David see the burial site, but she had been so wrong about how to tell him about Cecilia's death that I no longer trusted her judgment. We decided not to take David to the funeral or the burial.

Because David had come home with Herb and me, all the decisions about David began to fall on me. Mom talked to me several weeks later and said that she thought she was too old to raise David. She felt strongly that he needed younger parents and that he needed a man in his life. She wanted Herb and me to take David and raise him. Then my other nieces and nephews began to ask me, "Who's going to be David's Mom now?" I reassured them that I would be. Before he moved in with us, there was a transition period where David was with my mom at her house during the week and then with us on the weekends. We gradually kept him for longer periods.

The year was difficult for all of us. Mom took Cecilia's death so hard. She had lost an adult child, and she was trying to raise this very angry little boy. She didn't have the physical strength to restrain him. She

would call me sometimes and beg me to talk to David and try to per-
suade him to go to bed. His school would call us, and I would have to go
in and have a conference about his behavior.

My boss was very kind; he gave me one day off a week to go to Mom's
and go through Cecilia's effects. I went through her things so that a legal
inventory could be made for her estate. I didn't want Mom to have to do
that, but it was rough on me.

I had my own problems besides the death of Cecilia and beginning to
raise David. I had been to a dentist who had butchered my teeth. I wasn't
sure if they could ever be fixed; I was in a lot of pain and, as a result, not
in good physical shape.

*Elena's dental problems began in 1977 and continued almost nonstop for
six years. Three ill-formed crowns had been installed. In an attempt to correct the problems that these crowns caused, the dentist almost ground one
molar off.*

*Herb called his childhood dentist to get a referral, and one week later
Elena started seeing Dr. Coulon. When he took an X ray of Elena's jaw, he
found out that she has an unusual formation where her jaw bones connect. He
explained that the angle of her jaw is so shallow it doesn't come apart the
way it's supposed to, and that her teeth stayed in contact instead of coming
apart.*

He told me, "I'm going to have to create a new mouth for you." He
began by making me a set of temporary crowns, which were beautiful. I
knew I was in good hands. It took him eleven years to correct all the
problems I had.

He thought this condition was probably inherited. He asked me to
bring in one of my sisters. He x-rayed Silvia and found that she had the
same jaw formation. He still uses our X rays at the symposiums he gives
around the country to describe unusual jaw formations and the conditions they create.

There were so many problems with my teeth that I didn't get better
right away. I was in the middle of Dr. Coulon's treating me when Cecilia
died. He had to treat me for a number of years before I felt any improve-
ment.

In spite of my teeth hurting so much, at the beginning of the summer
I taught David how to swim. We knew he hadn't had any swimming lessons. He was almost afraid of any physical activity. I guess he was afraid

if he did anything, he would die, too. My aunt invited us to use the pool at her apartment complex. I taught him to float and get confidence in the water. It was part of the bonding. The next year he took swimming classes.

I felt we all needed a vacation in a beautiful, warm spot, that that would help us all heal. I began looking into where we could go as a couple with a seventy-year-old lady and a seven-year-old child. I knew we needed a house, not hotel rooms. I joined a club, Hide-Aways International, where you could find houses for rent. We settled on a house on Tortola, one of the Virgin Islands, for the month of July in 1984. It had a great beach. It was the most expensive vacation we've ever taken, but it was worth it.

Elena shows me some photographs taken on the vacation.

When I first saw this village of Cane Garden Bay, I felt like I was Gauguin discovering the South Pacific. It was so beautiful. I knew that as part of the healing process we needed to do the things we enjoyed. Mom began writing poetry again. I had taken my watercolors and began painting again. I hadn't done any art since my father died. Together we took care of David, who spent most of his time on the beach. In some ways this was a new beginning for me and my artistic career.

Because his skin is so fair, Herb can't be in the sun for long. So he came for the second part of the month, and Mom went home. Herb started scuba diving and got his certification.

I wasn't able to do it on this first trip. I was still mourning for Cecilia. I was so aware of the dangers and risks of doing a lot of things. Diving was one of them.

When we got back from Tortola, we felt that the psychological transition of David coming to live with us was completed. He moved in with us.

Raising David; Rediscovering Tai Chi

The first vacation on Tortola led to a second one the next summer. At Herb's
urging Elena began to dive.

That year I was a little calmer, so on the second trip, I was able to do
it. I was dazzled by the underwater.

On the second trip to Tortola, David was eight. He had had swimming
lessons, but he was still not a very good swimmer. Elena was terrified of los-
ing him. He had become fearless and thought he could swim.

I was calling him every five minutes. He would get mad at me. If I
didn't get a response, I was ready to run outside and make sure everything was O.K.

Soon after we returned from the second trip, David got a bike, so he
could also wander around the neighborhood. One of his friends was taking karate. We felt this would be good for David. After a while, he was
doing well. It was one of the few times he was able to focus his attention.

There was an adult karate class right after David's; Herb started in this
class. When a studio opened in Glenmont, closer to where Elena and Herb
lived, they went there. By that time David and Herb could take the same class.

When David was nine, he began to catch up with his motor skills. In the
summer of 1986, the family went to the Keys for a vacation. David started
scuba diving. Elena was still scared of his doing anything involving risks, so
he did this in a swimming pool.

The reason he wanted to learn to dive was to look for treasure underwater!

On that trip I developed an abscessed tooth because of all the corrections that had to be done in my mouth. I called Dr. Coulon, and he gave me the name of a dentist who prescribed antibiotics that took care of my problem. In spite of the abscess, I got my certification as a scuba diver.

My diving instructor, John, who certified me, was testing out an underwater videocamera for Sony. He made a video of us doing some fancy maneuvers underwater—holding hands in a circle with someone diving through, feeding moray eels and stingrays. That got me interested in underwater photography.

I've mentioned that when we moved to the townhouse, we knew it wouldn't be our permanent home. It was just too small. We had been looking at lots. I really wanted to design my own house, but it turned out that what I wanted was just too expensive. When Cecilia died, this had all been put on hold. All of our extra time was spent helping David adjust.

The swimming lessons, the scuba diving, the bike riding—all paid off for David; he became a real explorer. I remember wanting to explore my neighborhood when I was that age. He needed more space to ride his bike in the street. I worried about the traffic on Randolph Road, which was close to our townhouse. When he was almost ten, we saw that we needed to move to a bigger house.

It was in January that I saw an ad for houses and lots in Sandy Spring, Maryland. A friend had told me to always look at a lot in the winter, because that would be the worst time for the trees and ground cover. When we came out here to look at this development, there were no houses. The developers were going to build only as they presold the houses. There was a little bit of snow on the ground. I liked what I saw. I wanted a big yard—a place I could landscape and garden in. I kept thinking of Monet and Giverny.

By then Herb had settled his mother's estate, so we felt we could afford to make this move. The interest rates were starting to come down. We decided to buy the house—unbuilt—and the lot. We had to wait for them to build it for us, so that year was kind of exciting. We would come out on Saturdays and Sundays to see the progress. We sold the townhouse and moved here on December 30, 1986.

18. Elena, Herb, and David on vacation in Florida, 1986.

David celebrated his tenth birthday in the new house. He was going to a special school, Harmony Hills in Aspen Hill, and he finished the sixth grade there. At that point, the school system thought he was doing well enough to be mainstreamed. He attended middle school at Farquhar, which is near Herb and Elena's house.

He was well-oriented and had only a few problems. There were only a few incidences of negative behavior; I thought he was outgrowing his provocative acting out. Basically he was doing well. His sixth- and seventh-grade years were good ones for him. In many ways he peaked academically.

For the first time in years, Herb and I could turn some of our attention to ourselves. In 1985, when Herb turned forty-one, he was beginning to get concerned about his health. He had stopped smoking and was after me to stop too. Herb was also on me to get in shape too, but I wanted to find something that was right for me.

Herb had been involved in tae kwon do or karate, as it is known in this country, since he was in his late teens in the early sixties. I actually took some classes when we first met and got my yellow belt. The first person to bring martial arts to the Washington area was Jhoon Rhee; Herb was one of his early pupils.

Herb has a great story about being one of the first Americans asked to join the Reverend Moon's church.[1] He got invited to dinner at Jhoon Rhee's house and heard all about the Reverend Moon, who was the sole survivor of a massacre in the Korean War. After that Moon felt called to do something spiritual with this life and started his Christian church. Herb turned down the invitation to join.

After we moved to Sandy Spring, I was still working in Rockville, and I noticed Dennis Brown's "Kung Fu Studio" had opened a site near my job. In small letters under the "Kung Fu" sign was a small sign, "Tai Chi." It took me six months before I decided to check out the instructor. All the problems with my teeth had really taken a toll on my body. Even with the scuba diving, I needed some kind of regular exercise.

One lunch hour I went to the kung fu studio and met the tai chi instructor, Bakari Alexander. He was an imposing, mysterious Afro-Caribbean from Jamaica. Because we were both from the Caribbean, I felt an immediate affinity with him. He demonstrated the kind of tai chi he did. I could see it was different from what I had done before.[2] He told me I could come to the first couple of classes free.

I went to the first class on a Saturday. I couldn't believe how active it was. Within fifteen minutes my sweats were drenched. We were working the warm-up drills for our legs. By the time we got to the "snake creep," I thought I was going to die. The next day I could barely walk. It took the whole week to get over it. I realized how out of shape I was.

Bakari gave the class applications immediately, showing them how to apply what they were learning to self-defense. He pushed the class, and the more they sweated and grunted, the happier he was. When the weather was nice they went to the park.

It was a great class. When you sweat together, you bond! When we had breaks, he would show us how to do seated meditation, fire breath, and some other things from yoga.

Elena explains these two things. Seated meditation is done in the lotus position or just sitting cross-legged. The idea is to get the body very calm, to think of nothing, and just focus on breathing. Fire breath is a forced breathing, taking in a lot of air and pushing it out quickly. This is done in a rhyth-

mic pattern. Elena says she found it interesting how Bakari combined things from other arts and brought it all into tai chi.

Later Bakari again brought up breathing. Some people knew how to do the rhythmic breathing he had demonstrated with the seated meditation, but I still didn't. He reexplained how we should breathe during the warm-up set. For the first time in my life, I felt the *chi* and how it was powered by your breath. I was bowled over. After all these years I had finally discovered it.

Herb can tell you how obsessed I became. I was doing tai chi while cooking supper, in the bathroom while I was brushing my teeth. I wanted to get the movement just right, and I wanted to feel the *chi*.

That summer in August, Dennis Brown, the man who owned the studio, put on a large tournament called the Capital Classics at the Washington Convention Center. He brought national figures; Ernie Reyes Jr. and his father were the headliners. Ernie Reyes Jr., a Filipino, is a martial artist who has played in the movies. He was one of the Ninja Turtles. His father is a well-known martial artist on the West Coast.

Because the school was sponsoring the competition, everyone was expected to enter. There was one category for all internal arts, which included tai chi.

Elena explains that the internal arts are a category that includes tai chi, qi gung, and a couple of other Chinese martial arts. They are considered internal because they use the projection of chi. *It's the projection of* chi *that creates the force.*

To get ready for the competition, we began practicing all hours to get ready. I didn't want to win anything; I just didn't want to look like a total fool. I ended up placing in the competition. Herb also placed—in the sparring competition. Sparring uses hands and feet, almost like kickboxing. In the old days there was no contact in sparring; now there are rules about how much contact is permissible.

Placing in my first competition made me want to do more. I knew I could win. Dennis Brown continually had intramural competitions with his other four schools in the area.

You started tai chi again in 1987. What was the year you started winning these competitions?

It was the same year—only four months later. That's what was unbelievable. People at the competitions would ask me how long I had been

19. Elena demonstrating the tai chi movement "snake creeps down."

studying. I told them I had studied some before, but recently it had only been four months. They were amazed. I told them, "I work very hard."

So how long did you do the competitions?

Until 1992, on and off. Part of what I really enjoyed about the competitions was the showmanship. I loved the contacts; I met some really amazing people.

In 1988, the "Taste of China" competition was held. Pat Rice and her partner Steve Rhodes put this on in Winchester, Virginia. That year the Chinese National Champion, Chen Xiao Wong, appeared at this competition. "Xiao" means little, and Chen is the family name, so his name is Little

Wong. He was the nineteenth generation in his family that had been doing tai chi in the Henan province.

Elena explains that there must have been some generations where there were only females born. To keep the martial arts from dying, they would teach these to their daughters.[3] She met elderly Chinese women, born way before the revolution, who told her that both their grandfather and grandmother were martial artists.

Why hasn't that part of the martial arts been more publicized?

It's hard to say. There were at the most only a few compared to the thousands of Chinese women who weren't trained. First you had to be from certain families even to receive the training. If your family was one of the martial artist families, then you would probably marry into a family that was also one of these families.

Now back to the "Taste of China" competition. The list of masters coming was impressive. I was dazzled by their performances. Even before this, Dennis Brown had announced that he was going to take a group to China later that year. As soon as I heard, I knew I had to go. This was the golden opportunity I had dreamed about.

We were there for one month. We flew to Tokyo and then to the mainland. It was the first of October; this was the Chinese national holiday, when they celebrate their Independence Day.[4]

We stayed at the Beijing Institute of Physical Education in the northwestern suburbs. The institute had gates that were closed and locked at night.

Elena shows me a photograph of the institute. It looks a small, walled town with roads and trees. Elena says the walls were quite high. One night some of the younger students in her group wanted to go to a disco at the Holiday Inn in downtown Beijing. They had to sneak over the wall and then climb back in at 2 A.M.

Because of the national holiday, the first three days we toured. We went to the Great Wall, to some temples, and to the Summer Palace.[5] They walked us hard. If anyone wasn't in shape when they came, they would be after those first three days!

I had tried to read in advance. Of course, I knew what communist regimes were like, so I had some idea of what we might expect. Some people who made that trip were much more unprepared. My roommate told me about a particularly oppressive instance. On one of the morning

20. Elena on the Great Wall in China, 1988.

walks around the Beijing Institute, some of our group saw this old man being beaten by two guards. No one knew why he was being beaten, but the guards were beating him so severely that one of the men in our group wanted to intervene. Everyone else in the group warned him not to intervene, because that could create an international incident.

As the group moved away from the area, one of them turned around and saw that one of the guards had gotten a thermos of boiling water. Everyone carried these—this was the only kind of water you could drink. This guard threw the boiling water on the man's face. Our group thought that maybe the man had been caught stealing food or drinking alcohol. At that time drinking alcohol in public was prohibited. If you drank, you couldn't show any effects in public. China functioned, I'm sure, just like Cuba, with the neighborhood committees of spies.

Tell me about the tai chi you did there.

The kind of tai chi we were taught there is different from what is taught in the West. There are five major styles.[6] What we learn in the U.S. is the Yang style. I know enough about the history of tai chi to know that the Chen style is considered the original style; that's what we were taught in China. I had seen this in some of the tournaments. Your stances have to be low to the ground; it is a more powerful, forceful style. When we got there, we were told the Chinese government was trying to popularize the Chen style.

I think that by 1988 the Chinese government realized that the martial arts were a marketable commodity. So the government tried to promote different styles, a kind of "flavor-of-the-month" approach.

Our class was gung ho in the beginning. We had asked for a three-hour class and had been assigned the top coach. The Chen style is extremely complex and has some demanding moves. They were teaching all foreigners a simplified version that they were trying to standardize. They told us they could only give us two hours. After the first class, everyone was grateful. That was about the limit of anyone's endurance.

The last week we were to be part of a large demonstration by the school for the president of the school. There was some tie-in with a national holiday or ceremony. Chinese students were to be part of this. Our coach started drilling us for an extra hour. We had to get up at 5:30 A.M. to work with our coach from 6 to 7 A.M., before we went to breakfast. We had our regular class at noon. His concern was that we should look better than the other coaches' students. He drilled us and drilled us. After our demonstration he came up and said, through an interpreter, "You looked better than the Japanese." They were one of the other foreign groups studying there. This was his ultimate compliment.

Dennis Brown had had silk jackets, like school jackets, made for his group. The group wanted to give their Chinese coach one of the jackets as a sign of our respect and esteem. Dennis asked Bakari to give him his. American clothes were greatly coveted, especially clothes that had English words on them.

Our last week we toured around Henan. Chinese trains are really something. To help prepare for the trip, I had read *Riding the Iron Rooster* by Paul Theroux, which is about his prolonged travels on Chinese trains.[7] In China, when I was there, everything was very segregated as far as what was for foreigners and what was for the Chinese. Foreigners expected and were given better food, train seats, and beds. When we got to the train station, it looked liked a scene from wartime. There were people camping in line; it looked like some had been there for a week. As foreigners, we were led to a separate waiting room; then our guide went

21. Tai chi students from Dennis Brown's studio in Chen jiago, Henan province, China, 1988. This is the village where the Chen family has lived and practiced tai chi for nineteen generations. *Left to right, front row:* Richard Gates, Elena Maza, Alice McElfresh, Ava Harmel, Shifu (teacher) Perry; *back row:* Barbara Murray, Chen Zheng Li (nineteenth-generation master), Larry Hawkins, Dennis Brown, William Stephenson, Chen Xiao Tin (nineteenth-generation master), Ken Nichols, unidentified Chen family master, Shifu (teacher) Bakari Alexander, and Pete Gabrail.

in and bought our tickets. We got the good accommodations where only four people slept to a compartment. We had mattresses about three or four inches thick. There weren't enough compartments, so Dennis Brown had to be in one with five Chinese. Below this was the coach class, where all you got was a hard bench.

The only problem we had when we were leaving was that our flight was delayed. When the plane took off, it circled around like it might return. When we asked what was happening, an attendant said there was someone on the flight the government didn't want to leave. I never knew if this was true or if the attendant was joking.

You must have thought back to your leaving Cuba.

Yes, it was very much like that.

While you were there, were there parallels going though your mind about Cuba and China?

I tried not to let that happen.

We've talked a little about how different your life would have been if you had stayed in Cuba. Would you, in your wildest dreams, have ever gotten into tai chi there?

Probably not. Cuba did have a very large Chinese community. They had come over as indentured servants. The group that came was mostly men to work in the fields and sugar mills. Some became the cooks for the sugar mills. Mom has told me that when they paid off their indenture, they often opened grocery stores. I had never heard of anyone teaching tai chi. I'm trying to find out, but so far, I can't track anything down.

I want to push my question back a bit further. Suppose Castro hadn't taken over and that your family had stayed in Cuba. How would you have found this deeper connectiveness that tai chi has brought you?

I think I would have used traditional arts, probably painting or music, because that's what would have been available to me as a woman.

So there would have been some restrictions about what you could have done?

That's right. Here in this country I've had a lot of freedom to make more choices for my life.

Elena's Art; Return to Cuban Heritage

Elena's choices were many; increasingly they determined how her life began to play out. In 1991, she started teaching tai chi in the ground floor studio in her Sandy Spring house, a large L-shaped room that seems to have been designed for this. One wall looks out on the backyard that backs up to the one acre of uncultivated land. Elena calls this their "meadow" and hopes that in not too many years it will become a woodland.

Meanwhile David was having difficulties with his social and school life, resulting in brushes with the law. After a year in juvenile detention, he has been able to get his life on course. As well as adults can when a young person defies authority, Elena and Herb stood by him during this difficult time.

Elena and I talk about her hopes for David's future.

You know he is very, very bright; he's been tested and has a high IQ. I've kept everything.

She doesn't have to add that she is proud of him and what he has been able to accomplish. Her smile says it all.

During the fourteen years that Elena devoted so much time and attention to David's problems, she was still able to hold on with amazing tenacity to her personal goal of becoming a recognized, professional artist. She tells how she realized this goal.

In 1989, I had begun translating the letters of my cousin Alejandro for Charles White. These letters had a real effect on me. The few stories I had heard about Alejandro had always made me want to find out about

22. David, Herb, and Mrs. de la Maza, Christmas, 1997.

him. When I started translating the letters, the story of his life unfolded. I found I really identified with him, especially with the conflict he felt between his artistic ambition and having to support his family. I saw what he had done and how much he had accomplished. He showed so much courage and guts. I said to myself, "You put your art off to the side. You could have done a lot more if you had been like Alejandro."

I realized there was no way I could make a living doing art. I could see that artists had to get real-life jobs to live on. After 1978, when I started having all the problems with my teeth, I didn't do much art.

On our 1984 vacation to Tortola, after Cecilia died, as I've mentioned, I started working with watercolors; this was the first art I had done in years. Watercolor is a difficult medium, and my first paintings were awful; the colors were muddy. When we got back from Tortola, I saw a show of Winslow Homer's. I bought the catalogue. I was inspired and wanted to keep working.

For the next several years I just worked on watercolors. Our townhouse was near Brookside Gardens, one of the Montgomery County parks. I would go there to sketch and paint. I noticed they had shows in the lobby of the greenhouse. After talking to the person who organized these, I got on their calendar. In 1986, I had a small show there. That was my first solo show. My watercolors sold pretty well. A Russian man bought two. My aunt bought one. I would have given it to her, but she insisted on paying for it.

That got me going with my art. Nicholas, the Russian, asked me why I was working for an engineer, why I didn't just paint full-time. I began to wonder about this myself, and in 1991 I quit my job. I had worked for Cobb Engineering for fifteen years. I was feeling stale—seeing the same people day in, day out. I would look out the window and think, "What the hell am doing in here? I wish I was out there."

I decided to focus on my art. I had been hanging out at Rockville Arts Place since they opened.[1] I had taken a watercolor course there, and I was in the middle of taking a life drawing class. In fact, I had arranged it so that I could leave my job on Thursday afternoon to take this class.

About a month after I quit my job, Patricia Dubroof organized the "Artists Meet Artists" evening at the Rockville Arts Place, which interested me because I realized that I didn't know any artists, and that if I were going to make it as an artist, I needed to begin to make contacts and build up a network of artist friends. When Carmen Trujillo got up to talk about her work on one of those evenings, it was like looking in the mirror. I realized how alike we were—both Cuban exiles who had been here almost thirty years, both doing our art on the side, while she raised her family and I worked.

When Carmen and Elena talked afterward, Carmen couldn't believe they hadn't met. She asked Elena what she had been doing. Elena told her she had been working, because that seemed the easiest way to summarize everything she'd been doing besides working: painting, raising David, studying tai chi, getting her teeth fixed, as well as being a wife, daughter, and sister.

Carmen is a very outspoken artist/activist in the D.C. area. If Cuba is mentioned, the next question will be, "Do you know Carmen?" or, "Have you talked to Carmen?"

She offered to introduce me to a group of women artists who were going to meet in a couple of weeks. I went to her house a couple of hours early so we could chat. Even though she is eight years older, it was amazing to me that our lives were so parallel.

The meeting was at Karen Gallant's house. It was right after the national conference of the Women's Caucus for Art (WCA) was held here in Washington.[2] There was still a lot of free-floating enthusiasm and energy. I was very impressed. Toward the end of the meeting, I agreed to work with Carmen's multicultural committee and to work with the exhibitions committee.

The next show sponsored by WCA in 1991, Visible Differences, *was an open show at Martin Luther King Jr. Library in downtown Washington.*[3] *Alice Sims had come up with the theme of* Visible Differences *to reflect one of the goals of WCA: to provide exhibitions that reflect the ethnic, cultural, and artistic diversity of its members. Lillian Hamlin, an artist from Argentina who was serving as the WCA exhibitions chair, curated the show by making studio visits.*

Once I got going, I realized this was the way my life was supposed to be, that I really was an artist. After the Martin Luther King show, I started doing volunteer work at Rockville Arts Place. Jack Rasmussen, who was the director at that time, was such an interesting and professional person. I was accepted in a show there called *Three Acts,* which included painting, sculpture, and photography.

Soon after I saw an article in *Koan* about a new gallery in Georgetown, the Parish Gallery.[4] The article said that the gallery planned to feature African-American and Latino artists. By now I had learned that you just don't wander into any gallery and expect them to show your work. I had tried that in the seventies.

I went to talk to Norman Parish, the gallery owner, and I brought my portfolio of Afro-Cuban work. He encouraged me, explaining that if I wanted to have a show with his gallery, I needed to put together fifteen pieces of consistent quality on the Afro-Cuban theme, then come back with some of the new pieces. Our conversation made me realize that I had become more professional about discussing my work with a gallery owner. We tentatively agreed that I would get these done in the next year or year and a half.

I ask Elena, who by now was a Cuban exile of almost thirty years, how she had developed or maintained an interest in Afro-Cuban themes, especially the Santeria religion that was developed by the Africans slaves in the Caribbean.[5]

In the seventies, when Herb and I were in our hippie, psychedelic phase, my mother noticed that I was losing touch with my Cuban roots. I was speaking almost entirely in English; when I tried to speak in Spanish I made many grammatical mistakes. She would correct me pleasantly.

Mom started getting me subscriptions to Spanish magazines. One of the magazines had an article about Landaluze, a Spaniard who transplanted himself into Cuba. He painted in a classic style.[6] He did a lot of street scenes, but his paintings of all the beautiful mulattoes on the cigar bands and cigar boxes was what paid the bills!

That figure in the striped costume is really stolen from one of his paintings.

Elena points to a painting over the piano.

These are people who do Afro-Cuban rituals. When Landaluze painted this figure, there was little real understanding of who they were and what they doing, but they would be seen on the streets. Landaluze called them the *diablitos* (little devils). Later he was criticized as being racist for sometimes portraying the Afro-Cubans as monkeys. In spite of his prejudices, he was able to catch a lot of their movements and costumes. His work was so highly thought of that a book of lithographs of his paintings was published. His work falls into a period of Latin American art called *Costumbrismo*.[7]

This term refers to the period when national identity developed. In Latin American this took the form of each country's trying to express its particular customs. The painters and writers tried to accurately portray the dress, manners, and customs of their own area or country.

My grandfather had this book of Landaluze's art; it was published in 1867 or 1868. My Aunt Sarah told me that when they were getting ready to leave, she couldn't bear to let the Castro government have this book. She cut out part of it. When she sneaked the prints in letters, unfortunately she had to fold them. She kept a few for herself and sent me and my sisters each one.

Elena brings out the framed print of Landaluze's diablitos. In spite of the fold marks, it is an excellent print with the detail and sharpness of a photograph. Elena says many Cuban exiles have used this figure in paintings and drawings. The lithograph is titled El Ñáñigo. *Elena explains that this term relates to one of the Afro-Cuban sects, either a part of or the entire sect. Landaluze recognized this sect by giving the same name to the lithograph of the* diablitos.

The central myth of the Ñáñigo sect is very complex.[8] The central deity announces that he is going to speak to the members of two rival tribes through a tiger fish. The chieftain's daughter accidentally catches the fish.

That the first person to hear the voice of the deity/fish is a woman is the ultimate irony, because Ñáñigo was an all-male sect. The woman becomes scared, drops the fish, and it dies, meaning the deity was dead. To pay for this, she is put to a sacrificial death. This event is reenacted by sacrificing a goat or another animal. The voice of the deity is heard through a drum.

In Miami I found this book, *Los Negros Brujos*, by a well-known Cuban ethnologist, Fernando Ortiz.[9] My mother remembers that he presented lectures at the Lyceum in Havana. He is credited with starting the study of Afro-Cuban culture. He was the first person to want to know what was behind the costumes and strange rituals. He brought street vendors into his lectures to demonstrate classical African chanting.

In 1905, there was a famous case in Havana of a white girl who was kidnapped. When her body was found, her heart was missing. Professor Ortiz published a monograph soon after this about how traditional African beliefs were influencing the Afro-Cubans to commit criminal acts. He researched the case in Havana and found that the heart of a virgin was believed to help an infertile woman conceive.

Ortiz began to study the African cultures of Cuba. He was able to cultivate friendships with Afro-Cubans so he could witness some of the rituals and ceremonies. Lydia Cabrera was the other important person who studied this area. She was a painter who had studied in Paris. Cabrera talked to Ortiz about his research. When she began to listen to the stories of her servants, they began to confide in her, and she was able to put together their whole universe of beliefs. Cabrera gave up her painting entirely and devoted the rest of her life to researching the Afro-Cuban culture.

After I read the Ortiz book, I wanted to find out more. Then I got into Cabrera's book *El Monte* (The bush).[10] It was from these books and the Landaluze paintings that I discovered the Afro-Cuban culture. I tried to grasp it all with those two references. As I got older and more into it, I saw the mistakes and misinterpretations I'd made.

Elena and I get up from the couch and walk over to one of the paintings that was in her Parish Gallery show. Elena explains what is happening in one of the paintings. The Santeros were originally from Nigeria, from the Yoruba culture. They believed in a pantheistic universe where all the deities embodied different physical forces. Elena had gone to the Smithsonian's National Museum of African Art to see a video about Oshún, one of the goddesses, who is associated with a river there. In the African mythos, Oshún

EMBRACING AMERICA

had to be a virgin forever, not marrying or having any kind of relationship with a man, but in Cuba, this changed. Oshún became the classic seductive mulatto and the lover of Shangó, the god of thunder. In Cuba, Oshún became the goddess of all freshwater rivers. Oshún is also associated with other elements and colors.[11]

I comment that Elena has carried the water motif through the painting. Water is actually shown, and then there is a feeling of water in the textured green and orange paint that sprays across the canvas like a fog or moving clouds.

What does the orange represent?

Oshún's color is saffron. She is also associated with honey. People who believe in her wear amber beads. The lizard is her animal. You'll notice that there is a lizard emerging from the green water on her right.

There is a small white girl in the painting. Is that you?

It could be. I meant it to represent all of humanity that isn't African.

And the angel?

That's the angel of death. Notice that there is blood dripping from her sword. In spite of the way you are describing it, this is a dark painting—not the colors, but the message. Oshún has dropped the mirror she has just looked in and is going into a swoon because of the tragedy she sees: the future of Cuba, which is represented by the swirling paint. Looking into a mirror as a method of divination comes from a Congo sect.

These are complex themes to develop in paintings. How was your show received?

It was received very well. I bought an ad for my show that appeared in the newsletter that *Casa Cuba* produced. The *Diario Las Americas*, a newspaper in Miami, did an article in advance of the show. They couldn't come to see it, but the article said that showing in the Parish Gallery was prestigious.[12]

Elena laughs.

Of course, this was based on the press release that Norman Parish wrote.

The only thing that went wrong was the weather. My show had originally been scheduled for the fall of 1993. In the summer, the gallery owner called me and told me that a Spanish artist was going be in town until November, and that he needed to use my slot for his show. He was a sculptor and didn't want the expense of shipping his work back for a show. We traded, and I took the January slot. I was disappointed. January is the worst month for a show. People have no money after Christmas, and the weather can be lousy.

In January 1994, we had a lot of freezing rain. The regular opening for the Parish Gallery is the third Friday in the month, which was right at the end of the exhibit. I had the wisdom to have one other opening for my show so that I could get more people to see it. The first one was January 7. The weather wasn't too bad for that one.

Norman had hung the show on January 6. The next day I went to the gallery in the late afternoon to get ready for the first reception. As soon as I walked in, I saw a red dot, which meant that one piece had already sold. Norman told me that at 4:55 P.M. a man had come in, looked around, and said he wanted to buy the one that I used on the show invitation. Since he couldn't afford it, he bought a smaller one instead. He told Norman that he worked for ABC and was leaving that night to go to eastern Europe to cover a visit there by President Clinton. He gave a deposit.

A friend, Rene, who has bought some of my work, came to the reception early. He had told me he wanted to have first pick. Rene wanted to buy the same one that the man from ABC had reserved, so he didn't buy any. Another old friend bought one, and someone from the tai chi school bought one.

A year later, the man from ABC decided he wanted to trade up. It was an unusual arrangement, but Norman and I agreed that he could bring back the one he bought, buy the larger one he had originally wanted, and pay the difference. Rene then got to buy the one he wanted.

The reception at the end of the month was scheduled the day after the mayor of Washington, Sharon Pratt Kelly, asked all the businesses to close down. Everyone was running out of fuel because the roads were so icy, and no trucks could get through. Norman Parish called Elena the night before to see if she still wanted to have the opening. He was very doubtful about having it, but Elena reminded him they had sent some seven hundred invitations and couldn't possibly contact all those people.

We did have it, and about twenty-five people showed up. I met Clark, who had just opened his gallery, the Museum of Contemporary Art (MOCA), next door. Norman and I were both pleased that in all I sold four pieces from the show.

23. Elena with Norman Parish, owner of Parish Gallery in Georgetown, at the opening of her solo show *Afro-Cuban Paintings*, 1994.

Two months later, in March, I met Elena for the first time. She was serving as exhibitions chair of the Washington Area Women's Caucus for Art. She had invited members of the WCA to come to her house for a meeting to plan for a show that would be built around the theme of the "five elements."

One of the strengths of the WCA is its overt policy of inclusion. All shows provide an opportunity for both professional and emerging women artists to exhibit together. Because of the diversity of the population of women in metropolitan Washington, this also means urban and suburban women who are Latino, white, black, Asian, and Native American.

Elena explains the origins of The Five Elements *show.*

I met a woman who was a student at the Traditional Acupuncture Institute in Columbia, Maryland, who wanted someone to do her clinical practicing on; she said she preferred someone who was already familiar with parts of Chinese medicine. She agreed to do a trade. I would get acupuncture treatments, and she would get a piece of my art.

She explained that the Acupuncture Institute focused on the five elements: water, wood, fire, earth, and metal. The elements correspond to the seasons and are related to various internal organs. As long as your body maintains a balance among the elements, you are healthy; when they are unbalanced you get sick. A good acupuncturist can tell a lot about your organs just by feeling your pulse.

She gave me books to read, and I got involved with their approach.[13] At the institute, in the first year, students do artwork that relates to the five elements.

Around this time Kathy Oettinger, who was president of WCA at the time, called me and said that the Rockville Mansion was soliciting proposals. She hoped that I could write one for a show by WCA members. That's when I got the idea that the five elements would make a great art show.

Elena patiently explained the theme of the show to the WCA members who came to the first meeting. She told them that everyone in the West tends to think in terms of four—the four seasons, the four directions. She said that the Chinese conceive of five elements and five seasons because they make a distinction between early summer and late summer. To the Chinese, the early summer is fire—the height of growth. The second part of the summer is associated with the earth and the harvest.

The idea of elements was already being used by some artists in both individual work and in some group shows. Using five elements put a new twist on it. The way I sold it at the Rockville Mansion was that it would both introduce the artists doing the work to the public and introduce the public seeing the work to a different way of dealing with a familiar theme: all would be exposed to the thoughts of another culture.

Elena was pleasant, poised, and very organized in her presentation. Elena is proud of the fact that nineteen artists were selected by the juror to be in the show, the most the local WCA has ever had in one show.

As I have mentioned, I went to Elena's house three times to help her photograph the work that would be in the show. The photography was somewhat tedious because of the different sizes and surfaces of the artworks, but Elena was easy to work with. The same traits I had observed during the first meeting were still in evidence: Elena was always enthusiastic and well organized. During these mornings I learned that she was a Cuban exile and a painter, and that she taught tai chi.

The Rockville Mansion is an estate on spacious acreage that had been bought by the city of Rockville, Maryland, as a space for visual and performing arts.[14] The Five Elements *show was a success. There was a well-attended opening on a Sunday afternoon. Kathleen Moran, the arts programs specialist, had installed the work in four large rooms. Several weeks later, the artists in the show gathered with a few friends to discuss their work and how it was tied to the theme. The evening closed with the participants sharing a collective sense of a show well done.*

The next time I saw Elena after this gathering was in February 1995 at the national conference of the Women's Caucus for Art. I spent some of my time getting ready to be a panel participant and to have a book signing where the catalogue of my Valued Women *exhibition was being sold.[15] I saw Elena only briefly. She explained to me that she was staying with a dear friend of many years, and that because she wanted to spend time with the friend, she wasn't able to go to all the meetings.*

In November 1995, nine months after the San Antonio conference, WCA sponsored another exhibit in a space on Seventh Street in Washington, D.C. Elena and I were both in it and ended up gallery sitting together on the Sunday after Thanksgiving, near the end of the show. It was a very quiet day. Only a few people came into the gallery.

I was effectively immobilized that day, on crutches from a fractured ankle, so that afternoon provided an ideal time for me to ask Elena more about her life. Elena started by telling me about leaving Cuba at thirteen; slowly she filled in the years between then and now.

I was amazed at the complexity of her life's story. I asked her if she had ever thought about writing her life's story. She laughed and said she wasn't a writer. A week later I surprised Elena by proposing that we work together on her biography or a memoir. With some reluctance, she agreed that we could at least give it a try.

In January 1996, when I did the first interview, I realized how little I knew about Cuba. Elena lent me Cuba: the Pursuit of Freedom *by Hugh Thomas, a long and detailed history of that country.[16] I spent January reading it and taking notes. I conducted the first of many taped interviews in February 1996. Over the next two years, we made our way through the years of Elena's life. After I would transcribe and edit each session, more questions or details about what she had told me would arise. Slowly the pieces began to fit together.*

I asked Elena about her working as a curator for the Dover Art League soon after her show at the Parish Gallery. How did that happen?

In the spring, after my show at Parish, someone put me in touch with a young man who was running the Centro de Arte in the Mount Pleasant area of D.C., a Latino arts center. In turn, he asked me to curate a show of Latina women as part of the twentieth anniversary celebration of the center. The center is a small place sandwiched between two buildings. Although the show never happened because the only exhibition space available at the center turned out to be too small, I was recommended to the Dover [Delaware] Art League.

Phyllis Levitt, who represented the Dover Art League, had gone to a conference of state humanities councils in 1990 in Portland, Oregon. Her consciousness was raised when she heard that for an art league to become more than a private club for members, it needed to be involved in community outreach. Back in Delaware, Phyllis held meetings with representatives of various ethnic and cultural groups. A series of exhibits titled A Collage of Cultures *were planned. At one of the meetings, Clémence Overall, Gloria Fernandez, and Gina Miserendino suggested that the first show focus on the migrants, the seasonal agricultural workers on the Delmarva peninsula.*

Flyers in English, Spanish, and Creole were distributed to the work camps and the churches where the African-American, Puerto Rican, Mexican, Guatemalan, and Haitian workers could be found.

Elena brings out the catalogue, A Collage of Cultures: Many Visions, One Community: Works by Migrant Seasonal Agricultural Workers.[17] *In this catalogue, Phyllis states that she was keenly aware that the worker/ artists who came together for meetings and workshops were coming "from diverse cultural traditions into a community that is also diverse."*[18]

Phyllis also wrote that "in order to make the Dover Art League into a cultural institution, we would need to open our doors to those artists who might never feel welcome to enter our portals without an invitation."[19]

Clémence called the Centro de Arte, and they gave her my name. *The Five Elements* exhibit really helped me get the job. I took the book of the slides that you and I made, the artists' statements, and the invitation to show them I could organize a complex and comprehensive exhibit. They were very impressed. In addition, I submitted the low bid to curate the show. They had talked to one other artist/curator who wanted five thousand dollars. I wanted to do the show as much for the experience as for the money, so I had asked for only seven hundred dollars.

I learned so much. I had never even seen a migrant worker before. I wasn't sure if I could talk to them, if they would trust me. Phyllis and Clémence were fabulous to work with. They helped me in every aspect of the show. They had already located one artist by the time I was hired. That was Fegaintz, a Haitian painter. I was so impressed with his work that I thought if we didn't find anyone else, his work was good enough for a solo show.

Let me add a few things about Phyllis. When Phyllis retired from teaching, the Dover Art League hired her as a fundraiser. She had told them she would take the job only if they let her build it into a major organization. She felt that that part of Delaware needed a major arts organization; everything in Delaware takes place north of Wilmington. She's told me that the art league used to be an organization of about twenty-five artists, and that most of the shows were of their work. She wanted to change that so that the arts league would be more inclusive and would serve the parts of the community that were underrepresented. Clémence had been working a hot line for the county, working with the Latinos and Haitians. She had met several who were artists.

How long did you work on getting the show ready?

Almost a year. I went for my first meeting in October 1994, and the show was in September 1995. Once they selected me, I put together a schedule of how we should proceed. Mostly I would go there on Sunday. That was the day I could find most of the artists at home. My first field trip was to the Haitian church in Laurel, Delaware. Father Guy, a Haitian minister who had volunteered to help, came with us. After the service we met with some of the artists. Marie, who did the quilts, was one. Then I met Fegaintz.

Elena describes the other artists in the show.

Many of the people in the show were what are called "outsider," or self-taught, artists. Some of them didn't even think of themselves as artists. The art of theirs that we chose for the show was often, to them, just what they did. Many didn't realize their talent. There were fourteen artists in the show.

She opens the catalogue and points to the text and photographs of some of the artists and their artwork.

Marie Benoit from Haiti designs hats. Jorge Luis Berberena from Puerto Rico did wooden sculpture. Willio Castry from Haiti had adorned a bright yellow apron with drawings of Christ. Teresa Conde from Mexico did crocheted work. Margarito Diaz Oritz from Guatemala showed landscape and water scenes. The paintings by Fegaintz Gustin were based on his Haitian life and beliefs. Felix Joseph, another Haitian, did paintings. Catarina Jimenez Pascual, whose mother was a Kanjobal Indian originally from Guatemala and who was once part of a Los Angeles street gang before coming east, showed drawings. Carlos Eduardo Morales Gómez, whose family belongs to one of the Mayan groups in Guatemala, showed a *cortina*, a curtain that originally adorned one of the buses used to travel to market. Estebán Perez López, a Guatemalan Indian, presented some of the photographs he has taken over the past twenty years; he also photographed some of the artists for the catalogue. Juan Perez Morales is the Guatemalan artist who did the paintings of the massacres he witnessed. Maria Silva learned crocheting and knitting in a Mexican orphanage and showed some of her work. Jacqueline St. Pierre created a collaged table, a traditional art form from northwest Haiti. Franck Weche, also from Haiti, showed wood sculpture; this is a photograph of him working on one of his pieces.[20]

I always stayed with Phyllis. She housed and fed me during the entire year. She knew how much work I was doing and how little I was being paid. There really wasn't a lot of money up front for the project. The state arts council had given the art league fourteen hundred of the five thousand dollars the art league had asked for. When the league presented a symposium for the State Humanities Council, they got an additional ten thousand dollars; that's how the catalogue was produced.

We had a two-day opening because some of the artists had to work on Saturday. Both days were festive and well attended. Father Guy brought his wife and their new baby and other children. There were a lot of children. It was like a village square with so many people. They all felt very appreciated.

Some of the Dover Art League members disapproved of the show and chose not to attend because the migrant worker artists were self-taught and weren't really good enough to show in the art league. Some of the members thought they were so much better than the artists being shown.

Their attitude was in direct contrast to that of the agricultural workers. For most of them, this was the first time in their lives they were being recognized and appreciated for their artwork. Maria, one of the Mexican artists, grew up in the orphanage and learned to knit using bobby pins and wire hangers. I was so moved by her. No one outside the community of agricultural workers had ever befriended her or become interested in her. She brought her whole family with her to the opening. When she thanked us at the end of the show, there were tears in her eyes.

The art league began getting good publicity about the collage show. The show went to the Rehoboth Art League, and was well received. Then it went to Wilmington, Delaware, and got some good press there. The next year when the art league applied for a Native American collage show, they got twice as much funding. Now they are working on a show of the art of Asians and Pacific Islanders.

Are there enough people of that heritage in Delaware to do a show?

Oh, yes, Hiro, the Alexandria artist—you probably know her—is going to be the curator.

You really helped launch a winning idea. You are to be congratulated for tackling a big, amorphous idea and bringing together a fine show.

Elena smiles and nods her head.

Very immodestly I have to agree with you. Phyllis wrote me recently that the Delaware Department of Tourism gave my *Collage* show an award. That meant a lot to me. The best part may be that all the people in the art league who were disgruntled about the outsiders' art are now solidly behind the show. They can see how much their art center is benefiting.

Later you had your own solo show at the Dover Art League. How did that happen?

It was really a payback for doing the *Collage* show for such a low fee and delivering a show that has received so much acclaim.

I drove to Dover on a Sunday afternoon in April 1996 to the opening of Elena's show. There were two impressive parts of the afternoon reception in the art league. First was Elena's art. I had only seen her paintings and two beaded heads in her living and dining room, displayed in the informal way most artists use at home. She had had several of pieces in The Five Elements *show, but they had been engulfed by the work of the other eighteen artists. At the Dover Art League I saw for the first time a careful arrange-*

ment of her art: the landscapes together; the Santeria, Afro-Cuban—inspired paintings in proximity with the two Afro-Cuban beaded heads; several of the underwater paintings of Caribbean coral reefs grouped; and a stunning new painting that framed the entire show: a crocodile and a turtle at an underwater stand-off. This painting was used on the front of the invitation. It was a titled A Fable.

I asked Elena at the show if this painting was based on a Cuban fable. She took the time from the crowded opening to explain that this was her own fable, a visual metaphor for present-day Cuba: the crocodile represents Castro—fierce, swift, aggressive.

The crocodile is smiling a big, insincere smile, just like Castro. The turtle is the Cuban people. We are resistant, hard-shelled, and able to retreat easily from any serious threat. There is no way the crocodile can bite through the turtle's shell. In the end, the Cuban people will survive even the long years of Castro.

The second impressive part of the show were the people attending the reception. There was a room crowded by some of the art league's members, who were white and very upper-class; there were Latino friends and college professors; there was Father Guy, the Haitian minister who had helped with the collage show, and his beautiful, large family; and there were some of the migrant artists who had been in the first collage show. It was a wonderfully cosmopolitan group that could have been plucked from the neighborhoods of Georgetown, Adams Morgan, Mount Pleasant, and Dupont Circle in Washington, D.C., except in the capital city these people are hardly ever in the same room together.

At the show, I met Elena's mother for the first time. I was standing by the refreshment table eating a delicious pastry when Elena introduced us. That morning Mrs. Maza had made these pastries, cangrejitos, *for the opening. The word translates as "little crab" and refers to the shape.*

It's my favorite. I always ask her to make it for my openings.

Mrs. Maza was in her early eighties. The grace and beauty I had seen in photographs of her when she was married almost fifty years before still shone through. She took my arm and guided me through the exhibit, carefully explaining Elena's interest in the Afro-Cuban culture and her special love of nature and the water: "We lived close to the water. When Elena was only months old I would take her swimming. I made her a tiny bathing suit. Sometimes she swam without one. She's never been afraid of the water."

24. Elena and her mother, Olga Caturla de la Maza, at the reception for Elena's solo show *Various Splendor* at the Dover Art League, Dover, Delaware, 1996.

There was a crucifixion, a painting of a woman on a cross that I had never seen before. A small boy was bent over in agony at the base of the cross. To one side was a green VW. Paintings of small photographs of the woman on the cross surrounded the edge of the painting on two sides. Although she looked at it for a few minutes, Mrs. Maza didn't make any comments about it. Later that afternoon, I was standing by Elena when someone in a group of people asked her about it.

It's a painting about my sister Cecilia, who committed suicide. The boy at the base of the cross is her son, David. Those photographs of her around the edge are from different times in her life. The green car is hers.

I could only guess at the self-control it must have taken, but Elena's voice never broke in the five minutes she talked about the painting.

Later we talk about the show in detail. Elena explains why the beaded heads were part of it.

They are made from clear plastic Halloween masks. The features of the masks originally were very European. I recontoured them into Afro-Cuban ones. I used acrylic paste to do this. It was fairly tedious. When the paste dries it is rough, so I would have to sand it extensively between the layers. It was almost like making a sculpture.

You did a very professional job. I was sure these were made from a mold.

I had gone to see an exhibit of Yoruba art at the Smithsonian's National Museum of African Art. Clay masks from the seventeenth century were part of the exhibit. They were beautifully crafted pieces. I bought the catalogue, and in it I saw photographs of the famous sculptures of the Obas [Yoruba kings] with the beaded crowns.[21] I had just gotten interested in beading. I used some of the motifs from their crowns—the abstracted leopard for strength, the bird for his wide vision. I made them because it was important for me to have something that honored the Yoruba roots of my own Afro-Cuban paintings.

I ask about the crucifixion painting.

I did the painting in 1995 after the WCA conference in San Antonio. I was very moved by some of the presentations of the Latina women's group. One of the poems read was about the poet's sister who had died an alcoholic, a kind of slow-motion suicide. When she finished the poem, I burst out crying. I really identified with the poet and her pain over her sister's death. I vowed that I would do a painting about Cecilia. I left the conference with that idea. I knew it would have no marketability, but I knew I needed to do it for myself.

A Cuban friend, Zamorano, was curating a show to be held at the Moscoso Gallery around Easter. Since most of us Latinos have been raised Catholic, he thought that the crucifixion would be a good theme. When he called me up and I found out that *The Crucifixion* show he was proposing wouldn't be for a couple of months, I knew I could do it. I showed the painting in that show and then in the Dover show. I've talked to a curator in Jersey City about its being in a traveling show. I'm still waiting to hear about that.

Is it important for people to know the story of the painting?

While it makes more sense if people know the story, I've found that different people can get something from it without knowing the details.

Someone who saw it in Delaware, but who hadn't heard an explanation, told me recently, "I was so moved by that painting."

In the middle of serving as curator for the Dover Art League, Elena was contacted by another of the "Peter Pan kids."

That's what we call anyone who came over on the Operation Pedro Pan airlifts. He is able to go back to Cuba frequently through the channels open to scholars and educators. He believes we should lift the embargo, and that the flood of western goods would topple Castro quicker than anything else. He told me that a group of his friends were coming to this country to make a film. They were independent filmmakers, but some of them were members of the Institute of Cuban Film and Cinematography. To work there they have to belong to that; the government really controls so much.

One of the women had been at the University of Havana. She had lost her job because of something she had done. She and her husband had come to this country and lived in New York. Because of her filmmaking work, she had been awarded a very nice grant by an American organization. She was going to use this grant to underwrite a film about Cuban exiles who had come to this country when they were very young.

When these people asked my Peter Pan friend if he knew anyone that would fit this profile, he recommended me. I was a little concerned about them coming to my house. I knew one of them would be from the government security organization, a combination of our FBI and CIA. I showed them around my house. When they saw my tai chi trophies, they insisted that I put on my official silks to do a demonstration. This was in August, so I did a fifteen-minute demonstration outside. They were surprised at how much I sweated, at how strenuous it was.

They also interviewed me about being an artist. At that time I was in the middle of doing a painting about the *Balseros* (the raft people); this was when they were coming over, and I had all the press clippings around in my studio.[22]

What was their reaction?

They were pleased that this was receiving so much press attention. Cuban friends of mine say that the people in Cuba still think that American foreign policy revolves around them. There is a kind of amazing self-centeredness.

The film crew said to me, "Oh, you are still thinking about Cuba."

I told them, "Just because I'm an American citizen doesn't mean I've lost my Cuban roots and interest in the country." This impressed them.

Because they were late, they wanted to come back the next day and do the "talking heads" part of the tape. When I mentioned that I had two sisters and a mother in the area, they wanted to do a family interview. I wasn't sure. I called Silvia and Beatriz. At first Beatriz agreed to come, because she thought they were from Miami. When she found out they were from Cuba, she wouldn't come. Silvia said the same thing; she was sure they'd use us for propaganda purposes. When I called Mom, she said, "Yes. There are some things I want to say."

The next day Mom had her say. She got a little teary, and I was worried they might cut that out, but the cameraman assured me that we were restrained compared to some of the people he had filmed, who used the taping almost as a therapy session to relive all their anxiety and distress about leaving their country and their difficulties during their first years in this country. He told me they wanted to use the video for reconciliation between the exiles and those who stayed. I actually believed him.

When I had started interviewing Elena that day, she had showed me a charming article that Herb had written about the videotaping for the magazine Inside Kung Fu.[23] *Photographs that accompany the article show Elena demonstrating tai chi and working on a painting in her studio.*

So what was finally produced?

We were told that this video would be on public television in this country. They had to go back to Cuba for the final editing, which had to be approved by the government. My friend saw parts of it when he visited Cuba. He told me later that they cut out the interviews with all the normal people and focused on four people who were the most emotionally disturbed. It turned out to be a self-serving piece for the Cuban government. As far as I know, it's being shown only in Cuba.

I guess it's just as well my interview wasn't part of it. They could have shown my house and made a point about the materialism of Americans: "Twenty Cuban families could live in this house. These people are living like lords and aren't willing to share with the rest of the world."

In 1995, Elena won a three-hundred-dollar second prize in a show in Baltimore for two of her underwater paintings that were based on the photographs she had taken while scuba diving in the Caribbean. She was able to show more of these in the spring of 1997 at the Martin Luther King Jr. Memorial Library, a high-tech boxlike structure designed by Mies van der Rohe. The show, Cuando Calienta el Sol *(When the sun warms) featured the work of Marlene Napoles from Venezuela and Jerry Scott, whom Elena descibes as an honorary Latino. He worked at the American Interest Section in Cuba and in other Latino countries for a number of years. Elena showed her underwater paintings, some of which had been shown in the Dover show. The main gallery at the Martin Luther King Library is a large, gray-carpeted room, one floor below the lobby. The cool, subterranean space was perfect for her paintings of the sea. They shone like small beacons: the deep blue of the Caribbean offset by alizarin coral and golden reflections on the surface of the water.*

Included in the press release is Elena's descriptions of these paintings, written with the great passion she feels for what her heritage may contribute to the greater good:

> These paintings are meditations on primordial intimations, the origins of life on earth in the oceans, its infinite variety and richness. They may become elegies to what will someday disappear from the planet. Created in a traditional format, they are sometimes scorned by curators and galleries who think that only current art trends of disturbing, cutting-edge, or "socially significant" art are worthy of being exhibited. And yet the world is badly in need of such poetry right now. People need to look at these images as a way of cultivating the serenity and inner calm necessary to counteract the constant bombardment of artificial stimuli that our nervous systems are subjected to. My paintings, I offer to the world as a way of sustaining and healing the viewer's body/spirit.[24]

In 1996 Elena was elected to a two-year term as president of the Greater Washington, D.C., Women's Caucus for Art. The president of this organization officiates at general meetings, oversees the work of the exhibitions and multicultural committees, and assists with the newsletter. In addition to fulfilling her presidential duties, Elena chaired the membership committee.

In the middle of her two-year term with WCA, Elena was asked to help form an organization that would organize cultural events for the Cuban community in metropolitan Washington, D.C. This organization, formed in the summer of 1996, was named the "Cuban American Cultural Society." Dur-

ing our interviews Elena has mentioned several other Cuban organizations. I ask her to talk about these first.

The first one I heard about was *Casa Cuba*. This group had been active since the early eighties, after they had fled Castro. They wanted the Cubans who were here to maintain contact. Once or twice a year they had a dinner dance. They would get a Cuban band. I never attended any of those because Herb isn't really into dancing. But I did try to attend their cultural events. In addition to those, they organized several demonstrations in front of the Cuban Interest Section to protest some of the things going on in Cuba. It's on Sixteenth Street, below Columbia Road, near the Mexican Cultural Institute. This is in effect the Cuban embassy in Washington. They are not allowed to have a real embassy.

Elena explains that the United States has the same thing in Cuba, that there is an American Interest Section in Havana. She reminds me again that Jerry Scott, who showed with her at the Martin Luther King Jr. Memorial Library, was stationed there.

Some people in the Cuban community had gotten together to raise money for the Brothers to the Rescue, the group in Miami that assists Cubans fleeing Castro.[25] They had an art auction. Someone from this group got in touch with me. I don't even know how they got my name. I was just getting started as an artist in 1993. A very nice Cuban psychiatrist, Rafael Garcia-Barcenas, bought one of the things I offered the auction. He invited me to the Black Bean Coalition.

The Black Bean Coalition isn't a real organization—it's just a group that gets together once a month. We started calling ourselves the Black Bean Coalition to define who we were. Raúl Sanchez, who used to own La Plaza restaurant in Adams-Morgan, opened the Cactus Cantina on Wisconsin Avenue. Once a month he would offer us a buffet of Cuban food. There was always black beans and rice, which gave rise almost automatically to our name. He also always had *ropa vieja*, a traditional Cuban dish. The name translates as "old clothes"; this is a flank steak that is cooked for a long time in a sauce until it is very tender.

This group, which had been meeting at another restaurant for many years, was very informal. The first time I went was early in 1994. At that time there were fifteen or twenty of us; we had been able to chat because the group was that small. By the end of 1994 the word was out: fifty to sixty people began showing up. I went to the Christmas 1995 meeting and there were a hundred people there.

These are all Cuban exiles?

Yes. People would bring friends. I met Robin Myers there. She worked at the American Interest Section in Havana and got thrown out of Cuba because of her contacts with Cuban dissidents.[26] Someone in the State Department had told her about the Black Bean Coalition.

The only activity is the dinner?

That's right. It was a bargain. When we started Raul charged us only five dollars for dinner. Of course, he did make money off the drinks. Later he raised the cost to six dollars. When the group got so large, he moved the dinner to Tuesday night. I haven't been able to go because I teach a tai chi class on that night.

I ask if her mother's generation comes to the Black Bean Coalition. She replies that only a few attend.

There were other Cuban organizations. At one of the meetings of the Black Bean Coalition I heard about a concert given by Círculo Cubano de Maryland. I knew nothing about them but went with Mom to a concert they sponsored by the pianist Zenaida Manfugas, who turned out to be extraordinary.

Of Human Rights is an organization that dates back to the late seventies or early eighties; their mission is to help the political prisoners in Cuba. They have brought attention and pressure, through other governments, on Cuba and have eased the conditions of some of the prisoners. Oilda, Sergio's sister, [Elena's brother-in-law] has been active in this organization.

In 1995, she helped bring a company from Miami called Pro-Arte Gratelli. This is a reincarnation of the Pro-Arte Society in Havana where I studied ballet and where my parents went for concerts. The Miami group is a very well established company. I had seen an operetta they did in Miami that was first-rate.

Of Human Rights was able to rent Lisner [Auditorium] for this production, which featured the main singers in their costumes. They couldn't afford to bring the entire company with all the sets. The production was a big hit. The person that I thought was the top voice was a Cuban tenor, Armando Terron.[27] He's large like Luciano Pavarotti, and he has the same type of magnificent voice. He was the star of the evening.

Let me add this—Armando Valladares, who wrote *Against All Hope* in 1986, was held for a number of years as a political prisoner.[28] His book contributed a lot to the worldwide recognition of the problem of the large number of political prisoners in Cuba and the intolerable conditions under which they are kept. His book convinced liberal circles of what was going on.

In 1982, four years before Against All Hope *was published, Susan Sontag had caused some major ripples among New York intellectuals. At a rally in support of the Polish workers' party Solidarity, she gave a speech in which she accused "people on the left," herself included, of being unwilling to support anticommunist positions for fear of seeming to align with McCarthyism. She said that "fascism [is] the probable destiny of all communist societies—especially when their populations are moved to revolt."[29] Although she was criticized for including the entire left—many of whom had years before expressed displeasure with Stalinism and other ideological forms of repression—there was acknowledgment that too many in liberal circles had excused or overlooked the excesses of communism, particularly in regard to human rights.*

La Casa Cuba just ran out of steam. They thought they weren't getting enough support from the Cuban community, especially for the dinner dances, so they disbanded. Felix Pages had been doing the newsletter; he's not going to continue it.

You've mentioned the Cuban American Cultural Society; it seems to have come along at the right time to fill the void created by the demise of these other organizations. How did it get started?

We had our first meeting the summer of 1996. Lucia Vasallo was the moving force behind this getting started. She has tremendous energy. She is very sociable and knows everyone. She is not at all shy about calling a performing artist she barely knows and inviting him or her to come to Washington to perform.

We wanted to sponsor events. Everyone felt that culture and cultural events were really what held the community together. Some of the people wanted to do it on a very small scale—like a piano concert in someone's home. There are many older Cuban exiles, like my mother, who haven't established as many American friends and ties as people my age. Some of them would rather speak Spanish in social situations. The Cuban American Cultural Society brought back Armando Terron, who had appeared in the zarzuela that Of Human Rights had sponsored.[30]

Among the really fun things we've done for the members of the Cuban American Cultural Society is to have receptions to meet the artists after the concerts. I had the one for Zenaida. That's when I got my piano tuned. I would have died if she had decided to play it and found it out of tune.

She's the pianist that you first heard when the Círculo Cubano de Maryland sponsored her?

Yes. Her second concert was just as popular as her first.

I remind Elena that when we were talking about her moving to the large house in Sandy Spring, she told me that she had had a dream of re-creating the kind of salons that existed in Havana; she had mentioned the tall windows, the chandeliers, the gas lights.

Oh, yes, the *tertulia:* this is the traditional salon, particularly of my mother's generation and before. If you were of a certain class, this was what you did for entertainment. You invited interested friends and relatives to hear someone play the piano, sing, or recite poetry. I'm not sure that I had the *tertulia* in mind when we bought this house, but I wanted a house where we could entertain.

There was a concert of Cuban music at Mount Vernon College in 1996. Did your organization sponsor that?

No. That was part of the college's regular concert series. Last year was the centenary of Lecouna.[31] Everyone wanted to do something to honor him. Mount Vernon decided to do a concert of his music. I've heard from several people that it was their best-selling concert. They actually had two concerts because the singer they had advertised became ill; they gave people a rain check and she appeared at a later concert. I went to the first, but the second one was the same night as the concert by Armando Terron. These three concerts were well attended. The organizer of the Mount Vernon concerts asked me, "What is with you Cubans? Whenever there's a Cuban event, all of you show up to support it!"

Elena and I are almost finished. Her life continues, but this part of her story is told. We meet for the last of two sessions to check a few facts and dates.

I couldn't find that photograph I'd told you about—the one Herb took in 1986 when we visited Key West.

Earlier Elena had described a photograph of her in front of a sign in Key West that pointed two ways: pointing one way, the sign read, "Cuba 90 miles"; pointing the other way, it read "Miami 150 miles." At the time, Elena had said, with a sigh, that may be as close as she would ever get to Cuba.

However, I did find something else I wanted to show you.

She shows me a candle she bought in a Giant grocery store. The yellow candle is in a glass container that has an illustration of the patron saint of Cuba on it.

I bought this before one of the two times I almost went to Cuba.

I shake my head in disbelief. I am incredulous. You almost went to Cuba twice, and we haven't talked about this before!

Elena laughs in an apologetic way.

I'm sorry. Because it never worked out for me to go, I guess it wasn't as important to me as the other things that did happen. Let me explain about this candle. It has to do with Oshún and the Santeria religious sect. In Cuba, Oshún became associated with the patron saint of Cuba, *Nuestra Señora de la Caridad Del Cobre,* who comes from a seventeenth-century legend.[32] Three fisherman—one African, one Spanish, and one Indian—are out fishing. The sea becomes very rough, and they are about to capsize. They pray, and the Virgin, who is a mulatto in this legend, appears. She walks on the waves and calms the sea.

Virgin de la Caridad Del Cobre *is written on the glass candle container. The illustration makes the Virgin look Spanish. She is holding Baby Jesus. There are angels and putti on either side. The three fishermen are in a boat under the Virgin. A prayer to "Our Lady of Charity" is on the back, asking for strength to withstand enemies and blessing for the house where this image is "exposed."*

The candle was made in Laredo, Texas, but it is definitely for use by Cubans. The fact that the candle is yellow—for Oshún—and that it portrays the Virgin Del Cobre tells me it was meant to be used in Afro-Cuban ceremonies. A key tenet of the Yoruba sect is to protect the believer from evil.

Elena smiles.

I had considered going to Cuba with the Smithsonian—either in 1992 or 1993. I can't remember the exact year. They had asked for volunteers to go on a project investigating Afro-Cuban religions. I sent them all my qualifications.

Were you worried about going back? You've told me that a lot of people in Cuba don't like the "exiles."

No. I felt under the prestige and protection of the Smithsonian I'd just be seen as another one of the American tourists/scholars who were permitted to travel there. I couldn't have gone as an individual, but as part of a group I didn't think I'd stand out. As it turned out, the Smithsonian canceled the trip. They felt the political situation was getting too volatile to sponsor the project.

Then in 1995 I found a Canadian group giving a tour of Cuba. The tour was going to take us to an Afro-Cuban sect in the middle of the country at Las Villas. From there we'd go to Santiago for what is now called the "Fiesta de Fuego"; this is the old Santeria carnival. They were asking one thousand dollars per week plus the airfare.

What happened with the second trip?

I bought this candle before this trip. I decided to light it and ask the question, "Should I go to Cuba?" Even though it was perfectly still in the room, the candle went out immediately. I'm not ordinarily superstitious, but I felt that it was no coincidence that the candle went out after I asked that question. So that was my answer: "Don't go. Not yet."

Will you ever go?

I would never go back to live permanently. First, because Herb would never feel comfortable there. I know that if I went back I would be a stranger. I try to stay informed, and I have a pretty good idea of what's going on, but there is a whole generation that has become the "new man" in Cuba that I don't know at all.[33] If Cuba became free, I would definitely like to go back, stay for a while, and help them rebuild the country. Herb would go with me for that—a short-term visit.

I talked recently to a young man who is able to go back to Cuba from time to time. He told me that the people there have very mixed feelings about the Cuban exiles in the U.S. On the one hand, they resent us; they feel if we had stayed, there would have been enough collective weight to depose Castro. On the other hand, they feel that we should be helping them to survive in the very bleak conditions. They feel that when Castro dies or whatever, that we will come in and flood the country with money.

I ask if David or Elena's nieces or nephews might feel they want to be part of the new Cuba—whenever that happens.

David says he's an American. Of course, his father is American. Beatriz's children speak Spanish perfectly, but I'm not sure they would ever want to claim Cuban citizenship. But I can see how our talent could be of use to Cuba. This all ties in with why we started the Cuban American Cultural Society. Lucia and I feel that our Cuban culture has been completely destroyed by Castro; he has tried to rewrite our history through communism. The "new man" from the revolution doesn't necessarily know the old culture that I grew up with. Part of the reason the cultural society is trying to preserve the old Cuban culture is because this will provide the seed that can be taken back to Cuba; it will also provide an important identity for the young people who have grown up here. We will have this to offer the new Cuba when it rises from the ashes. There are such riches in our culture.

Last Saturday the Cultural Society had a lecture about a Cuban poet, a woman from the nineteenth century, Gertrudis Gomez de Avellaneda. She was known as "La Avellaneda." She was an amazing figure who towers over so many. She wrote plays and poetry. Hearing about her life meant so much to me. I could identify with her. She left Cuba when her father died; she was young and went to Spain with her mother. She still considered herself Cuban. She was nominated to the Royal Academy of Letters, but she was turned down for membership because she was a woman. Then she became a real feminist. She lived an unusual life; she had love affairs. She had a daughter who lived only a few months. The father of the child refused to acknowledge that it was his. Later she married another man, and he died in six months. She married again. All during this time she was writing poetry and plays. I found out there is a biography about her by the woman who delivered the lecture and a book of her poetry.[34] My mother had studied "La Avellaneda" in high school. This poet is the perfect example of the vast gaps that exist in the knowledge of our culture for those of us who have grown up in exile. God knows if the young people in Cuba today have ever heard of her.

I am reminded of another event sponsored by the Cuban American Cultural Society. They recognized and honored Mrs. Olga Caturla de la Maza, Elena's mother, for the poems she had written.[35] The luncheon celebration was a special afternoon and seemed to complete some kind of circle for Elena and her family. Most of the Maza family was there: Silvia and Bill and two of their three children; Beatriz and Sergio and five of their six children; Herb, David, and Elena; and many friends of the family.

Selections of Mrs. de la Maza's poems were read and praised in Spanish. Toasts were made, most often with water or coffee. By the end of the afternoon, all seemed sated with the tributes. Some had left; some were lingering to give one more congratulation to Mrs. de la Maza.

As the room cleared, Mrs. de la Maza saw David across the room fixing himself another cup of coffee. He and Herb had arrived late, and Mrs. de la Maza hadn't had a chance to speak to him. She called to him, "Cuquito!" "Cookie" was the pet name she had given David as a child. He turned, smiling. He knew who was calling him. No one had to prompt him to cross the room to her.

During those few seconds before he reached her, I thought of Mrs. de la Maza's conclusion when she wrote about the imprisonment of the many women and children in the "Blanquita" near her house, days after the Bay of Pigs: "[T]here was only one way towards freedom . . . exile."

Those words—exile and freedom—hung in a delicate balance as the afternoon came to an end.

David reached down and gave his grandmother a big hug.

Herb was to one side of them, his hands folded on his chest, a look of quiet satisfaction on his face. Elena turned when she heard "Cuquito." As she turned, one of the recessed ceiling lights illuminated her face, already radiant with an expression of serenity and happiness.

In the air above, the balance shifted: exile receded and freedom moved slightly forward.

Appendix

The Painting "The Prophesy of Ochun"
To my daughter Elena Maza Borkland

Now the goddess raises her illuminated hand,
to conjure lights and ancestral rituals,
transparencies of water, fluvial attributes,
in forests of mystery, of entwined branches.

Greens and wild energy, in bold brush strokes . . .
A man and two women pray for their sins,
chameleons, snakes, tropical symbols,
life in its beginnings: children of ghostly silhouette.

I salute you, Cuban painter of the diaspora,
who bring life to the myths of African culture,
brought by slaves, in cuffs of iron!

You understand why their gods were not forgotten:
you always keep love for your Antillian homeland.
And through the magic of art, in your painting they arose.

OLGA CATURLA DE LA MAZA

Reprinted by permission of Two Eagles Press International, Las Cruces, New Mexico

To Cecilia

You flew towards the portals of dawn,
dove of softest kindness,
you who loved everything that wept,
today because of hate, wounded without pity.

To live without the love of the adored one,
darkened your sweet clarity,
and the fury that dwells in vile people,
was, towards you, implacably cruel.

Your tormented suffering has ended,
the barb of evil you no longer feel.
At last, beloved daughter, you are calm.

On my knees at your side,
the founts of grief have opened,
and run overflowing through my soul.

OLGA CATURLA DE LA MAZA

Reprinted by permission of Two Eagles Press International, Las Cruces,
New Mexico

All the Sea for my Dreams

Thank you, Lord, for giving me
all the sea to float my dreams!
Rocking on its liquid hammocks
Loomed of waves and foam,
I will sing, to the beat to my nostalgia.

Beating its wings,
in silky evasion of whiteness,
a heron that passes
has saluted me: "Sister!"
I answer: "I love you!"
From a soul that shines,
because I am a sailor and Cuban . . .
And I have all the sea for my dreams!

OLGA CATURLA DE LA MAZA

Reprinted by permission of Two Eagles Press International, Las Cruces,
New Mexico

Notes

Preface

1. Harriet L. Beinfield and Efrem L. Korngold, *Between Heaven and Earth* (New York: Ballantine, 1991).

2. "Castro would have seen Operation Pedro Pan and Cuban emigration in general an efficient way to get rid of at least part of his domestic opposition. The brain drain devised by the United States was for Castro a 'purification effect.'" Victor Andres Triay, *Fleeing Castro: Operation Pedro Pan and the Cuban Children's Program* (Gainesville: University Press of Florida, 1998), 31. It was only years later that emigration became an embarrassment and was effectively stopped by the government.

3. Yvonne M. Conde, *Operation Pedro Pan* (New York: Routledge, 1999), 47, 53.

4. Margaret Paris-Stevenson, ed., *Cityscape: A Journal of Urban Life* (Washington, D.C.: Western High School of the Arts [later Duke Ellington School of the Arts], 1974–83). Eliot Wigginton's book *Moments* (New York: Doubleday, 1975) explains the "Foxfire learning concept": As students tape record their interviews of older community members, the experience of the interview and subsequent transcribing and writing of an article helps students appreciate their own local history while teaching them to write in a meaningful way. Wigginton's book *You and Aunt Arie* (New York: Doubleday, 1976), to which Paris-Stevenson contributed, drew from the first thirteen Foxfire projects—including *Cityscape*, the first urban project—and explained how each used the Foxfire learning concept. Hundreds of such oral history/writing projects have been conducted worldwide since this book was published.

5. Mirta Ojito, "Cubans Face Past as Stranded Youths in U.S.," *New York Times,* January 12, 1998, sec. A, pp. 1, 16. Donald Baker, "A Journey Out of the Past for 'Pedro Pan' Project," *Washington Post,* January 26, 1998, sec. A, p. 19.

6. Conde, *Operation Pedro Pan.*

7. Triay, *Fleeing Castro.*

8. Margaret L. Paris, *Valued Women: A Photo Essay in Celebration of Women over Forty* (Rockville, Md.: Self-published, 1994).

Chapter 1. Leaving Havana; Resettling in Albuquerque, New Mexico

1. "[The] glass-enclosed area [was] nicknamed *la pecera* (the fishtank)." Victor Andres Triay, *Fleeing Castro: Operation Pedro Pan and the Cuban Children's Program* (Gainesville: University Press of Florida, 1998), 72.

2. Hugh Thomas, *Cuba: The Pursuit of Freedom* (New York: Harper and Row, 1971), 1296.

3. Triay, *Fleeing Castro,* 15–16.

4. Thomas provides details of the Agrarian Reform Law in *Cuba,* 1070, 1215–33.

5. Russell Baker states in the preface of the 1956 edition of George Orwell's *Animal Farm: A Fairy Story* (New York: Penguin, 1956) that the book is "a passionate sermon against the dangers of political innocence," vi.

6. Conde, *Operation Pedro Pan,* 26.

7. Christmas was reinstated as a holiday in Cuba after almost three decades. "The declaration was a major concession to the Catholic Church, which is pushing to expand religious freedom in this tightly controlled Communist country." Serge Kavaleski, "Havana To Reinstate Christmas," *Washington Post,* December 2, 1998, sec. A, pp. 31, 36.

8. It was only much later that Elena knew the airlift as *Operation Pedro Pan.* The term was created in 1962 by a reporter for the *Miami Herald.* Conde, *Operation Pedro Pan,* 47, 53.

9. Beatriz Maza del Castillo, "Memoirs" (n.d.), 8.

10. Ibid., 9.

11. Triay, *Fleeing Castro,* 24–54.

12. Maza del Castillo, "Memoirs," 9.

13. Ibid.

14. Ibid.

15. Conde, *Operation Pedro Pan,* 89–90.

16. Triay, *Fleeing Castro,* 69.

17. Sugar was one of Cuba's major exports, and the sugar industry, which had many American investors, had been taken over by the revolutionary government. An invasion was on the minds of both Americans and Cubans because of

Cuba's nationalization of the sugar industry, a move that Richard Nixon termed "economic banditry." Cuba became part of the debate between John Kennedy and Richard Nixon during the 1960 presidential campaign. "In Cuba all believed an invasion was inevitable. Castro talked of it all the time." Thomas, *Cuba*, 1298–1301.

18. Elia Kazan, director, *Viva Zapata*, with Marlon Brando, Jean Peters, Anthony Quinn, Joseph Wiseman, Arnold Moss, Margo and Frank Silvera, 113 min. (1952). In the movie, Emiliano Zapata, an Indian tenant farmer, leads an army of Indians in the Mexican revolution in hopes of repossessing the land.

19. Elena Maza Borkland, "Memoirs" (n.d.), 7.

20. So many children continued to come that in early 1962, Secretary of Health, Education and Welfare Abraham Ribicoff asked Americans to open their homes to the Cuban children. "We can think of few better ways to 'fight communism' than to care for the children who flee from it." Conde, *Operation Pedro Pan*, 138.

21. Triay writes that Albuquerque, New Mexico; Yakima, Washington; and Helena, Montana, were the most responsive. Those cities did not have large caseloads of dependent children, and homes in the west tended to be larger and therefore better suited for foster care. *Fleeing Castro*, 67.

22. *The Newcomer Book: A Photographic Guide Book to Albuquerque for the New Resident of 1953*, 48 pages.

23. Paul Wendkos, director, *Gidget*, with Sandra Dee, Cliff Robertson, James Darren, and Arthur O'Connell, C-95 min. (1959). *Gidget* is a lighthearted coming-of-age film about an American teenager in the fifties.

24. Thomas, *Cuba*.

25. Ibid., 100–101, 111, 209–32, 469–70. The idea of Cuba's becoming annexed or a state was tied at first to the slave trade and to Cuba's being admitted as a slave state; later it was connected with Cuba's production of sugar, since many of the sugar mills were directly tied to American investors.

26. Thomas, *Cuba*, 1359–71.

27. Victor Andres Triay, *Bay of Pigs: An Oral History of Brigade 2506* (Gainesville: University Press of Florida, 2001), 6, 38–42, 73–82.

28. Chopin became an exile when the Russians captured Warsaw in 1831. "[H]is music represents the quintessence of the Romantic piano tradition." *The New Grove Dictionary of Music and Musicians*, Stanley Sadie, ed. (London: Macmillan, 1980), 4:292–312.

29. Marie Françoise Portuondo, *Ups and Downs of an Unaccompanied Minor Refugee* (Miami: Ediciones Universal, 1984). Marie Françoise Portuondo was born in France and raised in Cuba; when she was seven, she came to the United States as part of Operation Pedro Pan. Her memoir is filled with the same an-

guish, however understated, that Elena experienced in her first months in this country. Ms. Portuondo worked for several years with the Community Action Agency, Hialeah Center, in Miami to help Cubans arriving on the Mariel boatlift. She has taught Spanish at the Duke Ellington School of the Arts in Washington, D.C.

Chapter 2. De la Maza and Caturla Family Histories in Cuba

1. Carlos Márquez Sterling, "What Maza y Artola Represented in Cuban Politics," trans. Elena Maza, *Diario Las Americas,* March 11, 1984, pp. 5, 15.

2. Ibid.

3. José Martí, the Cuban patriot, organized the 1894 uprising. Hugh Thomas, *Cuba: The Pursuit of Freedom* (New York: Harper and Row, 1971), 305–6.

4. José Martí signed the order for the rebellion to begin on this day. Thomas, *Cuba,* 305–6.

5. William Branigin and R. Jeffrey Smith, "U.S. Took Steps to Curb Flights by Exile Group," *Washington Post,* February 27, 1996, sec. A, pp. 1, 5.

6. Chapter 25 deals with this division of power in Cuba and the rise in influence of Martí. Thomas, *Cuba,* 293–327.

7. Thomas, *Cuba,* 249, 254, 324.

8. Ibid., 400–402.

9. Ibid., 601–2.

10. Ibid., 1119, 1432–33. Eugene Robinson, "Cuba Begins to Answer Its Race Question," *Washington Post,* November 12, 2000, sec. A, pp. 1, 30. This recent article reassesses the idea that Cuba has done away with racial prejudice.

11. Nadia Boulanger was an internationally recognized teacher, conductor, and composer.

12. Alejo Carpentier, *La Música en Cuba,* 2d ed. Colección Popular (Mexico: Fondo de Cultural Económica, 1972). In addition to writing about music, Carpentier wrote novels. On the jacket of Carpentier's *The Harp and the Shadow* (San Francisco: Mercury House, 1990), originally *El Arpa y la Sombra,* is this quotation by Carlos Fuentes: "Alejo Carpentier transformed the Latin American novel. He transcended naturalism and invented magical realism. He took the language of the Spanish baroque and made it imagine a world where literature does not imitate reality, but rather, adds to reality. . . . we owe him the heritage of a language and an imagination. We are all his descendants."

13. Carpentier, *La Música en Cuba,* p. 318.

14. Thomas, *Cuba,* 544–63.

15. Elena Maza Borkland, "Portrait of the Author," in *Todo el mar para mis sueños* (All the sea for my dreams), by Olga Caturla de la Maza (Las Cruces, N.M.: Two Eagle Press International, 2001), 145.

16. This encyclopedia, published almost one hundred years ago, is now out of print.

17. In an e-mail to the author on November 18, 2000, Elena wrote:

My father wrote this book [Aquiles de la Maza, *Eutimio Falla Bonet: su Obra Filantrópica y la Arquitectura* (Geneva, Switzerland, 1971)] at the request of Maria Teresa Falla de Batista, Eutimio's sister, as a posthumous tribute to his patron; she published it at her expense as a small private edition. It contains Dad's recollections of the entire process of restoring the church, which was carried out over a fifteen-year period. My dad and Falla had studied architecture at the University of Havana, although Falla, being a few years older, was not in the same class. They became friends, and this resulted in a long collaboration where Dad functioned as the architect. Falla never practiced his profession as an architect, preferring to devote his life to philanthropic work. My Dad also did another restoration of a colonial house in Remedios for him, a modern hospital in Las Villas, and a swimming pool with a waterfall in a relative's home in Havana. I remember being taken there as a child. Falla never married or had children.

A photograph of the altarpiece in the church that Mr. de la Maza restored appears on page ninety-seven of Rachel Carley's *Four Hundred Years of Architectural Heritage* (photographs by Andrea Brizzi [New York: Whitney Library of Design, 1997]), although there is no mention of his name.

18. A documentary that shows contemporary footage of Elena's Miramar neighborhood and vintage footage of the beach club that she mentions was broadcast in July 2000 on the public television program *P.O.V.* on Channel 26, Washington, D.C. Stephen Olsson, director, *Our House in Havana*, with Silvia Marini Heath and Horton Heath, C-55 min. (Sausalito, Calif.: Soros Documentary Fund Open Society Institute, Cultural and Educational Media, 1999).

19. In an email to the author from December 2, 2000, Elena provided the following information, which she said that she picked up from family conversations:

"Vedado" is the section of Havana to the west of the center of the city (Habana Vieja/Old Havana) that extends towards the Almendares River. It gets its name from the word that means "prohibited." This particular parcel of land was set aside during the early colonial era as the private hunting grounds of the Spanish Governor Generals and their associates, therefore it was vedado/prohibited to everyone else. The name stuck. To give a better idea of the geography, Miramar then would be on west bank of the Almendares, Vedado on the east bank.

20. Olsson, *Our House in Havana*.

21. "One of the most celebrated ballerinas for fifty years, Alonso has combined a true sense of romanticism with a Latin boldness of feeling and the suppleness and high extensions of the Russian school with the brilliant footwork of the Italian." Marilyn Hunt, "Alicia Alonso (Alicia Ernestina de la Caridad del Cobre Martínez y del Hoyo)," *International Encyclopedia of Dance* (New York: Oxford University, 1998), 48–50.

22. Photographs of the Valley de Viñales with the *mogotes* are on pages sixty-two and sixty-three. Fred Ward, "Inside Cuba Today," *National Geographic* 91, no. 1 (January 1947): 32–69. There are photos of the town of Viñales in Maritza Betancourt, Eduardo Dobeson, and Vicente Soleto's *Los Pueblos Mas Bellos de Cuba* (Madrid: Agualarga Editores, S.L., n.d.).

23. Maza del Castillo, "Memoirs," 4–5.

24. Ibid., 6.

25. Ibid.

26. Thomas, *Cuba*, 691–99, 709, 718–25, 789, 1033. Although Fulgencio Batista did not officially become president until 1940, he had been wielding power behind the scenes since the fall of the dictator Machado in 1934. There was so much concern about the sugar crop during a series of strikes in 1934 that some of the more affluent Cubans suggested to U.S. Ambassador Jefferson Caffery that Batista should become a military dictator. When Batista first became president in 1940, he was welcomed as a savior with cheering crowds and bands in the streets, ironically the same way Castro would be welcomed almost twenty years later. After Batista became president, he ruled with an increasingly repressive military force until Fidel Castro took over the government in 1959. On April 9, 1952, *Time* magazine featured Batista on its cover with the Cuban flag behind him. The photo caption read: "Cuba's Batista: He got past Democracy's sentries."

27. Maza del Castillo, "Memoirs," 7.

28. Thomas, *Cuba*, 793.

29. This show of support did not include most Catholic priests and many devout laymen, including the de la Mazas. Thomas, *Cuba*, 724.

30. Frederico Laredo Bru was president from 1936–40, and a cabinet member in two previous Liberal (party) administrations. He "understood that his role was to be a mediator between the civilians and the military." He proposed a constitutional convention, held in 1940, that established a constitutional and civilian government. Manuel Marquez Sterling, "The Cuban Republic and Its Presidents, 1902–1959," *Herencia* 8, no. 1 (2002): 80–81.

31. Elena's father is mentioned in the bibliography (page 140) of Martha de Castro's *El Arte en Cuba* (Miami: Ediciones Universal, 1970). In a November 22,

2000, email to the author, Elena wrote: "In the same book is a photo of Juan José Sicre's statue of Martí that was probably intended to accompany my father's project in the competition for the monument to Martí."

32. Carley, *Four Hundred Years*, 150. This book has an excellent photo of the monument to Martí nicknamed "La Raspadura." The caption states: "The monument to José Martí in Havana's Plaza de la Revolucion was a collaborative effort, built between 1938 and 1952. The 450-foot modernist obelisk dwarfs a more traditionally interpreted statue of the Cuban independence leader." On page 138: "At the center of the trapezoidal plaza, almost a kilometer in length, was the monument to José Martí, with a star-shaped base and statuary that combined elements from two earlier competitions." No mention was made of the names of the winners of these earlier competitions. A photograph of "La Raspadura" that includes the statue of José Martí accompanies an article in the *Washington Post*. Ironically, "La Raspadura" has become a roosting place for vultures. Ken Ringle, "Letter from Cuba: To the Autumn of Their Discontent," *Washington Post*, August 3, 2001, sec. C, pp. 1, 4.

33. During Batista's rule, there was continuing unrest by students at the University of Havana and by members of various political groups. Fidel Castro fit into both categories. He was a member of the left-wing Ortodoxos Party, and he spent most of his time at the University of Havana—where he was supposed to be studying law—involved in political activity and ferment. He began his revolution in 1953, when he was twenty-seven, by attacking two barracks in Santiago and Bayamo, in the province of Oriente, located in the far southeastern part of Cuba. His attempted takeover of the barracks did not succeed. He was sentenced to fifteen years and his brother Raúl to thirteen years in the Isle of Pines prison, but a significant amount of public opinion was for Castro and against the continuing repression of Batista. Castro even became an unofficial candidate in the 1954 elections. In May 1955, Castro, his brother, and some of their followers were released under an amnesty law. Castro traveled to the United States and then to Mexico, where he was able to raise funds and troops for a revolutionary force that stationed itself in the hills of the Sierra Maestra in the southeastern part of Cuba. Castro's movement was supported by university students and others who, while not in direct contact with him, staged an unsuccessful attack on Batista's palace in Havana. In 1957, Castro began his own war for three months in the Sierra Maestra. In 1958, Batista began an offensive against Castro and his forces that was singularly unsuccessful. After many small battles and assaults in the southeast, in other provinces, and in Havana by groups and individuals, it became apparent that Batista was on his way out, and that Castro's revolutionary forces would take over. Thomas, *Cuba*, 800–803, 824–44, 862–63, 876–908, 924–31, 966–1019.

Chapter 3. Mrs. de la Maza and Cecilia's Flight to the United States; Together in Albuquerque, New Mexico

1. "But it had become clear that the only opposition candidate [to Batista] of any status, Márquez Sterling, had no hope." Hugh Thomas, *Cuba: The Pursuit of Freedom* (New York: Harper and Row, 1971), 1014–15.

2. "Castro had chosen Manuel Urrutia La, with whom he'd worked in the Sierra Maestra camp, to be the revolutionary president of Cuba, a puppet position whose strings were pulled by then Prime Minister Castro." Yvonne M. Conde, *Operation Pedro Pan* (New York: Routledge, 1999), 11.

3. Thomas, *Cuba*, 1032–33.

4. Ibid., 1073–74.

5. Ibid., 1076–77.

6. Ibid., 1215–33.

7. Ibid., 1365.

8. Conde, *Operation Pedro Pan*, 58–59.

9. Olga Caturla de la Maza, "The Caravan of 'The Blanquita,'" trans. Elena Maza Borkland (April 1961). Elena Maza describes this document by her mother as a historic snapshot from the "Week of Terror" in Havana during the Bay of Pigs Invasion in April 1961.

10. Conde, *Operation Pedro Pan*, 34.

11. In September 1999, Elena visited Albuquerque, New Mexico, and found the house on Roma Street. Although it was slightly improved—it had been painted, had shutters, and rested more firmly on its foundation—it still was the small two-bedroom house that she and her mother and sisters lived in for more than six months.

12. Letter to Olga Margarita De [*sic*] Caturla from Marshall Wise, U.S. Cuban Refugee Program, Department of Health, Education and Welfare, Social Security Administration, March 19, 1962. For reasons unknown, this letter uses Mrs. Maza's maiden name.

13. Letter to U.S. Cuban Regugee Program, Department of Health, Education and Welfare, Social Security Administration from Olga Caturla de la Maza, March, 1962, unsent.

14. "Comédie-Française played *Le Médecin Malgré Lui* (The doctor in spite of himself) one hundred and thirty-one times between 1680 and 1700." Anthony Levi, "Molière, known as Jean-Baptiste Poquelin, 1622–1673," *Guide to French Literature, Beginning to 1789* (Chicago: St. James Press, 1992), 514–28.

15. Aquiles de la Maza to Elena Maza, February 1962.

16. *Perry Mason* was a CBS television series of courtroom drama that aired from 1957 to 1966 and starred Raymond Burr in the title role of criminal defense

attorney Perry Mason. The series was based on the character created by Erle Stanley Gardner.

17. Thomas, *Cuba*, 574.

18. "[T]he most vociferous and dangerous opponents of Machado remained the students, led by men who were themselves no longer at the university or by professors." Thomas, *Cuba*, 577–91.

19. "Machado began to use the army in effect as an extra civil service, officers becoming overseers in all government departments, national and local, in a kind of parody of the Russian commissar system. Even the meat and milk monopolies were run by the army." Thomas, *Cuba*, 582–83.

20. Thomas, *Cuba*, 1371.

21. Ibid., 1322.

22. Opa Locka was used later to house the older of the young males from the Pedro Pan airlifts. Conde, *Operation Pedro Pan*, 98–99.

23. When the author wrote that paragraph, she shared the conventional understanding about when interstate commerce was integrated; however, a recent article in the *Washington Post* details how Irene Morgan integrated an interstate bus in Virginia in 1944, eleven years before the Rosa Parks incident. Thurgood Marshall took the Morgan case all the way to the United States Supreme Court, "resulting in a landmark 1946 decision striking down Jim Crow segregation in interstate transportation. She [Morgan] inspired the first Freedom Rides in 1947, when sixteen civil rights activists rode buses and trains through the South to test the law enunciated in Morgan v. Virginia." Carol Morello, "The Freedom Rider a Nation Nearly Forgot," *Washington Post*, July 30, 2000, sec. A, pp. 1, 10.

24. Dale W. Jacobs et al., eds. *World Book Encyclopedia*, 22 vols. (Chicago: World Book, 2000). The first edition of this encyclopedia was published in 1948.

Chapter 4. Starting Again in Arlington, Virginia

1. Morris Cafritz's construction company grew to become one of the largest in the Washington, D.C., area. In 1948, he created the Morris and Gwendolyn Cafritz Foundation, which has become an important philanthropic institution for metropolitan Washington. In fiscal year 1999, this foundation awarded $16 million in grants to 339 nonprofit organizations. *Cafritz Foundation Annual Report*, May 1, 1998–April 30, 1999, p. 2.

2. Hugh Thomas, *Cuba: The Pursuit of Freedom* (New York: Harper and Row, 1971), 1406.

3. Ibid., 1385–94, 1399–1415.

4. More information about the Cuban Missile Crisis is provided in Evan Thomas, "Bobby at the Brink," *Newsweek* (August 14, 2000): 49–59. The article

is an excerpt from Thomas's book *Robert Kennedy: His Life* (New York: Simon and Schuster, 2000).

5. "[T]he stage musical *Brigadoon* was the first major success of the songwriting team of Alan Jay Lerner and Frederick Lowe." Colin Larkin, ed., *The Guinness Encyclopedia of Popular Music*, 2d ed. (New York: Guinness, 1995), 1: 547–48. This musical love story, originally produced in 1947 and starring David Brooks and Marion Bel, was about two Americans who come across a quaint Scottish village only to discover it had disappeared years ago and returns for one day each century.

6. Maza del Castillo, "Memoirs," 6–7.

7. Ibid., 7.

8. Thomas, *Cuba*, 1404–6.

9. Ibid., 599. "He [Castro] accomplished something previously unheard of in Cuban politics—unity." Yvonne M. Conde, *Operation Pedro Pan* (New York: Routledge, 1999), 4. This was written in the first months after Castro took over.

10. "[Jessye Norman's] sumptuous voice [is] one of the richest and most expressive of recent decades." John Quinn and Les Stone, eds., *The St. James Opera Encyclopedia* (Detroit: Visible Ink Press, 1997), 567–68.

11. "The city's oldest musical institution, the Friday Morning Music Club, was approaching its centennial when I came to town. It is still Washington's most active source of free concerts and a cornucopia of imaginative programming." Joseph McLellan, "Final Touches: A Columnist Files His Concluding Notes," *Washington Post*, January 21, 2001, sec. G, p. 11.

12. "Pianist Ernesto Lecuona was one of the most internationally famous composers to come out of Cuba." Larkin, *Guinness Encyclopedia of Popular Music*, 3: 2431. Lecuona lived from 1896 to 1963.

13. George Orwell's novel *1984*, first published in 1949, satirizes a future totalitarian state. Orwell's satire was directed mainly against Stalin's Russia, and the novel is the source of the phrase "Big Brother is watching you," which is now commonly used in reference to inappropriate government oversight of citizens.

14. Aldous Huxley's satirical novel *Brave New World*, first published in 1932, is set in a completely government-regulated future world in which citizens are educated to believe that their duty to society lies in supporting its economic productivity and in which the practice of spirituality or the exercise of moral choice is seen as subversive and primitive.

15. "[Lawrence] Ferlinghetti was a leader in the American poetry revival in San Francisco in the fifties, a movement whose primary purpose was to bring poetry back to the people." Barbara Harte and Carolyn Riley, eds., *Contemporary Authors* (Detroit: Gale Research Company, Book Tower, 1969), 5–8: 373–

75. "[A]ll the poets around Ginsberg share the intense idealism, the social naiveté, the centering on the lyric of the self, the use of familiar linguistic materials—all of this is expressive of Ginsberg's concerns." Samuel Chartes, "Allen Ginsberg," *Some Poems/Poets: Studies in American Underground Poetry Since 1945* (Oyez: 1975), 71, cited in Carolyn Riley, ed. *Contemporary Literary Criticism* (Detroit: Gale Research Company, Book Tower, 1975), 4:181.

16. Radclyffe Hall, *The Well of Loneliness* (New York: Doubleday, 1990). This book, which in 1928 was both self-published and published by Doubleday, was for many years the only book available about the coming of age of a lesbian in a homophobic society.

17. *The Fountainhead,* Ayn Rand's popular, polemical 1943 novel, concerns an architect—supposed to be modeled on Frank Lloyd Wright—who emerges triumphant in his battle to realize his own personal vision through his design principles. Rand was an ardent defender in her novels of capitalism and of the rights of self-interested individuals.

Chapter 5. Introduction to Art; the Hippies' Life of the Sixties

1. William C. White, Bernard Prettier, and Harriet Prettier, *Flowering Trees of the Caribbean* (New York: Rhinehart, 1959).

2. Many Cuban songs, particularly those of Ibrahim Ferrer, use the names of Caribbean flowers as a metaphor for love. *Buena Vista Social Club,* a 1996 movie directed by Wim Wenders and produced by Ry Cooder (with Ibrahim Ferrer, Omara Portuondo, and Ruben Gonzalez, C-105 min.), features Cuban musicians who were popular in the forties and who have recently experienced an amazing comeback, due in some part to the impact and influence of this film.

3. A photocollage illustrating the concepts of Archigram appears in Spiro Kostof's *History of Architecture* (New York: Oxford Press, 1995), 748, fig. 29.7.

4. Keinholtz's exhibit at Washington Gallery of Modern Art is noted in Colin Naylor and Genesis D. Orridge, eds., *Contemporary Artists* (London: St. James Press, 1977), 474.

5. "Master of Monumentalists," *Time* (October 13, 1967): 80–86, and cover photograph.

6. *Washington Post,* April 5, 1968, sec. A, pp. 1–16.

7. James Kendrick. Home page. *I am Curious Yellow,* 1998. 23 August, 2000; available from http://www.q.com/movie/IamCurious.html; Internet; accessed August 23, 2000. This recent review of the 1968 movie confirms the opinions of both Elena and the writer.

8. D. A. Pennebaker, director, *Don't Look Back,* with Bob Dylan, Joan Baez, Donovan, Alan Price, Albert Grossman, and Allen Ginsberg, 96 min. (1967).

9. The Beatles, the phenomenal British pop/rock group, were already popu-

lar when they first appeared on television on the *Ed Sullivan Show* in 1964. "In common with Bob Dylan, the Beatles had taught the world that pop music could be intelligent and was worthy of serious consideration beyond the screaming hordes of teendom." Their movies *Help!* and *A Hard Day's Night* brought their antics and music to increasingly wider audiences. When the LP *Sergeant Pepper's Lonely Hearts Club Band* was released in 1967, it became a "cultural icon embracing the constituent elements of the 60's youth culture: pop art, garish fashion, drugs, instant mysticism and freedom from parental control." Colin Larkin, ed. *The Guinness Encyclopedia of Popular Music*, 2d ed. (New York: Guinness, 1995), 1:432–37.

10. D. A. Pennebaker, director, *Monterey Pop*, with Jimi Hendrix, Otis Redding, The Who, The Animals, Jefferson Airplane, Janis Joplin, Country Joe and the Fish, The Mamas and the Papas, Booker T. and the MG's, and Ravi Shankar, C-72 min. (1969). "This was the concert that kicked off the 1967 'Summer of Peace and Love' . . . that culminated in Woodstock." Mick Martin and Marsha Porter, *Video Movie Guide 2000* (New York: Ballantine, 1999), 746.

11. "Along with the Grateful Dead, the [Jefferson] Airplane are [*sic*] regarded as the most successful San Francisco band of the late 60's." Later this band evolved into Jefferson Starship. Larkin, *Guinness Encyclopedia of Popular Music*, 3: 2150–1.

12. Henri-Louis Bergson, a philosopher and essayist, had a poetic style full of metaphor and imagery that influenced imaginative writers and earned him the Nobel Prize for Literature in 1928.

13. "Smaller companies seeking a part of the long-distance telephone market challenged AT&T's monopoly in the 1970's. In 1982 the U.S. Department of Justice allowed AT&T to settle a lawsuit alleging violations because of its monopolistic holdings." Theresa Lippert, ed., *West Encyclopedia of American Law* (St. Paul, Minn.: West, 1998), 10: 45.

14. Robert Draper's *Rolling Stone Magazine: The Uncensored History* (New York: Doubleday, 1990) is a history of this magazine that was launched as a counterculture publication in November 1967 and is now a mainstream publication.

15. Joan Baez was the "queen of folk to Bob Dylan's king—her sweeping soprano is one of the most distinctive voices in popular music." Larkin, *Guinness Encyclopedia of Popular Music*, 1: 326–27.

16. Gerald Marzorati, "Altamont: End, and Beginning," *New York Times*, August 13, 2000, sec. 2, pp. 11, 16.

17. Michael Wadleigh, director, *Woodstock*, with Joan Baez, Richie Havens, Crosby, Stills, and Nash, Jefferson Airplane, Ten Years After, Santana, Country Joe and the Fish, John Sebastian, Jimi Hendrix, The Who, Janis Joplin, and

Canned Heat, C-184 min. (1970). *Woodstock* won an Oscar at the 1970 Academy Awards for "best documentary." Jimi Hendrix, a rock guitarist, was "one of music's most influential figures; he brought an unparalleled vision to the art of playing the guitar." Larkin, *Guinness Encyclopedia of Popular Music*, 3: 2489–92. Hendrix made a sensational appearance at the Monterey Pop Festival, where he played the guitar with his teeth, then burned it with lighter fluid.

18. Ellen Willis, "Steal This Myth: Why We Still Try to Re-Create the Rush of the 60's," *New York Times*, August 20, 2000, sec. 2, pp. 1, 18.

19. Aldous Huxley, *Doors of Perception* (New York: Harper, 1970). "[Huxley] endorses the use of hallucinogenic drugs as a means of heightening one's spiritual and aesthetic awareness." Milton Birnbaum, *Aldous Huxley's Quest for Values* (Knoxville: University of Tennessee Press, 1971), cited in Riley, *Contemporary Literary Criticism*, 4:239.

Chapter 6. Discovery of Tai Chi; Grandfather and Aunts Leave Cuba; Other Family Events

1. Channel 20, WDCA, an ultra-high-frequency station, now the United Paramount Network television station in the metro Washington, D.C., area, was a low-budget station that showed mostly reruns and old movies. It is located on River Road in Bethesda, Maryland, near Walt Whitman High School. Presently it is a popular station because it shows reruns of *Star Trek*.

2. Vincent Furnier changed his name to Alice Cooper, which became the name of the rock band. Dafydd Rees and Luke Crampton, *Encyclopedia of Rock Stars* (New York: PK Publishing, 1996), 215–16. "A teenage prodigy, this powerful, if inflexible drummer [Buddy Miles] was a veteran of several touring revues." Colin Larkin, ed., *Guinness Encyclopedia of Popular Music*, 2d ed. (New York: Guinness, 1995), 4: 2816–17. Miles formed his own Buddy Miles Band and collaborated with Jimi Hendrix and Carlos Santana, among many others.

3. "[Charles Manson] probably received more publicity from 1919 to early 1971 than any other in California's criminal history" because of his gruesome murder of five people in director Roman Polanski's house and of two in another household. Robert Jay Nash, *Bloodletters and Badmen: A Narrative Encyclopedia of American Criminals from the Pilgrims to the Present* (New York: M. Evans, 1995), 422–23.

4. "Once a psychology professor at Harvard University in the 1960's, [Timothy] Leary became one of America's most controversial and influential figures for his outspoken advocacy of the use of LSD." Hal May, ed., *Contemporary Authors* (Detroit: Gale Research Company, Book Tower, 1969), 107: 278. Aldous Huxley, *Doors of Perception* (New York: Harper, 1970).

5. José Silva and Burt Goldman, *The Silva Control Method of Mental Dynamics* (New York: Pocket Books, 1988).

6. Cheng Man-ch'ing and Robert W Smith, *Tai-Chi: The Supreme Ultimate Exercise for Health, Sport and Self-Defense* (Rutland, Vt.: Charles E. Tuttle Co., 1972); Cheng Man Ch'ing, *Cheng Tzu's Thirteen Treatises on T'ai Chi Ch'uan,* trans. Benjamin Pang, Jeng Lo, and Martin Inn (Berkeley, Calif.: North Atlantic Books, 1985); Mark Hennessy, *Cheng Man-ch'ing: Master of Five Excellencies* (Berkeley, Calif.: Frog, 1995).

7. In the television series *Kung Fu,* which aired from 1972 to 1975, David Carradine starred as Kwai Chang Caine, who prefers nonviolence but uses his skills in martial arts when necessary. Alex McNeil, *Total Television: The Comprehensive Guide to Programming from 1948 to the Present,* 4th ed. (New York: Penguin, 1996), 458–59.

8. Elena has chosen these three books as representative of the many she has on tai chi: Dai Liu, *T'ai Chi Chuan and Meditation* (New York: Schocken, 1986); Herman Kauz, *Tai Chi Handbook* (New York: Doubleday, 1974); Waysun Liao, *T'ai Chi Classics* (Boston, Shambhala Publications, 1980).

9. Marcel Carné, director, *Les Enfants du Paradis* (Children of paradise), with Jean-Louis Barrcult, Asletty, Pierre Brasseur, Albert Remy, Maris Casarés, Leon Larive, Marce Herr, and Pierre Renoir, 188 min. (1944). *Les Enfants du Paradis* was made during the Nazi occupation of Paris. "Long beloved by connoisseurs the world over is this rich and rare film of infatuation, jealousy, deception, grief, murder and true love last(ing) forever—set in pre-1840 Paris." Mick Martin and Marsha Porter, *Video Movie Guide 2001* (New York: Ballantine, 2000), 191.

10. "[E]xistentialism became a catch-all term for the cultural and artistic avant-garde and for radical critiques of universal principles and absolute values." G. B. Madison, "Existentialism & Beyond: Jean-Paul Sartre, Simone de Beauvoir, Albert Camus and Maurice Merleau-Ponty," in *The Columbia History of Western Philosophy,* ed. Richard Popkin (New York: Columbia University Press, 1999), 698–705.

11. Marshall McLuhan, *The Medium Is the Massage* (New York: Random House, 1967). In an opening statement McLuhan states that the "medium" of our time is "electric technology": that it "is reshaping and restructuring patterns of social interdependence and every aspect of our personal life." He says the type of media is more important than the content of what is being communicated. *The Medium Is the Massage* supports this thesis; it is a book of short, often radical (for its time of 1967) statements combined in a surprising and confrontational way with a wide range of photographs and images and widely different typefaces or fonts.

12. Norman Mailer's *Armies of the Night* (New York: New American Library, 1968) deals with the storming of the Pentagon and the early anti–Vietnam War efforts. Articles in the *Washington Post* from October 15, 1967, to 22 October 22, 1967, describe the building dissatisfaction and unrest about the Vietnam War.

13. In 1964, two destroyers were sent to patrol eight miles from North Vietnam and four miles from its islands in the area of the Tonkin Gulf. Most countries at this time had a twelve-mile limit for foreign vessels. The destroyers were attacked by fast, smaller North Vietnamese crafts, but there was no significant damage to either of the American ships. Several days later in foggy weather and rough seas, there was the perception by those on the two U.S. destroyers, one of which had been in the first attack, that another attack was imminent. Even though no attack was ever definitively verified, President Johnson ordered reprisals through what is called the Gulf of Tonkin Resolution. Although there was some opposition in the Congress to this resolution—which was the formal declaration of America's involvement in the Vietnam War—defenders of the resolution believed that the United States was too committed to the war to pull out, and that whatever mistakes had been made would have to be absorbed into the general war effort. Stanley Karnow, *Vietnam: A History* (New York: Viking, 1983), 366–72, 374–76.

14. The famous photo of the young woman bending over the body of a student shot by a National Guardsman is on page one with related stories. *Washington Post*, May 5, 1970, sec. A, p. 1.

15. Carl Bernstein and Peter Osnos, "U.S. Permits Use of Ellipse for War Rally," *Washington Post*, May 9, 1970, sec. A, pp. 1, 7.

16. Galt MacDermot, music, Gerome Ragini, and James Rado, book and lyrics, *Hair*, with Lynn Kellogg, Melba Moore, Sally Eaton, Diane Keaton and Lamont Washington. "[*Hair* was the] first musical of the hippie peace and love generation." Larkin, *Guinness Encyclopedia of Popular Music*, 3: 1792.

17. *Washington Post*, July 4, 1970, sec. A, pp. 1, 4; and July 5 1970, sec. A, pp. 1, 21.

18. *New York Times*, May 7, 1970, sec. A, p. 19.

19. Enigmatic and mercurial, David Bowie was a musician who appeared in "outrageous costume(s) and . . . experimented with diverse ideas, themes and images that coalesced effectively, through not necessarily coherently." Larkin, *Guinness Encyclopedia of Popular Music*, 1: 512–15.

20. Hugh Thomas, *Cuba: The Pursuit of Freedom* (New York: Harper and Row, 1971), 1424–25.

21. "This was a web of neighborhood watchdogs, usually one per block,

whose sole function was to spy on and denounce their neighbors." Yvonne M. Conde, *Operation Pedro Pan* (New York: Routledge, 1999), 22–23.

22. Thomas, *Cuba*, 1437.

23. Ibid., 1322.

24. Toya died in 1998, several years after this interview.

25. *Washington Post*, April 5, 1968, sec. A, pp. 1–16.

26. St. Albans is a prestigious boys' private school adjacent to the Washington Cathedral in Washington, D.C.

Chapter 7. Cecilia's Dilemma

1. In the column "Divulgación Ciudadana," Mrs. Maza wrote a tribute to her husband and his accomplishments in architecture on the tenth anniversary of his death. Olga Caturla de la Maza, "En Memoria de Aquiles de la Maza," *Diario Las Americas*, October 1, 1989, sec. A., p. 10.

2. *Washington Post*, May 10, 1983, sec. C., p. 4.

Chapter 8. Raising David; Rediscovering Tai Chi

1. The Unification Church was founded in 1954 by Sun Myung Moon. ". . . the Unification Church has drawn considerable attention from anticult movements and the media. Among the many accusations leveled at it are that it uses brainwashing or mind control techniques to recruit and keep its members, that it breaks up families, that the leaders live in luxury while the rank and file membership is exploited and oppressed by its authoritarian organization." Mircea Eliade, editor in chief, *The Encyclopedia of Religion* (New York: MacMillan Library Reference USA, Simon and Schuster MacMillan, 1995), 15: 141–43.

2. In an email to the author on October 29, 2000, Elena wrote that Bakari taught her the Yang style of tai chi, an un-lineaged style of unknown origins that came from Willy Lin. Lin taught it to Dennis Brown, then Dennis Brown taught Bakari. Bakari also taught the "Secret Yang" style, learned from Mfundishi Talo-na (née Ray Cooper) of Chicago, who learned it from Professor Ho Chi Kwan.

3. "*Crouching Tiger* [*Crouching Tiger, Hidden Dragon*, directed by Ang Lee] is drawn from a series of martial-arts novels familiar to Chinese children. The plot involves a young impetuous noble woman, Jen, . . . who has a secret talent as an expert warrior and energy to spare. . . . 'We've grown up with this genre, of legends and myth about heroes and heroines able to fly,' says Yeoh [the movie's heroine]." Sharon Waxman, "The Director Who's Giving Martial Arts a New Kick," *Washington Post*, December 20, 2000, sec. C, pp. 1, 19. During the Boxer Rebellion, "a group known as the Red Lantern Society [was composed of]

young women, who it was said could ride on clouds and kindle fire to burn the warships of the Westerners." J.A.G. Roberts, *A Concise History of China* (Cambridge: Harvard University Press, 1999), 202.

4. In October 1911, over a period of weeks, China became a republic. Roberts, *A Concise History of China*, 206.

5. Ibid., 189.

6. In an email to the author on November 15, 2000, Elena provided this information about the five known styles of tai chi:

> Chen style is believed to be earliest; the clan traces itself back nineteen generations to the late seventeenth century in Chen-jia-gou, Henan province. This style is characterized by its low stances and emphasis on showing fa-jing in the form. Fa-jing, or fang-chin, is defined as a discharge or release of energy (Chen Wei Ming, *Questions and Answers on T'ai Chi Ch'uan* [T'ai Chi Ch'uan Ta Wen], trans. Benjamin Pang, Jen Lo, and Robert Smith [Berkeley, Calif.: North Atlantic Books, 1985]).
>
> Yang Style, the best known and most commonly practiced in the United States, traces its origins to Yang Lu Ch'an in the nineteenth century. Yang spent eight years in the Chen village studying their taiji, then went to Beijing, where he began teaching members of the court. He created his stylistic innovations supposedly because the effete nobles couldn't do the more strenuous Chen taiji. A good account of the family lineage is found in *T'ai-chi Touchstones: Yang Family Secret Transmissions*, compiled and translated by Douglas Wile (Brooklyn, N.Y.: Sweet Chi Press, 1983). This is one volume of a three-volume set. Wile has been repudiated by the Cheng Man-ch'ing family and associates for publishing an unauthorized translation [of] *Chen Tzu's Thirteen Treatises on T'ai Chi Chuan.* "Taiji" is another way of spelling "tai chi"; this spelling uses the pinyin system of phonetic spelling in English as opposed to the older Wade-Giles system.
>
> Wu Style is the next, and I know very little about this style, other than it is different from the other two. The Chen family said the founder of the clan studied at the Chen village for some time. There are a number of practitioners of this style in this country, which is characterized by repetitive sort of wind-up movements when starting certain postures.
>
> Sun Style was the invention of Sun Lu-tang, a martial arts master who became a legend in Beijing in the 1920s and 1930s. The Chen family claimed that they never taught him their taiji, and that it has no knowledge of how he had learned it. The story that I had heard from Diosdado Santiago is that Sun Lu-tang was actually a master of Hsing-I,

a very different internal martial arts, who decided to take up taiji in middle age. He evidently did not understand some taiji principles very well, and the form he devised clearly shows this. It is not well known; in fact, I've never met anyone who claimed to know it or to have seen it, except one young woman in China, a French-Canadian who had lived in Beijing for several years and who had met someone who claimed to have been a student of Sun's.

I know nothing about the fifth style: Wu, pronounced differently from the first Wu.

7. Paul Theroux, *Riding the Iron Rooster* (New York: G. P. Putnam's Sons, 1988).

Chapter 9. Elena's Art; Return to Cuban Heritage

1. Rockville Arts Place is a nonprofit arts center in Montgomery County, Maryland, that was incorporated in 1987.

2. "The Women's Caucus for Art is the major national organization for women actively engaged in the visual arts professions." "WCA (new, proposed) Statement of Purpose," *Women's Caucus for Art of Greater Washington Newsletter*, Summer 2000, p.4.

3. Martin Luther King Jr. Memorial Library, the main library for the District of Columbia, is a modern building designed by Mies van der Rohe and opened to the public in 1972.

4. Ken Oda, ed., *Koan (Ken Oda's Arts Newsletter)* (Washington, D.C.). This arts newsletter was published for the metropolitan Washington, D.C., area by Ken Oda from 1992 to 1998.

5. Migene Gonzalez-Wippler, *Santeria: African Magic in Latin America*, 5th ed. (New York: Original Products, division of Jamil Products Corp., 1989).

6. Guillermo De Zéndegui, "Landaluze: A Great Spanish Costumbrista in America," *Americas Magazine* 27, no. 9 (September 1975): 16–23. Illustrations are on the inside front and back cover. On page 21 is a watercolor titled *Dance of Ñáñigos*.

7. Ibid., 16–23.

8. Ibid.

9. Fernando Ortiz, *Los Negros Brujos* (Miami: Ediciones Universal, 1973).

10. Lydia Cabrera, *El Monte (Igbo—Finda: Ewe Orisha. Vititi Nfinda)* (Miami: Ediciones Universal, 1975).

11. Hugh Thomas gives a detailed description of the Yoruba religion's influence in Cuba in his book *Cuba: The Pursuit of Freedom* (New York: Harper and Row, 1971), 517–24.

12. Maria Victoria Caturla, "Una Nueva Pintore Cubana: Elena Maza" (A new Cuban-American painter: Elena Maza), *Diario Las Americas,* January 8, 1977, sec. B, p. 15. *Diario Las Americas* has given extensive coverage to Elena's subsequent exhibits. "Pintora Cubana Expone sus Obras en Washington, D.C." *Diario Las Americas,* January 1, 1994, sec. B, p. 11. Maria Elena Saavedra, "Exponen por primera vez en Miami los Artistas Cubanos Elena Maza y Santiago Caballero" (Cuban artists Elena Maza and Santiago Caballero show for first time in Miami), *Diario Las Americas,* July 2, 1998, sec. 1, p. 2. (A photograph with the last article was taken when Zenaida Manfugas gave a concert for the Cuban American Cultural Society. With her are Lucia P. Vasallo, president of the Cuban American Cultural Society; Olga Caturla de la Maza; and Elena Maza.) Guillermo Cabrera Leiva, "Exhiben Obras de Elena Maza y Santiago Caballero en Coral Gables" (Exhibition of Elena Maza and Santiago Caballero in Coral Gables), *Diario Las Americas,* July 17, 1998, sec. 3, p. 2.

13. Harriet L. Beinfield and Efrem L. Korngold, *Between Heaven and Earth* (New York: Ballantine, 1991).

14. "Rockville Mansion" is the popular designation for Glenview Mansion, which is part of the Rockville Civic Center, a nonprofit arts center of several buildings in Rockville, Maryland. The mansion and surrounding land was bought by the city of Rockville in 1957. Kathleen Moran is the arts program specialist.

15. Margaret L. Paris, *Valued Women: A Photo Essay in Celebration of Women over Forty* (Rockville, Md.: Self-published, 1994).

16. Thomas, *Cuba.*

17. Phyllis Levitt et al., *A Collage of Cultures: Many Visions, One Community: Works by Migrant Seasonal Agricultural Workers.* An exhibition and catalogue funded by Delaware Humanities Forum, a state program of the National Endowment for the Humanities, 1995, published by Dover Art League, Dover, Delaware.

18. Phyllis Levitt, "An Invitation to Build Community," in *A Collage of Cultures,* by Phyllis Levitt et al., 1.

19. Ibid., 2.

20. Levitt, *A Collage of Cultures,* 15–20.

21. The catalogue of the exhibit Elena mentions is by Henry Drewal, John Pemberton III, and Rowland Abiodun and is titled *Yoruba: Nine Centuries of African Art and Thought* (New York: Abrams, in association with the Center for African Art, 1984). Richard Farris-Thompson, *Flash of the Spirit* (New York: Vintage, 1984).

22. Anders Gigi, "The Latin Beat," *Washington Post,* September 29, 1995, "Weekend" sec., pp. 6–8. On page seven is a reproduction of Elena's painting with

this caption, "Elena Maza's *Tribute to the Balseros/Raft People* is among Latin art celebrated at the Fondo de Sol Gallery." This gallery is devoted to Latin American and Caribbean art and is located at 2112 R Street, Washington, D.C.

23. Herb Borkland, "Eating Black Beans with Chopsticks," *Inside Kung Fu* (April 1995): 56–59.

24. Elena Tscherny, "Paintings by Maza, Napoles and Scott on Exhibit at the Martin Luther King Jr. Memorial Library: *Cuando Calienta el Sol* (When the sun warms)," District of Columbia Public Library press release, April 10, 1997.

25. William Branigin and R. Jeffrey Smith, "U.S. Took Steps to Curb Flights by Exile Group," *Washington Post*, February 27, 1996, sec. A, pp. 1, 5.

26. Thomas Lippman, "Surviving a Nightmare inside Castro's Cuba," *Washington Post*, November 1, 1996, sec. A, p. 23.

27. "Antología de Zarzuelas," with Armando Terron, Lisner Auditorium, George Washington University, Washington, D.C., October 29, 1995.

28. Armando Valladares, *Against all Hope* (New York: Knopf, 1986).

29. "Susan Sontag Provokes Debate on Communism," *New York Times*, February 27, 1982, p. 27. Sontag's controversial speech, in which she calls communism "fascism with a human face," is printed is its entirety in the *Nation*, February 27, 1982, 230–31.

30. The word *zarzuela* is defined in the *Oxford English Dictionary* (Oxford: Clarendon Press, 1989) as "a traditional form of popular musical comedy in Spain."

31. Colin Larkin, ed., *The Guinness Enclyclopedia of Popular Music*, 2d ed. (New York: Guinness, 1995), 3: 2431.

32. Thomas, *Cuba*, 520. *Nuestra Senora de la Caridad Del Cobre* is also known as the *Virgen de la Caridad del Cobre* or *Caridá*, familiarly *Cachita*, the patron saint of Cuba.

33. "Castro began to develop at greater length the concept of the free 'new man' who would, as Guevara had hoped, be no longer alienated from society, unsullied by contact with the profit motive, but conscious, like Alain's peasant, of the country rather than the corrupt city, and living for the community from the cradle to the grave." Thomas, *Cuba*, 1446.

34. Florinda Alzaga, *La Avellaneda: Intensidad y Vanguardia* (Miami: Ediciones Universal, 1997).

35. Three of Mrs. Maza's poems are included in the appendix. One is a tribute to Elena, one is a mourning for Cecilia, and one is a tribute to her identity as a Cuban poet. They are included in *Todo el mar para mis sueños* (All the sea for my dreams), a book of Olga Caturla de la Maza's poetry that was published by Two Eagles Press International of Las Cruces, New Mexico, in 2001. Elena was the editor of this publication.

Margaret L. Paris is a photographer and writer in the Washington, D.C., area. She teaches at Duke Ellington School of the Arts, Washington's arts high school, and at Georgetown University.